RECENT DEVELOPMENTS IN READING

RECENT DEVELOPMENTS IN READING

Proceedings of the Annual Conference on Reading Held at
The University of Chicago, 1965

VOLUME XXVII

Compiled and Edited by
H. ALAN ROBINSON

THE UNIVERSITY OF CHICAGO PRESS

Supplementary Educational Monographs

Published in conjunction with THE SCHOOL REVIEW and

THE ELEMENTARY SCHOOL JOURNAL

NUMBER 95   DECEMBER 1965

Library of Congress Catalog Card Number: 65-26068

THE UNIVERSITY OF CHICAGO PRESS, CHICAGO & LONDON
The University of Toronto Press, Toronto 5, Canada

PREFACE

*

THE THEME of the Twenty-eighth Annual Conference on Reading, "Recent Developments in Reading," is almost identical with that of the Second Annual Conference and first published proceedings (1939), "Recent Trends in Reading." When the two programs are compared, three striking similarities appear: (1) We were concerned this year with the role of reading in education, as were the conference participants in 1939, although we placed a little more of our attention on the functions of reading and the tremendous significance of reading in today's modern and complex society. (2) We devoted almost as much attention to reading in the content areas as was given in the 1939 conference. It is interesting to note that although numerous papers related to reading in the content areas were presented at the 1939 conference there are a number of contemporary educators who seem to think that the emphasis on reading instruction in the various subject disciplines is a brand-new idea. (3) Both conferences highlighted corrective and remedial reading, although in 1939 this topic occupied a large block in the proceedings as contrasted with the rather integrated treatment in this year's proceedings. Perhaps this occurs because remedial and corrective practices in reading were relatively narrow and dichotomous in 1939; in 1965 the innovations and experiments by design tend to treat both developmental and remedial aspects of reading instruction as parts of one total framework.

As there are striking similarities, there are also major differences in the two conferences. The 1965 conference placed much greater stress on experimental and novel approaches to the teaching of reading and on the great variety of new materials on the market. Some of the approaches obviously are not new when one views the total reading spectrum through the years, but they are being presented to educators and the public today with greater vigor than ever before. On the other hand, the multitude of materials is quite new and presents many problems to educators who need to develop criteria for selection and utilization. Some of the materials are so much a part of a "new" approach that teachers, supervisors, and administrators need to view both approach and materials with extreme care.

Hence, this year's conference focused on evaluation of recent developments in reading. The conference opened with a view of the significant role reading plays in our society. Recent developments in materials and procedures were then explored and evaluated, with particular emphasis on the roles of linguistics in reading instruction and of reading in the content areas. The development of effective, flexible readers was given a great deal of emphasis. The conference concluded with a review of the present status and a look into the future of reading instruction.

Almost all general sessions were followed by meetings at different grade levels from the primary grades through the junior college and of special interest groups. Two additional sections provided for corrective and remedial teachers and for administrators, supervisors, and reading consultants. A general evening session in collaboration with the International Reading Association dealt with recent developments in reading in Sweden.

Proceedings of twenty-eight conferences have been published under the following titles:

I. Recent Trends in Reading, 1939
II. Reading and Pupil Development, 1940
III. Adjusting Reading Programs to Individuals, 1941
IV. Co-operative Effort in Schools To Improve Reading, 1942
V. Adapting Reading Programs to Wartime Needs, 1943
VI. Reading in Relation to Experience and Language, 1944
VII. The Appraisal of Current Practices in Reading, 1945
VIII. Improving Reading in Content Fields, 1946
IX. Promoting Personal and Social Development through Reading, 1947
X. Basic Instruction in Reading in Elementary and High Schools, 1948
XI. Classroom Techniques in Improving Reading, 1949
XII. Keeping Reading Programs Abreast of the Times, 1950
XIII. Promoting Growth toward Maturity in Interpreting What Is Read, 1951
XIV. Improving Reading in All Curriculum Areas, 1952
*XV. Corrective Reading in Classroom and Clinic, 1953
XVI. Promoting Maximal Reading Growth among Able Learners, 1954
*XVII. Oral Aspects of Reading, 1955
*XVIII. Developing Permanent Interest in Reading, 1956
*XIX. Materials for Reading, 1957
*XX. Evaluation of Reading, 1958
XXI. Reading Instruction in Various Patterns of Grouping, 1959
*XXII. Sequential Development of Reading Abilities, 1960
*XXIII. Controversial Issues in Reading and Promising Solutions, 1961
*XXIV. The Underachiever in Reading, 1962
*XXV. Reading and the Language Arts, 1963
*XXVI. Meeting Individual Differences in Reading, 1964
*XXVII. Recent Developments in Reading, 1965
*XXVIII. Reading: Seventy-five Years of Progress, 1966.

The editor is deeply indebted to the great number of people who assisted with this year's conference. A conference of such magnitude could obviously not be undertaken without the active participation and co-operation of faculty members and many student helpers. I am particularly grateful to the members

* Copies of titles marked with asterisks are available. All other volumes are out of print.

of the advisory committee composed of faculty members at the University of Chicago. During the school year 1964–65, the advisory committee was composed of the following members.

Janet Emig, Education
Sara Innis Fenwick, Graduate Library School
John Ginther, Education
Helen M. Robinson, Education
Helen K. Smith, Education
Ellen L. Thomas, Laboratory School
Samuel Weintraub, Education

H. ALAN ROBINSON

TABLE OF CONTENTS

*

CHAPTER I

THE VITAL ROLE OF READING IN THIS COMPLEX SOCIETY

*

E. T. McSWAIN

*

IN AN article entitled "America, To-morrow: The Resources of Great-ness," John Lear shared with the reader this idea: "Among the animals of earth, only man can dream. Other species laugh and cry, love, rage, and kill. Man alone has the power to imagine to-morrow."[1] The weather and seasons are forces of nature; communities and societies, however, may be created, sus-tained, improved, or even destroyed by human beings. People, alone, by their individual and collective action have the opportunity to achieve their imag-ined social, economic, and political to-morrows.

One important role of reading in the schools is to offer materials and profes-sional instruction that will assist chil-dren and youth to acquire cognitive understandings, values, and innovat-ing goals for the imagined tomorrows they desire for themselves, their com-munity, and their nation. Reading in-volves more than the ability to see and to say words and sentences. Reading is the most productive process by which individuals may develop informed and imaginative minds and thus the proc-ess by which they may become the de-signers and controllers of the increas-ing technologic energy of their contem-porary, complex society.

As a conceptual process, reading can develop complacent minds, historical-ly indoctrinated minds, or well-in-formed, courageous, and innovating minds. The mental outcomes of read-ing depend more upon the kinds of materials read and the cognitive ap-praisal of what is read than upon speed of reading and amount of materials. An idea expressed by Julian Huxley merits critical appraisal by administra-tors and teachers, who, by their pro-fessional decision-making, determine the purposes, the instructional meth-ods, and the printed materials that con-stitute the reading programs offered in the schools: "The first and most obvi-ously unique characteristic of man is his capacity of conceptual thought. . . . Man has the possibility of mak-ing [progress] the main feature of his own future evolution."[2] Nuclear ener-gy, electronic automation, and ex-panded technological operations can serve man by providing ways to expand the annual production of material products and thus to increase the na-tion's gross national product. The lev-el of reading ability and reading ma-

[1] Saturday Review, XLIV (September 2, 1961), 35.

[2] Man in the Modern World (London: Chatto & Windus, 1950), p. 2, 21.

1

terials will determine the quality and productivity of man's cultural, political, and spiritual evolution.

Reading is the conceptual process that enables young people to develop ideas, understandings, values, and attitudes from the subjects included in a curriculum. Reading materials and the cognitive outcomes of reading can render a great service to the millions of children and youth attending school in the decade 1965–75 by providing a means of escape from a situation described by E. J. Trueblood in *The Dawn of the Post-Modern Era*: "Relatively few people seem to realize that we are living in the post-modern world, . . . in the beginning of the atomic age. The tendency to live in the past, amidst dead and dying issues appears to be as strong in our times as it has been in any previous period." [3]

CHALLENGES FOR TEACHING

The innovating frontiers of materials to be read and instructional methods to be offered in the schools in the next decade are the following: Young people must be helped (1) to acquire reliable understandings of the societal conditions, issues, and trends which characterize their nation's contemporary, complex society and (2) to find interest in these conditions in order to sustain the individual and collective requirements for advancing national and international societies during the last quarter of this century. Fortunate will be the children and youth who have the professional leadership of teachers who strive to upgrade their

[3] (New York: Philosophical Library, 1954), p. 149.

understandings of contemporary societies and who devote time to imagining social, economic, political, and educational innovations that will be required for productive work and intelligent citizenship in the approaching next five decades. Attractive, serviceable physical facilities and professionally structured organizational policies and practices are important, and yet the mental and moral productivity of each school system depend on the academic competency, civic sensitivity, and imagined tomorrows of each member of the faculty.

Members of each school faculty should be challenged to examine the implications for the choice of reading materials and instructional methods of the following realities: (1) Pupils now in the first grade will reach age sixteen in 1975 and age forty-one in A.D. 2000. These millions of potential adults can anticipate twenty-three years of employment, responsible citizenship, and more leisure time before arriving at retirement age in the third decade of the twenty-first century. (2) The young adolescents now in grade eight will reach age twenty-three in 1975 and age forty-eight in 2000. This group can look forward to seventeen years of employment, productive citizenship, and expanded leisure time before age sixty-five in the second decade of the next century. During the years 1965–75 reading programs in the elementary and secondary schools can be personally and culturally productive only in the degree they encourage these future adults to develop and accept the values and human-centered goals essential for

social progress in an era of unprecedented technological and affluent productivity. In a recent article Peter F.
Drucker has predicted that "by 1968
the mid-age will have dropped to twenty-five or lower." [4]

Teachers of all subjects now have
the opportunity to appraise their professional response to each of the following pertinent questions: (1) What
percentage of the materials assigned to
children and youth is concerned largely with historical yesteryears? (2) What
percentage of the reading materials is
related to contemporary societal conditions, issues, and trends? (3) What percentage of the reading materials presents information and forecasts concerning the values, human innovations,
and goals which should nurture in tomorrow's young adults the desire to advance beautification of metropolitan
cities, to expand the health services, to
improve educational programs, and to
provide adequate recreational facilities? Teachers have the opportunity to
use reading to develop minds which
will give greater value and support to
upgraded personal-social living environments than to increased consumption of material conveniences.

It is reasonable to assume that school
people who possess high abilities in
reading should be expected to have a
realistic interpretation of the implications for reading of today's complex
society. Their response to the question, "What may be the probable characteristics of the next quarter century?" should be as thought-provoking
as a reply given by David Sarnoff.

Personally, I am convinced that it will
be a period of drastic decisions. It will be
filled with events that, taken together, may
well determine the direction and even duration of man's destiny on this planet.
. . . The features of vital technical growths
can be discerned in the numberless em-
bryos in the womb of science. . . . But
these features will be matched by even
more significant developments in the political, social, and moral spheres. . . . This
means that the coming quarter-century
will be crowded with crises and climaxes.
. . . We will be confronted with great
challenges that call for dramatic commitments on our part. . . . But we do have a
choice: We can grovel in terror before the
mighty forces of science and historic adjustment. . . . Or we can face those forces
with courage, determination and calm intelligence.[5]

This penetrating view of Sarnoff's may
be adopted as the 1965–75 purpose and
goal of teachers of reading in each subject and at all levels. Productive innovations concerning reading materials
and teaching methods designed to develop courageous, intelligent, and responsible minds deserve higher priority than concerns such as when to begin to teach reading, rate of individual
reading, and amount of materials.

The most powerful instruments for
defending and advancing democracy,
nationally and internationally, are not
supersonic jets and intercontinental
ballistic missiles (ICBM) but imaginative, resourceful, and responsible
minds (IRRM). Education must develop in ever increasing numbers IRRM
that will be able to extract maximum
benefits from an expanding technology
and economy. Poorly informed and

[4] "American Directions: A Forecast," Harper's Magazine, CCXXIX (February, 1965), 42.

[5] "The Fabulous Future," Fortune, LI (January, 1955), 82.

narrowly prejudiced minds will be un-prepared to direct the forecasted changes toward human advancement. Poorly read and poorly informed citizens will become an increasing economic and political loss to our nation. Teachers of reading have the responsibility of developing minds, prepared and willing to work to eliminate costly unemployment, undemocratic racial discrimination, indefensible slums, and inhumane poverty. Reading programs must make the attempt to produce minds that will recognize the serious consequences that may result when greater concern is given to economic and technological advance than to the advancement of the personal and social welfare of every American.

During the next decade administrators and teachers have an obligation to recommend for approval by the board of education the textbooks and reference materials that will be read and studied. A critically important question for them to ask is, "How do the materials produce understanding, values, and goals related to contemporary and innovating societies such as the United States and her interdependent world-neighbors?" Teachers of all subjects, and especially teachers of reading, must face their moral responsibility to free young people from out-of-date ideas and information concerning America's crucial frontiers, the American Indians, the Eskimos, and peoples recently freed from colonial domination. Just as the idea of serving stale and poorly prepared food in the school cafeteria is repugnant, so should the practice of offering stale, non-realistic, and unreliable reading materials

in the classroom and library be repugnant. Reading and reference materials can best serve maturing minds in the last quarter of this century and the first two decades of the next century if they are focused on contemporary society and the inevitable tomorrows.

The United States Census Bureau forecasts that our nation's population will number about 220 million in 1975 and between 320 and 340 million in the first year of the next century. Equally significant is the prediction that by 1980 approximately 80 per cent of Americans will reside in about two hundred metropolitan centers, or megalopolises. Reading and reading materials will determine in large measure the educational, social, and self-renewing qualities of these gigantic centers. Whether people in the last quarter of this century will be privileged to benefit from the highest standards of personal, community, and megalopolis living will be strongly determined by the materials that are read in the schools during 1965–75. The challenge to reading is the development of minds competent and ready to build a new American heritage that will deserve the honor given to yesterday's American heritage. The explosion of new knowledge and the increasing size of America's megalopolises call for an explosion in appropriate reading materials. How can reading prepare minds to cope with the problem of creating approximately eighty thousand new jobs weekly for at least ten years so that young people may escape the degrading impact of joblessness? Only informed, socially and politically centered minds can create the conditions for an evolution of a new America.

How can the reading programs offered in today's schools help youth to understand the inescapable effects of an exploding world population? William P. Bundy has presented the idea that the decade 1965–75 may well decide whether most nations will choose the method of freedom and whether men can learn to live together constructively in a world of developing justice and order.[6] To extend a view expressed in the Preamble of the Charter of UNESCO — since wars begin in the minds of men, so too do the innovating purposes and actions toward the obtainable, if education (and reading materials) can produce informed, politically responsible, and courageous minds.

DEVELOPING UNDERSTANDING CITIZENS

Teachers of reading and reading materials have an opportunity to advance understanding among the people of free nations by assisting the children and youth to become globally exportable in an era of jet-propelled aviation. Engineers are directly responsible for the mechanical safety of each jet; education, teachers, and reading materials are responsible for developing culturally and morally exportable passengers. What is observed and understood by Americans when they deplane in another country depends in large measure on what they have read and talked about in home, school, church, and

6 "A Look Further Ahead," in *The Report of the President's Commission on National Goals* (Englewood Cliffs, N.J.: Prentice-Hall, Inc., 1960), pp. 361–72.

other educational institutions. Geographical distance is now measured in terms of number of flying hours. Each passenger's cultural exportability must be appraised in terms of his understanding of the geographical, cultural, educational, and political conditions that have arisen since World War II.

Teachers and reading materials have the opportunity to assist young people in learning to interact intelligently in an age of global radio and television communication. Satellites similar to "Early Bird" and "Telstar" will be launched in greater numbers and will improve in efficiency. Persons remaining at home will have the opportunity to visit with peoples and events around the world. They will interact daily with news about current happenings in various countries and will receive minute-by-minute word symbols and pictures of political and industrial events around the electronic-wave encircled world.

Satellite mass media bring words and pictures to the screen of each television set. The interpretation of what is seen and heard by each individual is conditioned by the conceptual results of previous education. A person whose reading has been limited is likely to interpret the televised words and pictures on a lower level than a person who is widely read and thinks critically. Reading materials and reading activities best serve young people and global communication when they encourage the development of a higher competency in psychological seeing, listening, and thinking. The need is imperative to remove from the curriculum materials and pictures which may retard a child's psychological ability to interact intelligently with others. Several faculty meetings to appraise the materials that should be removed from each classroom can be productive. Reading materials that are more up-to-date and more reliable about people in other countries, especially Latin America and Asia, should be obtained in greater quantities.

Faith in, understanding of, and intelligent readiness to apply in thought and action the foundational tenets of American democracy are other qualities that may be developed by reading programs in each school. Reading and discussion should assist a young adult's freedom of thought and action. The strength of democracy in a free society is dependent upon the readiness of each individual to understand and to accept his opportunity to participate in democratic decision-making in the community, the state, and the nation. The more affluent a society becomes, the greater the need for individuals who place a high premium on improvements in human and political affairs. An understanding of the basic requirements of a democratic society requires more than lip service. A complacent concern about raising the standards of applied democracy in housing, in race and religious relations, in employment, in education, and in voting can be as serious a threat to American democracy as the threat of communism or totalitarianism. Nonintentional assistance to various forms of totalitarianism may be given by individuals who are poorly informed, narrowly indoctrinated, and unreasonably self-centered.

Each classroom and each school should offer young people the opportunity to engage in a democratic laboratory. Reading and reading materials should contribute to a growth in understanding of the rights and responsibilities of the members of a society, of the ways to cope with issues without yielding to emotions and self-centered biases, of the proper democratic relation between a majority and minorities, and of the value to applied democracy of self-control, readiness to recognize ethical values, and a desire to help others. A people which desires to be free is obligated first to will to be free. Reading materials and discussions in the school can effectively prepare the millions of young people who will face the obligations and opportunities of adult citizenship in the years 1975–2010 by assisting each individual (1) to improve his understanding of democracy as a way of living, a philosophy of political decision-making, and a form of self-government; (2) to expand his understanding of contemporary conditions that are in conflict with the rights and responsibilities of a free people; and (3) to accept the obligation to participate in social and political discussion and decision-making to advance the standards and services of democracy in an era of unprecedented opportunities and complex problems.

Reading and reading materials now face the problem of a new dimension — the development of minds capable of using creatively and productively the time released by the reduction in the working day or a working week. Forecasts now predict a reduction in work hours for more and more persons as industry and the economy expand in the years ahead. How wisely these individuals will be prepared to use the non-working hours for personal enrichment, for more satisfying family life, for wholesome recreation, and for participation in various kinds of social services will be determined in part by understandings, appreciations, and values obtained during their years in school. The schools' opportunity is great to provide experiences, materials, and leadership that will motivate and assist young people to develop interests, appreciations, and skills in art, music, dramatics, handicrafts, literature, and physical recreation. These areas are as essential to a proper preparation for citizenship in the next five decades as are understandings and skills developed in the more formal subjects in the curriculum. Valuable learning may be experienced by children and youth when schools provide time and appropriate materials for self-exploring and self-directed activities in reading, in art, in music, in dramatics, in handicrafts, in literature, and in physical recreation.

Progress in this complex society will be conditioned by many factors: increased changes in technological production, solutions to problems arising from the explosion of new knowledge, continued growth of the nation's and the world's population, readiness of adults to participate in political and social decision-making, adequate funds (local, state and federal) for improvements in education at all levels, and innovating programs and materials in the schools designed to assist young people to understand and cope with contemporary society. Appropriate and adequate reading materials and programs can play a most productive role in motivating the millions of young people who will be attending school during the years 1965–75 to accept with courage, intelligence, and purpose the necessity of their participation in their society as mature and informed citizens.

CONCLUDING STATEMENT

I present two questions for appraisal: (1) Could teachers of all subjects and all administrative personnel become better prepared to serve children, youth, and society if for the next school year they reduced by 50 per cent the time usually given to typical school problems and used that time for reading and discussion of materials related to societal problems, issues, and opportunities? (2) What can be done by members of the teaching profession to increase the use and availability of materials that will upgrade the understanding of youth of their nation and interdependent world and will help them become creative, informed, and determined cobuilders of a better society? The responses to these questions will depend on the imagined tomorrows desired by each member of the teaching profession for youth, for schools, for reading programs, and for their own profession.

In conclusion, the following ideas expressed by Peter F. Drucker, may be of interest to teachers and especially to teachers of reading:

At some unmarked point during the last twenty years we imperceptibly moved out of the Modern Age and into a new and yet nameless era. . . . The old view of the world, the old tasks and the old center, calling themselves "modern" and "up-to-date" only a few years ago, just make no sense anymore. . . . An abundant and increasing supply of highly educated people has become the absolute prerequisite of social and economic development in our world.[7]

[7] *Landmarks of Tomorrow* (New York: Harper & Bros., 1959), pp. ix, 114.

CHAPTER II

MEETING CURRENT READING NEEDS

*

IN KINDERGARTEN THROUGH GRADE THREE

HENRIETTA KOMAREK

*

NO LONGER can it be said that the range of reading levels and abilities is narrower in the primary grades than in the higher elementary grades. Today a widened range of reading levels and abilities is present from the beginning of school experience and must be considered if we are adequately to meet reading needs. A kindergarten may contain levels of reading and reading readiness ranging from fluent, meaningful reading at third-grade level and above to a complete absence of reading-readiness experiences and language development. A kindergarten, whether in a low or high income area, may contain any or all of the following:

1. Children who can already read. Special provision must be made for these children if they are to be sufficiently challenged.

2. Children who have been exposed to newspaper reading programs by eager parents and who have developed negative attitudes. These children will have to be redirected and sometimes retaught.

3. Children who have had nursery-school reading-readiness experiences.

4. Children who have been read to and who have had many pleasant experiences with books at home.

5. Children who have had no readiness experiences in nursery school or at home.

6. Children who have superior language ability that has been developed in verbal homes where rich vocabularies are used and where meanings of words are discussed.

7. Children with poor language development who come from non-verbal homes where vocabularies are meager and substandard speech is the rule.

8. Children who have traveled or whose parents have traveled and have given the children the benefit of their widened horizons.

9. Children whose backgrounds have been expanded by intelligently controlled television viewing.

10. Children whose television viewing has produced fears and negative attitudes that have to be overcome.

11. Children who have never gone beyond their own neighborhoods.

12. Children in various stages of maturity — physical, mental, and emotional.

13. Children with special problems involving sight, hearing, speech, or physical handicaps.

14. Children who are emotionally disturbed or socially maladjusted.

Because of such widespread individual differences, we can no longer group children in kindergartens according to chronological age and adequately take care of the current reading needs of each child. All children in kindergarten and first grade, in a given school system, should not be put through the same readiness experiences and workbooks. If we require the child who can already read or who is ready to begin to learn to read to sit through these readiness experiences, we are not meeting his reading needs; we are also risking the chance of developing poor attitudes toward reading and school. We are likewise erring if we press a child into beginning reading when he has insufficient experiential background or maturity to be successful.

EARLY AND CONTINUAL DIAGNOSIS

If we are adequately to meet the reading needs of each child from the outset, we must have better programs of diagnosis that start earlier and continue throughout the primary grades. We need to know all we possibly can about a child, and we need to know it early. It is too late to commence diagnosis after children have been grouped according to chronological age in kindergarten in the fall. Diagnosis should start the previous spring when children are registered for kindergarten. A detailed questionnaire filled out by the parents can give the first indications of a child's readiness to learn to read. Individual conferences with parents at this time should be the second step in preparing for the proper placement of each child. If a parent indicates that a child can read, this child should be individually tested in an informal manner with graded reading materials. Selections from the preprimers and read-

ers of any good series can be used for both silent and oral reading. The child's comprehension should be checked with appropriate questioning. If the child seems sufficiently mature and advanced, the *Gray Oral Reading Test* (Bobbs-Merrill, 1963) may be used. If possible, the child should be given an individual intelligence test.

Tentative grouping should then be made on the basis of questionnaires, conferences, and chronological ages. No definite grouping should be made during the first few weeks of school. Careful observation of the children during group activities in this period should help teachers make further adjustments in the membership of the groups. The observation period will also enable teachers to place those children properly who did not register for kindergarten in the spring. Groups should be kept flexible so that adjustments can be made whenever necessary according to the changing needs of each child.

Parents should be thoroughly informed of the procedures used and the reading program followed. Much criticism from parents can be averted if they have sufficient understanding of how reading is being taught. This should be done through periodic group conferences as changes are made.

We can no longer justify the mass administration of readiness tests at the end of the kindergarten year or at the beginning of first grade. Children should be grouped so that those who have sufficient background and are able to advance more rapidly are tested earlier in the kindergarten year and started in a beginning reading program. Potential underachievers should also be identified at an earlier stage through teacher observation and a review of the tests that have been given. Too often the only part of the tests that are observed by the teacher are the final scores and ratings. More careful scrutiny may reveal problems that are hindering reading progress.

IMPORTANCE OF FLEXIBILITY

Much of the success of a reading program hinges on the personality and attitude of the teacher. An understanding teacher can succeed with poor materials, but a teacher who lacks understanding and feeling for children seldom succeeds even though she may have the best materials. Even the best teachers are guilty at one time or another of inflexibility in the teaching of reading. If one quality were to be isolated as most often standing in the path of meeting the present-day child's reading needs, it would be inflexibility.

The majority of schools use a basal reading program. In most instances these are good programs, with sequential development of not only word attack skills but also interpretative and critical reading skills. Too many teachers, however, try to fit the child to the program instead of adjusting the program to the child. In line with the general increase in academic learning, many of the new revised basic reading programs are greatly advanced. Vocabulary loads are increased at each of the primary levels. Skills formerly taught in second grade are now taught in first grade. Some primary teachers, consequently, have been complaining that the material is too difficult for slower

groups. What they are really saying is that they are still trying to fit all children into the same mold as in former years in spite of the fact that they know it cannot be done.

Some primary teachers still cannot seem to rid themselves of the idea that they have somehow failed if they have not succeeded in getting every child to read "up to grade level." Those children who do not fit into the mold must be given additional time with experience charts and simpler supplementary readers and materials. They should be taken only as fast as they can go successfully and comfortably, beginning at their particular stages of development.

If children can progress at a more rapid rate, on the other hand, teachers should be willing to make adjustments readily by shifting children from one group to another and by providing additional enriching materials at higher levels. To hold back a child whose reading has progressed beyond that of his group only for the purpose of finishing a workbook should be considered a cardinal sin.

With any basal reading program, a wide variety of trade books at reading levels that will challenge all readers within a classroom should be provided. Children should be encouraged to read widely along the lines of their interests from the time they start reading. Since today even children at the primary level have a closer contact with world affairs, primary teachers should be constantly searching for interesting books and supplementary materials that will stimulate the imagination. Opportunity should be given for individualized reading, and children should be allowed to select the books themselves. For this purpose, all schools must have adequately supplied libraries if they are to meet children's reading needs.

It is more important than ever that children be given a good basic foundation in word-attack skills so that they can independently attack new words like "sonic boom" and "guided missiles" that have become a part of our everyday speaking vocabularies. For some children this may mean the introduction of additional materials employing a phonic approach.

Our emphasis at the primary level can no longer be solely on the development of word-recognition skills. Even at the kindergarten level children must be stimulated to interpret and evaluate what they hear and read. This can only be done through stimulating questioning by the teacher and much discussion of reading materials. Primary children are no longer satisfied with just learning to identify words. We should not underestimate their ability to make judgments, to select main ideas, and to summarize what they read. Too often we are so intent on seeing that all children learn the short and long vowel sounds, for example, that we do not allow adequate time

for improving the thinking skills, which are just as important.

CONCLUDING STATEMENT

Because of the widespread attention given to beginning reading programs at the present time, it is important that primary teachers be well informed about all new methods and have clearly in mind their own goals. They should be ready to accept the changes in grouping and methods that will be necessary because of the wide range of individual differences now recognized at the primary level. They should know how to use diagnostic measures to reveal children's strengths and weaknesses in reading. They should be ready to make adjustments in their own plans when diagnoses reveal the necessity for regrouping to meet individual reading needs. They should be ready to use a variety of methods to meet the needs of individual children. If necessary they should be willing to attend reading workshops as well as in-service and university reading courses in order to be better prepared to teach the additional reading skills that may be required at their grade level. Much of the success of the expanded reading programs now being adopted at the primary level depends on the primary teachers and how well they adjust to the necessary changes.

IN GRADES FOUR THROUGH EIGHT

ROBERT EMANS

＊

IN HIS book *Nineteen Eighty-four* George Orwell predicts a future in which conformity among individuals abounds, freedom has vanished, and democracy exists no longer. Differences in points of view, creativity, thinking for one's self, and controversy are no longer allowed or even possible.

It is interesting to note that we are now, in 1965, about halfway between the time Orwell made his predictions and the time his predictions were to come true. Some of his predictions have so far failed to materialize. Whether his predictions have or have not come true, however, is not the real issue. The message of *Nineteen Eighty-four* is that there exist today the seeds which make the predictions of tomorrow possible. Orwell comments, for example:

> The invention of print, however, made it easier to manipulate public opinion, and the film and the radio carried the process further. . . .The possibility of enforcing not only complete obedience to the will of the State, but complete uniformity of opinion on all subjects, now existed for the first time.[1]

I am not suggesting we should necessarily believe that Orwell's predictions will come true. He has posed a challenge, however, not only for society, but also for our schools.

[1] (London: Secker & Warburg, 1949), p. 207.

Other writers have stated this challenge. Nila Banton Smith, past president of the International Reading Association, has said that "the most imminent *danger* of mass communication lies in its potency as a molder of public opinion."[2] And John Dewey wrote, "He who has learned as we call it to read without having learned to judge, discriminate, and choose has given hostages of dependence to powers beyond his control."[3]

The need for reading intelligently, thoughtfully, and critically is a need of our times. Much of what we know comes to us secondhand through print, radio, film, and television. Most of what we know, therefore, is sifted through someone else's eyes and mind, with someone else's beliefs and biases.

Learning to read critically, then, is a vital part of education. It must begin early so that it becomes interwoven with all aspects of intellectual and emotional life. The age of ten is an opportune time to enhance a child's critical skills. By that time he is apt to have an intimate and secure knowledge of his immediate world. His organized knowledge, extensive vocabulary, reading facility, and usually stable emotions make it possible to turn his

[2] *Reading Instruction for Today's Children* (Englewood Cliffs, N.J.: Prentice-Hall, Inc., 1963), p. 18.

[3] *Construction and Criticism* (New York: Columbia University Press, 1930), p. 17.

13

energies outward to question his knowledge and beliefs and to seek information.

The difficulty of learning to read critically is compounded by a tendency to accept anything in print as true. Most students do not learn to overcome this tendency. Mary C. Austin, in *The Harvard Report*, concludes that ". . . there is little evidence that schools are doing more than a minimal job in this vital instructional area." [4]

What is critical reading? Most writers agree that critical reading involves understanding and some type of reaction to what has been understood. Many writers indicate that an important requirement for critical reading is the possession of some sort of criteria on which to base judgments. In fact, William S. Gray defines critical reading as ". . . the evaluation of what is read in the light of sound criteria or standards." [5]

SOURCES OF CRITERIA

Where do we get the criteria to use in critical reading? They must come from at least three sources: the experiences of the reader, his beliefs, and his purposes.

Several writers stress the importance of experience in reading critically. This stress is warranted since most critical reading involves a comparison of what one thinks is real with what one reads. Since what we think is real is derived from our experiences, the teacher must help build experiences and select topics with which each individual has had experiences.

Much of what we read is not factual. Our evaluation of what we read must often depend on our beliefs. We must encourage the child to apply his beliefs while reading. We must listen to his views as well as express our own. Albert J. Harris makes this point when he says, "Children who spend years in school and at home learning to accept the authority of parents, teachers, and books in unquestioning fashion grow up to be receptive, easy victims of propaganda." [6]

A good reader compares his purposes with those of the writer. He also uses his purposes in selecting what to read and in deciding how thoroughly to read. Students need practice in answering such questions as: Does a specific piece of information answer a given question? Is the information important in light of the purpose? Students need opportunities to discuss what they have read both when they skim and when they read thoroughly as well as practice in these skills themselves. They need to compare their purpose for reading with the author's purpose for writing. They need to discuss the irony, sarcasm, and humor.

CRITICAL READING AND CONTROVERSIAL ISSUES

There are two general approaches in teaching critical reading, one direct and the other incidental. A direct approach was utilized by William Kott-

[4] *The First R: The Harvard Report on Reading in Elementary Schools* (New York: Macmillan Co., 1963), p. 41.

[5] "The Major Aspects of Reading," in *Sequential Development of Reading Abilities*, ed. Helen M. Robinson ("Supplementary Educational Monographs," No. 90 [Chicago: University of Chicago Press, 1960]), p. 17.

[6] *How To Increase Reading Ability* (New York: David McKay Co., Inc., 1961), p. 444.

meyer, who developed specific reading materials incorporating advertisements, editorials, and cartoons.[7] In an incidental approach, the various critical reading skills are not taught specifically, but the opportunity exists for them to be learned as students carry out some other purpose.[8] Little research has been done to establish the merits of either approach, although many authorities agree that there does need to be a planned program of instruction.

If controversial issues are used as a setting, the problem of the approach to the teaching of critical reading is lessened. The learning becomes more purposeful than in isolated practice exercises. And yet, it is also possible to stop from time to time to give specific help when individuals need it. Controversial issues are useful in teaching critical reading because they can be divided into three parts: information, argument, and conclusion. The criteria developed from experiences, beliefs, and purposes can, in turn, be applied to each of these three parts.

CRITERIA AND INFORMATION

When an issue has been identified, students need practice in finding pertinent information. They need to discuss the relative merits of the encyclo-

pedia, atlas, world almanac, and other resource materials in terms of their purposes. Once they have found a source of information, they need to determine whether it contains the information they desire. Students may be given practice in deciding whether materials answer specific questions by, for example, sorting newspaper clippings into specific topics or cutting up of a number of articles on various topics, shuffling the parts, and then sorting them back into the original articles.

Once the relevant information has been located, it is important to investigate the writer. Who is he? Does he write with authority? What is his background? What is his purpose in writing? Is his purpose similar to mine? A number of specific learning activities which can give additional practice are useful at this point. Authorities in a number of fields may be matched to various topics. Students may be asked to read about the background of an author and to state why he takes the stand he does. They may compare different authors' views, interests, and biases. They may locate and discuss the differences between editorial and news writing.

The next step is to examine the information presented. This may be accomplished through a comparison of the new information with past experiences, including those gathered through reading. Students may discuss which of a number of conflicting statements is most likely to be correct and be asked to explain the contradictions. Is the information accurate? Is it from observation, inference, or hearsay? Are enough facts presented? Is it up to

---

[7] *Handbook for Remedial Reading* (St. Louis: Webster Publishing Co., 1947), pp. 151–70.

[8] Charles B. Huelsman, Jr., "Promoting Growth in Ability To Interpret When Reading Critically: In Grades Seven to Ten," in *Promoting Growth toward Maturity in Interpreting What Is Read*, ed. William S. Gray ("Supplementary Educational Monographs," No. 74 [Chicago: University of Chicago Press, 1951]), pp. 149–53.

date? If not, is it important that it should be? Students can be given information from a number of different sources on the same topic, such as a news event, in order to compare their accuracy. Another useful activity is to discuss whether a headline in a newspaper is fact or opinion. Fact and opinion may also be studied in other types of reading. They can be asked to state whether a statement is false, true, or partly true, and if partly true, whether or not this makes the statement misleading. An interesting activity is to compare advertisements for the same commodity. Can all brands be the best?

CRITERIA AND ARGUMENT

The next step in dealing with a controversial issue is to analyze the argument. An important consideration is the choice of words. What emotional appeals are made? What words indicate anger, joy, relief? What words are used that will tend to make one want to accept something? Reject something? What words are used regarding patriotism — red-blooded, American, democracy, communists, fascists? What words are used regarding values — thrifty, clean, honest, time-saving, hard-working, achieving, progress, wasteful, dirty, lazy? What figures of speech are used? Are the words related to emotion or to reason? Does the writer consistently use the same meaning of a word throughout, or does he shift meaning? What use is made of the indefinite pronoun? Who are the "theys" to whom the writer refers? Students may be asked to restate what a writer has said using less emotional words.

They may also be given a chance to write their own propaganda in the form of advertisements for a play, a book, or an idea.

In addition to the choice of words, the steps of an argument should be studied. Students should have practice in identifying the main arguments and in telling whether or not the facts support the argument. Are there explanations or arguments, other than the one given, which could just as easily be made from the same information? Is the reasoning logical, or are there unfounded jumps? Are the relationships described by the writer really cause and effect? Are the relationships analogies? A possible activity for students is for them to discuss the sequence of an argument or a story to determine cause and effect. Predicting the ending of a story, or giving alternative endings, should help them develop an understanding of cause-and-effect relationships.

CRITERIA AND CONCLUSION

Finally, the conclusion should be examined. Is there enough evidence for such a conclusion, or should more facts be gathered? Is all the relevant evidence used, or is some ignored? What indirect means does the writer use to make the reader believe in his conclusions? Are these means acceptable?

Probably most important, a good critical reader asks, What are the consequences of accepting the writer's conclusions? Would accepting his conclusions support or undermine established beliefs? If the conclusions support established beliefs, it may be useful to review the argument to be sure students are not accepting the argument for that reason. If they contradict established beliefs, it may be valuable to re-examine those beliefs to determine if they need changing.

If students are going to become critical readers, they must develop sound criteria. These criteria come from their experiences, beliefs, and purposes. Controversial issues are a good, and perhaps crucial, setting for critical reading. Students should have practice in applying their criteria to the information, arguments, and conclusions found in various treatments of controversial issues.

In Orwell's *Nineteen Eighty-four* there seemed to be no hope — only despair. I doubt if there is any real cause for such despair. Our youngsters can, and will, become intelligent, creative, thinking individuals. Our job is to help them by alerting and educating them to be critical readers.

* * *

IN GRADES NINE THROUGH FOURTEEN

SISTER MARY BRIDE, O. P.

*

THE READING requirements of today's high-school and college students presuppose highly polished reading abilities progressing from the most basic level of comprehending fact or data through interpretation, or an active exercise of the mind upon the data, to evaluation — the self-conscious assessment by the reader of his reaction to a work. This progression does not occur in sequence. One cannot, or ordinarily does not, perform these operations in three separate readings. Nor can one decree that all works will be read in grade nine for data, in grade ten for interpretation, and in successive grades for evaluation. What makes the teaching of reading so enormously difficult is that all these operations are actually going on together and at different rates of speed and depth in accordance with the maturity and experience of the reader, which are not necessarily determined by his age and grade. The only control we can exert on the process is through the choice of works of a lesser or greater degree of complexity.

FACT OR DATA

A good practice in presenting any book to a class is to ask them first to survey it, that is, to read through rapidly just to get the broad outlines of the story. Unusual words or difficult passages should be marked for future attention but not delayed over any longer than is necessary to follow the thread of the action. This step might be begun in a silent reading period, during which the teacher should circulate, noting student rates of speed and study habits. The following period might then be devoted to a general discussion in which, through probing and prompting, the teacher elicits from the class the plot line, particulars of setting and characterization, and all information necessary to assure that every member of the class has a clear idea of the progression of events. Differences of opinion may arise, or the class's understanding of certain aspects or events may be somewhat hazy. This should provide an occasion for dividing the class into small discussion groups to reread together the debated passages and report their findings.

Another period or two might be devoted to familiarizing the class with the action and characters. The teacher's creativity and ingenuity will be taxed to keep these sessions alive and interesting. Comprehension of the basic facts is the most fundamental step in the whole process, because if the student has not been able to enter enjoyably into the experience presented in the story the subsequent exploration will be meaningless drudgery for him. If some students have seen a movie version of the story, a panel discussion or debate might be arranged on the advantages and disadvantages of the respective versions. A group of students who enjoy acting might present a dramatic reading of one of the exciting scenes, or the teacher might present an interpretive reading of a passage or play a recording of one. Having by these means become involved in the story, the students will now be ready to proceed to the second level — the interpretation of what the author is saying by means of the story, if, indeed, they decide he is saying anything else besides the story itself.

INTERPRETATION

To decide whether the author is saying anything besides the story itself, students should now be asked to make a close reading of the text, paying attention not only to *what* the author says but also to *how* he says it. If the teacher thinks it necessary — regardless of grade level and depending on class readiness — the class should spend one or more periods on this type of reading. The search for hidden meanings proceeds beyond the grammatical and logical relations into the realm of rhetoric — that level of writing in which we are concerned with the author's manipulation of language to influence the reader, not directly through attention to what he asserts, but indirectly by what he implies or suggests.

The first elements of rhetoric are "voice and address." To discover them, we ask: Who is telling this story? To whom is he telling it? What is his attitude toward the events in the story and toward his audience? The author's attitude sets up the tone of the story and is immensely important in dictating our response. Voice and address are the most important of all the rhetorical elements because they give the key to everything else that happens.

In Joseph Conrad's *Secret Sharer* (in *Great English Short Stories*, ed. Christopher Isherwood; Dell, 1957), for instance, a ship's captain tells a story about his experiences. He believes, and makes us believe, that he is a kindhearted conscientious man who is devoted heart and soul to his profession and to his fellow man. But the facts tell us that he is new and insecure in his job. He got his post by a means he does not want too closely scrutinized. He is suspicious and ill at ease with his crew — he considers the first mate a fool, and he feels that the second mate. is out to make trouble for him. The rest of the company are strangers to him. When he casually announces that he will undertake the first watch, the author is careful to show us, by the reaction of the crew, that this is unheard of among seamen. He is almost criminally careless in leaving a rope ladder hanging over the ship's side overnight in a strange port.

What all this adds up to is that, as the captain tells us one story — his view of the events — the author is telling us another. And if we really want to know what the author is saying in this book, we shall need to pay careful attention to both.

At this point the teacher may hope the class has scented an exciting detective chase, a mystery thriller all its own. The teacher has presented them with enough clues to send them in full pursuit through the book, checking every instance where the captain's account of events is subtly contradicted by the author's presentation of facts. Other rhetorical devices, such as inverted parallels, irony, symbols, climax, suspense, antithesis, contrast, and the common figures of speech, rest on and spring from this initial duality.

EVALUATION

Having made reasonably sure that the students know what the author is saying, while admitting that it is prob-

ably never possible to grasp the full content of any work of art, the teacher is justified in proceeding to the final stage in the act of reading. Evaluation is the reader's critical examination of the author's performance. We may question, for instance, whether he used the proper means for saying what he had to say — was the novel the best medium for presenting the problem of insecurity? Granted the means, has he made the best use of them; that is, has he written a good novel? And finally, we may ask if he has treated his materials with integrity; is his work morally acceptable?

The answer to the first question will depend, of course, on what the person making the judgment thinks a novel should do. This is where the subjective element known as taste enters in. If a person thinks that a novel should provide entertainment without bringing up vexing problems of human psychology, he will answer this question in the negative — and *de gustibus non est disputandum*. The second question has already been answered by our thorough explication; anyone who knows the norms of good writing will have to admit that this novel is well written.

The answer to the third question raises the most vexing problems and could form the basis for many such disquisitions as the following. It is a question not of the man's art but of his prudence. Since a writer presumably seeks readers, and since anyone who undertakes to share his innermost thoughts with another is to that extent a teacher, we have a right to challenge an author's interpretation of life. We may ask what assumptions he makes about human nature in his work and whether these assumptions are in objective agreement with what man throughout his long pilgrimage in time has more or less consistently thought and written about himself. If they are not, we have a right to ask the writer to prove his assumptions. If his assumptions are in agreement, we may ask whether the incidents he presents and the language in which he presents them are warranted by his purpose.

In this delicate operation the reader, too, must exercise integrity. And this is a very essential part of our teaching, particularly in modern times when external censorship, whether by parent, church, or state, is rendered practically impossible by the multiplicity of books and the ease with which they may be procured. No agency can pretend to be able to pass on all that is written today. Therefore, parents and teachers must accept the responsibility for developing principles of self-cen-

sorship in young people. Students must be taught how to distinguish between serious moral purpose and pornographic exhibitionism. In much modern literature, the dividing line is very thin.

We can also help students by pointing out that being shocked is not necessarily harmful. Shock in confronting human depravity is a healthy reaction; it is a proof that one sees the evil and undesirability of a particular form of activity. The time for concern is when one is not shocked, when one begins to accept depravity, not as a sad indication of man's natural proneness to evil, but as something to be condoned, even permitted. A student who sees Holden Caulfield's language and meanderings in *The Catcher in the Rye* (Little, Brown, and Co., 1951) as a proof of Holden's immaturity, bad upbringing, and disturbed emotional state and who derives from this experience a determination to profit by Holden's mistakes has been educated; he has, in Aristotle's words, experienced a catharsis.

* * *

IN ADULT LITERACY PROGRAMS

DANIEL E. LUPTON

*

THE REASON the schools so largely fail to serve as a means of social mobility for the undereducated adult from the culture of poverty to the culture of abundance is not any cultural barrier to learning but, rather, a very

real lack of opportunity outside school. This lack of opportunity and the potential failure of the "War on Poverty" are intimately related. The great enemy of the efforts of the poverty warriors is the "apathy of the poor." This is a well-known but little understood phenomenon. The poor have long memories. They remember the slum-clearance and neighborhood-redevelopment programs which cleared them out of their homes and placed them in other already overcrowded neighborhoods. They are familiar with the dehumanizing aspects of low-cost housing, which is often administered so that efforts to acquire middle-class values are penalized by forcing the more achievement-motivated occupants to move as their incomes rise above a certain level. They have experienced the "War on the Poor" for many years and under many guises. Understandably, they may be tempted to look the most recent gift horse in the mouth. This may be particularly the case since the representation of the poor in the planning of that program is so often conspicuous by its absence.

The undereducated adult may also be reluctant to participate in basic-education or job-training programs because of the psychic exhaustion engendered by the stresses of coping with daily life. Years ago, Eli Ginzberg pointed up the tremendous effort demanded of the undereducated to maintain themselves, even marginally, in a literate society.[1] Frustration and hostility are the inevitable results as society closes door after door in their faces. These feelings may be expressed dramatically in the form of revolution or riot or, more commonly, in the skepticism and apathy which have become characteristic of the "other Americans."

The hostility of the undereducated American is also directed inward. Strive as he may to reject the society that rejects him, he unconsciously accepts the very criteria by which he was found wanting and was rejected. In contemporary life there are many frustrations we all face which lead to self-devaluation, but in the case of the undereducated adult these stresses are greatly intensified. The low self-esteem of these adults is akin to that of many physically handicapped individuals, who are only barely able to escape seeing themselves as other than monsters unworthy of love and totally inadequate to the demands of life.

The undereducated American is thus the victim of his frustration. And in the case of the illiterate who had the opportunity to learn the basic skills in childhood and was unable to do so, this frustration is compounded. A survey of the previous educational opportunities of a group of individuals enrolled in basic-education classes in a large metropolitan program confirms this fact.[2] This survey also indicates that the adult who has been denied the opportunity to learn in childhood is not now troubled by this dual frustration — the original failure to learn and the consequent failure to succeed in society. It seems probable that those with the latter type of experience are the ones who pick up the skills of literacy with such astonishing rapidity and zeal — often in spite of the mate-

1 Eli Ginzberg and Douglas W. Bray, *The Uneducated* (New York: Columbia University Press, 1953), p. 172.

2 This survey was conducted by the writer among literacy teachers and program administrators during two in-service training programs conducted at the Center for Continuing Education, The University of Chicago, fall and winter, 1964.

rials and teaching methods. Their frustration and hostility is proportionately less and hence exercises a lesser inhibiting force on their ability to learn.

At present we are making a concerted effort as a nation to open up opportunities for employment, further training, and education for all our citizens who are the victims of the culture of poverty. This effort will be successful only in so far as it is able to mitigate their deep hostilities and thereby penetrate their apathy and skepticism.

MEETING ADULT NEEDS

Nothing succeeds like success. If we can introduce into our programs an air of accomplishment, a sense of achievement, cracks may begin to appear in the thick walls of apathy which surround the undereducated. The first experiences of the undereducated adult in a basic-education class are crucial. He will judge the program by the results, not merely by his own sense of achievement; that is, even before he himself experiences success, he can participate vicariously in the successes of others like himself.

Society is attempting a breakthrough, and the undereducated adult is even now being cajoled, coerced, enticed, and bribed into programs of basic education and job training. It is most important that these programs show results as quickly as possible. Obviously, then, the "hard cases" cannot be tackled first — not because they are of less importance, but because the success achieved with the more readily educable and employable adults can be used to instil hope in the others.

A basic-education program that comes to terms with the hostilities of the undereducated adult and with the anxieties of its middle-class instructional staff has gone a long way toward meeting the needs of the illiterate adult in a realistic and effective manner. This type of program should be given top priority because of its intimate connection with the adult students' readiness to learn. Such a priority will indicate that a total approach to the development of psychological readiness is at least as important as a concern for suitable materials and methods.

In the past, services for the poor have been provided by individuals and agencies drawn from the mainstream of our society, the non-poor. Planning has tended to be based on the very rejection which the poor have experienced at the hands of society. Whether educational or social, these programs tend to regard the poor as inferior and incompetent. There is a manifest reluctance to trust the poor to know what their problems are or how to remedy them. All decision-making is reserved for the professionals. It is evident that programs of basic education embodying such an approach cannot win the wide-scale acceptance among undereducated adults that is crucial to the success of the whole effort of the "War on Poverty." Far from recognizing and coming to terms with hostility, such programs actually increase them by the implied rejection built into the programs themselves.

This implied rejection, which the poor are quick to sense, is further compounded by the disillusionment of the staff, whose help is rejected or ignored by their potential or actual clients. A basic-education program that faces the fact that those it wishes to serve have been the objects of society's rejection for some time and are as a consequence slow to trust that society when it attempts to be the agent of social uplift will have taken a giant step toward effecting a change, toward educating its potential students, before even one class has been held.

How can we face the facts of rejection and hostility? We can recognize that these feelings are often a justifiable and normal reaction to an extremely difficult situation. An opportunity to express and desensitize these hostile feelings through individual and group discussions is imperative. Further, if the staff can be helped to see these feelings, not as a threat to themselves, but as the main block to learning among undereducated adults, their basic-education program will have a much greater chance of success.

CONCLUDING STATEMENT

To be effective, basic-education programs among the undereducated adults of America must be based on certain essential perceptions. These perceptions, which are the only realistic foundation for attempts to confront the hostilities and skepticism of the poor, may be stated as follows: (1) The undereducated poor do indeed have certain competencies. (2) The poor must be reached in ways that are acceptable to them. (3) The problems to work on are the ones which the poor and undereducated themselves perceive as problems. (4) An effective approach will be one which relates the instructional programs to meaningful activity.

This paper has attempted to recommend ways in which basic-education programs can come to terms with the hostilities of the undereducated poor. Vast sums of money are being spent and will continue to be spent over the next few years to alleviate their situation. Much of that money will go into the production of teaching materials and aids of many kinds; large expenditures will also be made for specialized teacher preparation. All of these are necessary beyond doubt. But the most important factor, the one which must have top priority and pervade all other concerns, is a recognition of the psychological state of the undereducated adult. Only if this factor is recognized and used as a basis can other efforts bear fruit and the "War on Poverty" end in the victory of a self-renewing society.

IN CORRECTIVE AND REMEDIAL CLASSES

CARITA A. CHAPMAN

*

WHICHEVER contemporary area in society may be identified as most significant — automation, education, integration, poverty, or space technology — there are certain basic underlying needs of youth that we must attempt to satisfy. Our children must be prepared for, first, maximum personal adjustment and, second, social participation with "social" understood to mean the interdependence of persons in the formulation of values, attitudes, and behavior that will contribute to a peaceful society. To be more specific, personal development comprises

1. an acceptable self-concept, or self-esteem;
2. social recognition among one's peers;
3. academic competence;
4. an understanding of our natural world;
5. an appreciation of the aesthetic features of life; and
6. a judicious use of leisure time.

Social participation demands

1. personal adjustment;
2. ability to work effectively in group situations;
3. an understanding of issues, people, and ideas;
4. respect for the rights of those of diverse national, racial, and religious origins; and
5. international awareness.

Neither the needs of society nor the reading needs of youth exist in a vacuum; they interact with each other. That is, reading is not an end in itself but is one means of realizing individual and group goals; and vice versa, individual and group goals provide the subject matter or purposes for reading.

What are the fundamental reading skills that we must help a student master in order to become an efficient and independent reader? The four most important are word perception, comprehension, critical reaction, and creative reading. The needs of disabled readers are essentially the same as those of students in regular classes, differing only in degree. For both levels of readers, the depth and clarity of their insights into their social world will depend in large measure on how efficiently they can handle the tools of reading and how effectively we guide them toward an understanding of the current social panorama.

METHODS FOR MEETING CURRENT READING NEEDS

The first significant method that utilizes the interrelationship between reading needs and societal needs commences with an individual diagnosis of a student's reading strengths and weaknesses as determined by formal and informal tests. On the basis of the individual's present reading level, long range instructional goals may be set which take into consideration reading needs and the group needs of society. The long-range goals may be implemented by daily evaluations and by assignments of short-term achievable goals. The latter provide immediate success, which the disabled reader desperately needs to build confidence in his ability to handle the tools of reading effectively. Informal diagnosis should be continuous and methods and materials constantly adjusted in accordance with evaluations. If the student is learning, he is changing, and so we, too, must change our methods and materials to meet his changing needs.

The teacher may learn indirectly how the school and the larger society impinge on the student and affect his views of his needs and interests by (1) asking periodic interest-inventory questions such as "After school I like ———" or "If I could have three wishes, I would wish for ———" and (2) maintaining an atmosphere of warmth, acceptance, and security in which the learner will be able to volunteer his felt needs. Knowing these felt needs will help in setting meaningful goals with which the student can identify. Involving the student in discussions of the results of a diagnosis and in the setting of goals helps him identify with and feel interested in our mutual job — to help him read better.

The second method of meeting current reading needs is to have accessible many varied materials appropriate to the ability levels and the specific needs of the students. Today the market is saturated with well-constructed materials, and our task is one of selection — selection of materials appropri-

ate to the goals established for our particular learners. Selection should also be understood to mean the elimination of compulsive plodding from cover to cover in any workbook; those sections not useful to the development of the particular needs of students should be skipped. This is not to say that practice in the basic reading skills sufficient to develop independence should be eliminated but to advocate a judicious and well-planned program based on goals rather than the pattern of the materials.

Remembering that the most important need of readers in remedial classes is to improve their reading to the level where they can effectively read classroom assignments, we must give them help in developing reading skills in the various content areas. Two series are particularly helpful, *Be a Better Reader* (Prentice-Hall) and *New Practice Readers* (Webster) . A practice worthy of consideration is the use of science and social studies textbooks that are not known to the student to provide practical application of reading skills simultaneously with information about our natural world and social heritage.

Reading materials that demonstrate the practical implications of reading are more necessary for the retarded reader, and we should not rely on books designed especially to develop reading skills. Such supplementary materials as the food and sports sections from local newspapers, job-opportunity announcements, and words of popular songs can be used with discrimination to provide practice in reading different kinds of materials for different purposes. Reading the daily newspaper may be a formidable venture for disabled readers who read below the sixth-grade level, but interest in aspects of the social scene can be stimulated by weekly current events papers written for their particular level, such as *News for You* (Syracuse University) . With such materials and those specifically constructed by the teacher, not only can word attack and comprehension skills be developed but they can become a mainspring toward personal and social understanding.

Workbook materials have been stressed in remedial classes as the primary tool for improving specific reading skills. However, recreational reading on varied subjects is also needed. A clinic or classroom should maintain a small library to whet the appetite of reluctant readers with easily accessible books at their reading levels. As a guide to students, the books in this library may have index cards with several questions about the story inserted in the charge-card pockets. These questions can also give students tools with which to evaluate future independent reading. The teacher's knowledge of books and annotated book lists may serve as guides in recommending special titles to youngsters to satisfy present needs and interests and to awaken new interests.

Another way to meet current reading needs is by developing backgrounds of experience for particular concepts, events, or places that are to be introduced in future reading materials. Although the maturity level of many retarded readers exceeds their present reading achievement level, it cannot be assumed that they have adequate experiential backgrounds for the materials. We must foresee areas that will require student preparation. A valuable aid is a picture file containing illustrations of unfamiliar concepts. Access to such a picture file can help students learn vicariously more about the world in which they live.

Students' backgrounds may also be extended by exhibitions of natural objects pertinent to materials they are likely to read or may be motivated to investigate. Such items as a dried starfish or a live cactus with new shoots stimulate the inquisitiveness of students, and they can then be guided to books on their reading levels giving factual information. This process also works in reverse — when reading about sea and plant life, for example, real objects enhance students' understanding and extend their interest.

Audiovisual media may be used to establish a "listening and viewing corner" where several individuals can work independently. Phonic and listening skills can be developed, and language and speech patterns can be improved by using a tape recorder with several earphones or a filmstrip projector adapted for short-range viewing. The possibilities for experimentation in this area are many, and it is frequently necessary for teachers to prepare appropriate materials to meet the particular needs of particular students.

Capitalizing on every opportunity at the time it presents itself to develop concepts, widen horizons, correct misunderstandings, and direct students to books or other materials is the teacher's most important task in making a start toward developing socially acceptable concepts. Such an opportunity arose in a reading clinic when a small group was reading in a basal reader the story of Jeremiah and a little black lamb that had been rejected by its own white mother and by Jeremiah's grandmother. Jeremiah befriended the lamb and accompanied it through its escapades. The story ends with the mischievous black lamb winning two prizes at the country fair, making everyone proud of it. At the completion of the story, a little Negro girl inquired, "Why didn't they like the lamb just 'cause he's black?" A discussion developed among members of the group concerning possible reasons why the black lamb was disliked, which evolved into a discussion of the fallacy of accepting or rejecting people simply on the basis of color and without understanding that anyone can possess good qualities. Here the social problem of racial prejudice was discussed as a natural result of reading and discussion. While using stories from the basal reader to develop word-attack and comprehension skills, teachers can simultaneously develop critical reading skills either by provocative questioning or by directing the questions raised by the students.

The art of questioning is one of the oldest and most effective means not only for developing better reading skills but also for motivating students' personal and social adjustment. Questioning about work or recreational reading should elicit more than recall or literal-meaning responses; attention should be extended from questions about "who," "where," "when," and "what" to well-formulated "whys" and "hows." Through directioned questioning, students can be helped to develop reasoned verbal formulations as a basis for their thinking instead of being allowed to stop at "I think" or "I like this." It is imperative in today's society that individuals be taught to think about what they read and to raise questions about its value. A free atmosphere for discussion is vital in developing critical readers. Current issues may be used as the subject matter for formulating criteria for rational evaluation. As students read about and discuss the issues of the day, they may be guided to additional books to answer their questions and extend their knowledge.

To meet society's needs for better intergroup understanding, retarded readers with like needs should be placed in small instructional groups to promote appreciation of or respect for the attitudes of others. This type of grouping aids oral communication skills and provides social interaction, since the members of each group can be encouraged to interchange ideas, experiences, and insights. It also provides an opportunity to integrate basic reading instruction with instruction focused on the common needs or problems of the group.

A PRACTICAL EXAMPLE

Controversial issues such as race relations require rational understanding, and the difficulty of maintaining objectivity precludes them as specific subjects in remedial teaching. Therefore, social awareness and respect for others can only be taught indirectly in a more neutral setting such as the United Nations — the diversity yet similarity of its member nations, its origin, its purpose, and its organizational operation. A prerequisite to the successful direction of any unit, and especially this one, is that the teacher maintain objective attitudes for the students to emulate. Other requirements of such a unit are the following: (1) It should be devoted primarily to improving the basic reading skills of the retarded readers and secondarily to developing group needs such as social awareness; (2) it should provide a cursory treatment of the United Nations; (3) it should utilize reading materials at the achievement and interest levels of the particular group, which may require special materials constructed by the teachers; (4) it should make use of supplementary audiovisual materials to enrich the students' backgrounds; (5) it should provide for class discussions; and (6) it should last a maximum of four weeks to maintain high interest. Thus, the ingenious teacher of retarded readers, attuned to the current social needs of a complex society, may interrelate the teaching of basic reading skills with the teaching of socially significant problems as a means of improving both.

CHAPTER III

RECENT DEVELOPMENTS IN INSTRUCTIONAL MATERIALS

*

ELIZABETH GRAF

*

WE ARE now in the midst of a great renaissance of instructional materials in the field of reading. At few times in our history have there been so many new ideas, such a rush to release certain new and revised types of materials, and such a desire on the part of publishers to satisfy the real and changing needs of the schools. This is a frustrating time to discuss recent developments, for what is up-to-date one day may not be the newest thing on the market the next.

During the spring, a large urban school district sent letters to one hundred twenty-five publishers of instructional reading materials requesting them to submit their publications for examination and possible adoption. Instructions to the companies were the following: (1) Instructional materials would be used to conduct a basal reading program. (2) Supplementary materials would be selected to complement and enrich the adopted basal series. (3) Only materials which were representative of many cultures and ethnic groups in American life would be considered.

Forty-four companies responded, this number being limited by the third criterion that only multiethnic materi-

als would be considered. Mountains of materials were received. This response reflected what had been evident for many months. The publication of reading materials is in a state of transition. Many new ideas are being advanced. Educators are issuing new demands. Materials are being published which seek to carry out these new ideas and new demands. We can anticipate a future date when even more exciting materials will be forthcoming. However, not everything is changed, and although there are points of difference, there is general agreement in many basic beliefs.

AREAS OF GENERAL AGREEMENT

Publishers are in agreement about some fundamentals concerning children and their development. Recently I heard a reading consultant from a well-known company talk of the philosophy of their basal series. Her presentation of twenty minutes could just as well have been made by representatives from other companies. She spoke, for example, about the importance of adhering to what is known about children at various ages and how they grow, about the importance of providing for individual differences, and about the necessity for a sequential and continuous program to develop in children the ability to read as well as the desire to turn to reading for information and pleasure. All companies emphasize skills programs, although they use a variety of methods to lead a child toward independence in attacking new words. Most programs also go beyond the goal of word recognition. Comprehension, interpretation, thinking, critical reading are almost universally emphasized as objectives in nationally known reading programs.

If you look at the title pages of the various reading series, you will see that well-known reading authorities are actively engaged as authors or consultants for the large publishing houses. With the consolidation of smaller companies, more human resources have become available to those who publish reading materials. A veritable flood of additional materials has been forthcoming. Supplementary materials representing the most famous authors of children's literature are now within budget limitations because of new paperback editions.

Publishers are cognizant of the findings of psychologists concerning the interests of boys and girls at various grade levels. They give attention to reading-readiness programs. Teachers' guides and manuals are fast becoming a more important consideration in any series adoption, for these are recognized as important factors in the development of improved teaching methods in the field of reading.

AREAS OF DIFFERENCE

There are, however, significant differences which mark series as unique and probably point the way to the future and to what we may expect from all companies. Some changes in basal programs continue to affect the kinds of materials being released: their content, their vocabulary, and their illustrations. The movement really started some years ago when the Great Cities School Improvement Program was initiated. Statistics coming from this group indicated that a high percentage of the children in our country live in the combined urban and suburban areas. Studies showed that this percentage would grow. A subcommittee of the great cities group recommended that some changes be made in both written content and illustrations of reading materials to reflect the contributions of the various ethnic groups making up the American population. This subcommittee met with publishers and discussed what changes should be made.

Gradually, and the movement is still going on, companies have included stories and illustrations which indicate a compliance with these requests in basal series as well as some supplementary materials. The content is more urban-oriented. In the older editions mother, father, and children live in a fine suburban single-dwelling community. The children are always well dressed. They are good, well-behaved boys and girls who live in the comfort of a well-protected environment. They have the happy experiences which the middle-class family provides for its children. One class of people is portrayed — middle-class white. The urban child who lives in a multiple-dwelling building in the center of a city is not able to relate to this family or its way of life. Today more and more companies are basing their stories on experiences which constitute the life of the urban child.

Some publishers include nothing else in their books. Their stories tell only of the experiences of the city child who plays on the street, who revels in the coolness of the water from the fire hydrant on a hot summer day. His home is one of a row of houses, and his grandparents (if involved in the story) live in an apartment house. Some publishers have avoided picturing a home with mother, father, brothers, and sisters. They know that many urban children are living in broken homes and on relief, and they have therefore sought to avoid a traditional middle-class family unit. They solve the problem by limiting the stories to activities on the playground and the street.

At the beginning of this movement, the Negro was the only ethnic minority represented. Gradually educators and publishers are recognizing the need to include other ethnic groups. America has many cultures, and many races have made contributions to her greatness. It is accepted more and more that they should all be depicted in our readers.

This multiethnic influence is also evident in the illustrations. In the best of them, the children and adults are real people, not illustrations from a previous edition with merely a change of skin color. They are not stereotypes or caricatures of the race to which they belong. One company avoids this problem by using real-life children as models. Photographs are taken of attractive youngsters seen on the street or in the stores, and line drawings are made from these pictures.

As we talk about proportions of urban and suburban, we must look at the total city realistically. Some people, quite mistakenly, would limit urban life to the experiences of a child in the inner city, which in many cases is hot, dirty, and squalid. Although it is true that many of the reading series are too suburban-centered, there is also a real danger that some companies today are erring in the other direction. Cities of today contain lovely residential sections which meld into the finest of suburbia. Suburbia itself is acquiring certain characteristics of the city. Balance is important. A child should know both types of living through the story and illustrative content of his reading materials.

In addition, we must not limit the experiences of the slum child to life as he knows it. We will not be giving him what will benefit him most or what his family may want for him. The American way of life encourages adults to expect for their children something more than they have had themselves. At the present time some companies are publishing two editions of their materials: a regular edition depicting a modified form of life, as in the past, and a multiethnic edition. Probably the best edition contains a balance of both.

Publishers are now giving more consideration to producing materials which present a sequential, continuous program for all learners in the same classroom. One company has introduced such a series for the slow learner who is over-aged for his instructional level and who therefore needs materials which are low in reading level but high in interest. This same material works well for the retarded reader of average intelligence who may not be able to use the regular series. This same company has recently released a reader especially designed for the above average child who is reading above his grade level. Eventually, both series, for slow and retarded readers and for above average readers, will extend from grade one through grade six.

INSTRUCTIONAL READING MATERIALS

Acceptance of the fact that not all children entering first grade are ready to read has resulted in publication of an abundance of materials designed for reading readiness. In districts which believe that kindergarten is the place for more formal activity, these reading-readiness materials are being presented to kindergarten children.

A real revolution in instructional reading materials is now going on in the first grade. There are many approaches; some are new, and some are renewals of interest in methods which had been used before. A few companies are cautiously experimenting with the Initial Teaching Alphabet (ITA). One company is transliterating its entire first-grade program. A publisher of paperbacks will have at least thirty titles ready this fall. Both English and American companies have published books written in ITA. One American group has materials ready for purchase through the third-grade level of difficulty. The approach deserves our attention, and research studies now being conducted should be followed closely by educators to see whether the promised results are forthcoming.

Words in Color (Encyclopedia Britannica) is another new and different beginning-reading instructional program. The student is encouraged to associate a definite sound with the color in which a letter appears. When he is able to make the association of sound and letter and no longer needs the association of color and sound, he makes the transfer to traditional printing and writing.

Linguistic principles are applied in many of the recently published basal reading series. One company, in fact, is now publishing a pure linguistic series. The names of the letters of the alphabet are taught until students know them from *A* to *Z*. Only then do they learn to read words or sentences. No experience charts are created; no written forms are presented except the letters of the alphabet. When students finally read, their books contain no pictures, for the pure linguistic approach to reading instruction holds that pictures interfere with the acquisition of basic knowledge.

One company is sponsoring a reading program based on trade books that may be used throughout the year as a student increases his ability to read. Each book in the program's kit is different. Special bulletins, which give suggestions to the teacher for individualizing sequential, practical, and effective reading programs, are also a part of the kit. Acceptance of this material has encouraged the author and his company to offer a more advanced kit. A third, which will be released soon, will be multiethnic in content, both text and illustrations. Other kits with individual titles will be flooding the market. Most of them will be produced to supplement the regular reading program published by the company.

Most teachers are quite familiar with reading laboratories, which have been on the market for some time. These are based on the well-established finding that individuals learn the various reading skills at different rates. Students are stimulated and motivated by this type of program because they can, through the testing and recording process, know their scores immediately and compare them with earlier scores. These laboratories have been particularly effective for retarded readers, although advanced readers are also challenged by them. High-school kits are available, which can be used to remedy deficiencies of individual students, to increase reading speed, and to help students learn to adjust reading skills to different purposes.

One of the most promising and certainly one of the most inexpensive movements today is the booming publication of paperbacks. It is important at all levels, and its importance is growing rapidly. For many years paperbacks of classics and modern authors have made these works available to millions of students at low cost. English courses at the high-school level have been enriched through the use of paperbacks. The intermediate grades have more recently been the benefactors of a host of titles. High-school students have been building up libraries of these books for some time through subscriptions to book clubs. Now even younger children can have similar advantages. They, too, have their book clubs and receive paperbacks monthly.

Library services are mushrooming throughout the country. Elementary schools now count school libraries as an essential part of their instructional facilities in addition to the room libraries which have been accepted as necessary for many years. Library books in quantities undreamed of a few years ago are now being supplied. Of course, the National Defense Education Act has had a role in this increase, especially in the fields of science, mathematics, and foreign languages. The extension of NDEA funds to the fields of English, reading, and social studies will similarly enrich these areas of study. When the Elementary and Secondary Education Act becomes operative, increases can be expected at all grade levels.

INSTRUCTIONAL MATERIALS OTHER THAN BOOKS

Films and filmstrips are constantly being improved, as are the instruments needed to use them. Tape recorders are being used with increasing effect. Tapes are being used by teachers for independent work by individuals and small groups. For example, a teacher may cut a tape giving instructions to students, who record their answers on a check list which has been provided for this purpose.

The crowning glory of these years is the overhead projector. This aid has been used very effectively for the development of reading skills. It has the advantage of focusing the attention of all the students in a class on the same problem and of assuring the teacher that everyone is looking at the right exercise. The flexibility of the overhead projector recommends it for many different purposes. Transparencies can be made. Overlays can be introduced to show changes in words and to demonstrate certain procedures. A clear sheet can be used by the teacher to prepare his own projections. Other aids are being used at the secondary level. The Controlled Reader, the Perceptoscope, the Rateometer, and the Reading Accelerator are examples of devices which pace the reader and push him along to improved habits and more effective use of skills.

Today the great emphasis on prevention of reading difficulties has resulted in the publication of materials specifically designed for the retarded reader. There is little excuse today for a school district's not supplying teachers with materials at all instructional levels. The abundance of materials should encourage teachers to let each child progress at this own pace. Tests are available to them to discover the specific weakness of each individual, and correction can be made before the case becomes chronic and much more difficult to remedy. Because we are dealing with human beings, subject to human frailties and the vicissitudes of everyday living, remedial cases will always be with us. Remedial teachers will find that there are effective materials from many sources.

WISE SELECTION OF
INSTRUCTIONAL MATERIALS

Teachers, administrators, and supervisors who must make a wise selection from the floods of materials are confused by the very abundance. There is more need than ever to use judgment, careful evaluation, and an analysis of the needs and objectives of their own school systems. Nothing is good for a school system unless it satisfies instructional needs. The following questions should be asked. What kind of a reading program do you have? Weaknesses? Strengths? What are the objectives of your reading program? What kind of school population do you have? What will your teachers be able to use?

An excellent way to make this kind of survey is to appoint an overview committee. Teachers from all elementary and secondary grades should be represented. From the resulting reports, a complete picture of the school reading program will evolve, demonstrating both weaknesses and strengths. Recommendations should be a part of the responsibility of this committee.

The next big step is to make a check list of criteria before beginning an examination of the materials. The following suggestions may be of some help.

1. *Philosophy and objectives.* Certain questions concerning philosophy and objectives must be answered. Have the authors built their reading program on a sound philosophy of reading instruction? Is this philosophy evident in the basal reading program? Are all steps in the program carefully presented and consistently developed? Is the series or the book consistent with

our present knowledge of child growth and development? Is it consistent with our present knowledge from research? Is vocabulary control evident?

2. *Content.* Another area for careful consideration is content, both text and illustration. Illustrations is a most important area for evaluation, especially in the primary grades where pictures become an integral part of the whole plot. Is the content varied and interesting? Are the stories vital — characterized by good plots, humor, realism, suspense, surprise, and action?

3. *Authorship.* Every adoption committee should make certain that the books and series it decides to order are written by scholars in the field of reading. Through training and experience, these persons should have proved their capabilities to create a program of instruction through which children will not only learn to read but will also develop a liking for reading. If a team of authors is involved, it should include at least one who knows how children learn and grow and a linguist who can give assurance that the materials are linguistically correct.

4. *Mechanical features.* The mechanical features of the materials should not be neglected. The paper must be of good quality; the type size should be suitable for the grade level; and the pages should be attractively arranged.

5. *Learning aids.* Today's teachers depend on the various learning aids which are frequently an integral part of basal programs. Filmstrips, films, big books, phrase cards, tests, and so on, are offered by the best of the modern programs to enrich and simplify the task of the teacher, and they should be carefully examined.

A very important consideration in the selection of materials is the teachers' guide or manual. The best of these are thorough and detailed. They contain a strong statement of purpose and philosophy, and detailed suggestions for each lesson. The modern teacher, particularly at the elementary level, has come to depend on this guide. Many of today's teachers are excellent teachers of reading because of the well-prepared manuals which guided them in their early teaching experience.

6. *Workbooks.* We have moved far from the day when workbooks were a series of dreary and monotonous drill pages, frequently so difficult that children could not possibly do them without constant help from the teacher. We now have workbooks that can be used independently by students at all grade levels to correct specific weaknesses. Programed learning has been applied in some workbooks so that students can work independently and progress at their own rates of growth. Workbooks should be evaluated both as an accompaniment to a basal program and as a supplementary aid for correcting weaknesses.

The difference between a good and a poor selection of instructional materials often depends on the use of a thoroughly and thoughtfully constructed evaluation sheet. A good adoption will be able to stand a test of the soundness of its philosophy, the practicality of its teaching guides, the quality of its content, the soundness of its mechanical features, and the richness of its learning aids.

CONCLUDING STATEMENT

This, then, is a time when masses of instructional materials are being published. It is an exciting time, for so many new ideas are being tried. Publishers have had meetings in various parts of the country with administrators and supervisors to inform them of their publications. A hint of an adoption, especially by a state or large city, brings the book men to talk about their programs and to promote their newest offerings. We educators must be wise in our selection. There are real dangers along the way which might interfere with the wisest choice.

Some educators are unfortunately not as selective or as discriminating as they should be. They "fall for" a program that claims to be a panacea for all ills. On the other hand, we must be on the alert for the values in the new materials. We may be skeptical about some of the "new"; for example, some educators have no interest in the new multiethnic materials. However, it would be better for all of us to adopt an open mind and an attitude of watchful waiting. When a movement looks promising, experiment with it. Try out some of these new instructional materials. We need much experimentation. We need research under controlled conditions to test new programs.

All of us, teachers, administrators, and supervisors, must keep up to date at this time of great transition in the field of instructional reading materials. If your books are old, ask yourself this question: Is this the time to adopt? Your answer will depend on your need and what is available from the publishers. No school district can afford to buy new books each year; so it must be able to live with the books it has selected for at least a few years.

In the meantime, we must think of movements in education which will affect the achievement of children in the years to come — the Operation "Head Start" programs, the Economic Opportunity Act of 1964, and the Elementary and Secondary Education Act. All of these will have a strong influence and will affect the learning patterns of the children in our schools.

Right now we have the best, the most numerous materials we have ever had. It is up to us to make wise selections and to use the materials in the most efficient manner. We know that change is inevitable. It is up to us to look ahead to what education will need in the future and to pass these findings on to our publishers.

CHAPTER IV

USING NEW INSTRUCTIONAL MATERIALS

*

IN KINDERGARTEN THROUGH GRADE THREE

LORETTA BYERS SAUER

*

T HE RECENT projects for educating culturally disadvantaged children have emphasized the crucial relation of experiential background and language development to school success, and especially to success in reading. Some children are completely ready for reading and may even have begun to learn to read before entering school, but most children need to have a readiness for reading developed. The number of children who do not succeed in reading and the number who verbalize from books without real comprehension indicate that more rather than less attention needs to be put on readiness instruction. The primary classroom must provide many opportunities for rich sensory experiences and a positive emotional tone toward reading. General readiness can be promoted by experiences in block play, painting, dramatic play, study trips in the community, construction, and group social experiences such as listening to stories, discussing, planning, and singing. The development of specific skills and abilities can be facilitated by some of the newly published materials. At the kindergarten level, readiness books such as *We Read Pictures* (Scott,

Foresman) can be used to help children acquire or clarify concepts basic to reading, to increase their hearing and speaking vocabularies, and to give practice in left to right direction. Kits for developing oral language skill, enriching vocabulary, and building concepts are now being published, for example, *Building Pre-Reading Skills* (Ginn). As a rule we have not made sufficient use of the excellent filmstrips which have been issued for concept and vocabulary building, such as *I Live in the Country* (Harper and Row). Whereas teachers formerly had to search for adequate pictorial material for readiness development, several publishers are now furnishing well-designed sets of pictures, for example, *Readiness Pictures* (Macmillan).

At the first-grade level, schools have a variety of choices in readiness materials in addition to those mentioned for kindergarten. For children with limited home backgrounds and meager English, some books, such as *We Read More Pictures* (Scott, Foresman), now stress the concepts and vocabulary needed in preprimers. Language development is promoted in books such as *Language Readiness* (American).

Primary teachers are keenly aware of the interrelatedness of the language arts. They realize that to be successful in reading children need experiences to develop listening skills, to improve their speech, and to build vocabulary. Children from lower and lower-middle socioeconomic levels, especially, need to work on language skills since they are not usually verbally oriented.

WORD RECOGNITION SKILLS

Since reading is a functional skill, it is important that it be taught from the beginning with primary emphasis on meaning and purpose rather than on process. The very first reading should be for the purpose of communication and should involve an integrated approach to word analysis so that the child sees word identification as a necessary step in unlocking meaning. Children will learn some words through configuration or shape, some from picture clues and context, and many through word analysis or from a combination of these methods.

Whether a teacher is using the basal reader approach, the language-experience approach, or individualized reading with books selected by the students, it is imperative that he have in mind the sequence in which basic skills in word analysis need to be taught so that he can present them at the appropriate times. Many of the new teacher's guidebooks for basal reading series have detailed information on the word-identification skills and the order in which they should be presented as well as many methods for their development. Although the guidebooks present the pattern of skill development the authors want teachers to follow, they are frequently so encyclopedic in content that they should not be followed slavishly. As the teacher becomes familiar with the framework of skills, he will select those techniques most appropriate for his pupils.

Although the basic teaching of word analysis should be a part of each daily lesson, filmstrips can help to clinch skills or to dramatize them. There are several sets of filmstrips on the market to implement the teaching of phonics. Records to assist in auditory perception of various elements have also been developed by several publishers. These are particularly beneficial for children who have heard inaccurate pronunciation in their preschool years and for those who have difficulty differentiating sounds.

A novel way to teach sentence construction and word building — by utilizing consonants, consonant blends, some consonant digraphs, and vowels — is contained in the *Linguistic Block Series* (Scott, Foresman). Pupils experiment with specially prepared blocks to discover facts about the structure and use of the English language. This series would seem to offer real possibilities for independent activity in conjunction with a basal reader program or an individualized reading program.

Although all basic reading series have planned frameworks for word analysis, some recent publications present a different approach to word identification. The various linguistic series, for example, tend to include in beginning reading textbooks only words that show a regular correspondence between spelling and sound. Emphasis is placed on regularly spelled words and occasionally on nonsense syllables. Learning words through their configurations or from picture clues is discouraged. Needless to say, it is difficult to produce interesting, meaningful books for beginners when the vocabulary is so severely controlled. There is a tendency for the emphasis to be on word-calling rather than on comprehension. Teachers who use these series will have to make an especial effort to make the reading meaningful.

The task of phonetic analysis is much simplified for children using the Initial Teaching Alphabet (ITA), since in that system a character is provided for each common phoneme and each letter has only one form. One reading series using ITA, the *Early To Read Series* (Initial Teaching Alphabet Publications, Inc.), utilizes the phonic method of teaching with little emphasis on sight vocabulary. Other series using ITA provide a broader attack on word recognition.

INDIVIDUAL DIFFERENCES

One of the most significant advances in the field of reading is the development of materials that meet the differing abilities, interests, and orientations of children from diverse backgrounds. For many years teachers struggled to interest all children in material which was primarily directed toward middle-class white children. Now multicultural readers are available that capture the interest of children of low socioeconomic status and of races other than white (Follett; Macmillan; Scott, Foresman). In these books several cultural groups are represented among the characters, and the content is often related to the out-of-school lives of city children. Some of the books are shorter so children experience accomplishment sooner, and there is a large ratio of running words to new words. A fringe benefit of great importance is that at least one series of these multicultural readers (a series of preprimers) seems to be of great interest to boys, who have long predominated in reading disabilities.[1]

To organize instruction to meet individual differences in reading, teachers have two possibilities: (1) a flexible grouping plan with different levels of reading plus independent reading, and (2) an individualized plan (in this division the language-experience approach is classified as an individualized technique). In both cases the teacher will probably utilize basal readers, being careful to see that each child has reading materials on a level at which he can succeed. If the teacher uses a grouping plan, he will probably use workbooks, teacher prepared follow-up materials he himself has prepared, or both. Follow-up work will be designed to reinforce comprehension and word-recognition skills rather than to test. The assignment and pacing of follow-up work should be adjusted to each child's readiness for the given task since no group is ever simultaneously ready for the same task.

For group or individualized reading, a well-stocked book table is essential. A wealth of attractive, interesting supplementary material is now available.

[1] Gertrude Whipple, *Appraisal of the City Schools Reading Program* (Detroit: Detroit Public Schools, 1963), p. 21.

The Reading Round Table (American) is in paperback and ranges from the primary through the sixth-grade levels. The *What Is It?* series (Benefic) answers many science questions for young children. *Gateway to Reading Treasures* (Laidlaw) is a unique supplementary series in that its vocabulary is correlated with ten basic reader series. The *Reading Caravan* (Heath) and the *Jim Forest Series* (Harr Wagner) provide vitally interesting supplementary material.

For the superior reader in the primary grades, several companies are developing special books. Ginn's *Primary Enrichment Series* and Lyons and Carnahan's *Curriculum Enrichment Series* are examples of these. Space does not permit listing the many well-designed readers, but teachers will have no difficulty in finding suitable ones to fit every pupil's appetite. In addition to readers, the book table will also need a changing supply of colorful, varied trade books and some of the children's magazines.

Introducing dictionaries to children in the primary grades for group and individual use can facilitate independence in reading and in writing and can help develop the dictionary habit. Beginner Books, Macmillan, Follett, and Scott, Foresman publish primary dictionaries. For third graders of superior ability a programed textbook, *Dictionary Discoveries* (American), teaches dictionary skills on an individual basis.

CONCLUDING STATEMENT

Since one of the major goals in teaching reading is the development of an enthusiasm for and an enjoyment of reading, it is fortunate that primary teachers have available a variety of reading materials from which to choose. Children form their attitudes toward reading in the primary grades; thus, their development of interest and skills at this level is very important. Enriching experiences, attention to all the language arts, varied lessons in reading utilizing appropriate materials, and constant evaluation of children's progress should lead to a successful primary reading program.

* * *

IN GRADES FOUR THROUGH EIGHT

ADELINE PRENER

*

TEN YEARS AGO — even five years ago — teachers were deploring the dearth of adequate instructional materials to supplement or replace the basal reader. Now there is a deluge of material, and the teacher is faced with a different problem: how to choose wisely from this flood. The key word here is "wisely." If we were in the habit of treating reading materials as we do prescription drugs, it might be helpful to affix cautionary labels such as "effective when taken as directed," or "if symptoms persist, discontinue use," or "use when needed."

AVAILABLE MATERIALS

Materials may be listed by grade level. This type of designation gives a sense of security to the neophyte. The experienced teacher has learned that grade designations are not always his best guide.

Materials may be listed by the skill they purport to develop. They may deal in part or completely with phonic analysis, structural analysis, comprehension, study skills, or content area skills. This type of listing is the one a teacher looks to when he wishes to find materials in an area that he has not been able to treat to his own satisfaction.

Materials may be divided by format. They may be conventional textbooks, multitexts, classmate editions, programed materials in any number of forms, boxed kits, or multilevel materials. There are no clear-cut divisions between types of material on the basis of format.

Let us take just one area — vocabulary development — as an example of new materials. Albert J. Kingston, in discussing methods of building vocabulary, suggests that words should be presented and studied in context and that pupils should be taught a technique for using context clues.[1] He suggests that pupils should be given a

[1] Kingston, "Vocabulary Development," *Journal of Reading*, VIII (March, 1965), 265–71.

structured teaching situation to enable them to encounter more words in a controlled context than they would meet in free reading. Both of the materials described below try to do this.

The *Word Clues Programed Workbooks* are a series of seven books, published by the Educational Developmental Laboratories, which present each word in context. The levels are from grades seven to thirteen at present; the publishers plan to extend the series to include grades four, five and six.

The *Reading Spectrum*, Macmillan's complex of instructional materials for the intermediate grades, contains six booklets of vocabulary development skills. These booklets also use the context-clues approach. They have sections on combining forms, affixes, base words, use of the dictionary, and figurative language.

Both of these vocabulary development materials are planned for the student to use at his own pace. The EDL material is programed instruction; the Macmillan material is partially programed.

SELECTING NEW MATERIALS

Sometimes we have no choice; new materials are thrust upon us. This has been the experience of many a teacher who has found himself required to teach the "new math" when he has no more than a nodding acquaintance with the old. At such a time, there is only one course: to assimilate the new material as rapidly as possible.

But if we are given a choice, we should approach new materials with definite criteria in mind:

What do I expect of it? If I am using a basal reader in which much of the content is literary, I may need to use other materials to give specific and abundant attention to vocabulary skills, locational skills, comprehension skills, and speed and study skills.[2]

How am I doing the job now? In what way is it unsatisfactory? I may be unhappy with my program because the good readers do not need it and the others are not benefiting from it. In such a case I will be asking myself: Is the new material multilevel? Are enrichment activities included? How much of my time will it take?

How much does it cost? We must think about the cost in money. Do not forget, however, the cost in time, teacher time and pupil time. Many programs are unfortunately conceived as five-day-a-week packages, and we may have trouble fitting such a program into the classroom schedule. Interruptions have become commonplace: assembly programs, special projects, snow days, testing, athletic events, music events, PTA events. As more and more is squeezed into the curriculum, time grows more and more important.

How will I know if it is doing the job? And more important, how will the pupils know? Is evaluation built into the program? Are there progress charts? If the children are to keep the records, are they cumbersome and demanding? Do they act as a brake to achievement or as an incentive? Some record forms resemble flow charts demanding the skill of an engineer — and take almost as much time.

Can I try it on a small group first? Inevitably, you will find ways to improve your techniques as you deal with a program, and changes are more readily made in a small workable group.

Is it suited to my group? If I am teaching an urban group, I should certainly make every effort to select from among the new offerings created for multiethnic populations in cities. Years ago we had little choice; today we do not have to pretend that every child lives in a freshly painted house in a tree-shaded neighborhood.

Have I the energy and enthusiasm to give it a proper start? Most of us would agree that teachers would do better not to try new material rather than present it shoddily. We have each encountered the child who says, in effect, "I had that. Ugh!" Another potentially useful piece of material ruined!

USING NEW MATERIALS

First, don't open anything — except to check to see that the order has been properly filled. Resist the urge to get going on the material at once.

Second, having shown such strength of character, go one step farther. One week end, say no to every temptation; take home the new material and steep yourself in it. Look through the materials as a pupil in your class might; ignore the manual. Try to imagine whether it will appeal to the pupils. Does it make you curious? Is it forbidding? Does it look like fun? Whatever the reaction, you will want to know.

[2] William D. Sheldon, "Reading Instruction in Junior High School," in *Development in and through Reading,* Sixtieth Yearbook of the National Society for the Study of Education, Part I (Chicago: University of Chicago Press, 1961), p. 314.

Now, be a teacher. Look at it in your most organized SQ3R way. Preview it. Ask yourself questions. Picture the pupil least likely to follow directions; where might he go astray? Picture the quick, impatient pupil; where might he start to fidget? How much of the material would your class take at one sitting?

Third, try a sample lesson. Be the teacher and be the pupil. Work through the entire exercise, answering all questions and doing all suggested activities. Did you peek at the programed responses? Did you come up with an answer different from that indicated?

Fourth, prepare your lesson. Decide how you will introduce the material and how you will take care of the mechanics of distribution, collection, storage, and record-keeping.

Let your class in on the planning. The combination of an enthusiastic teacher and a group eager to try something new is unbeatable. Together they have a strong purpose extrinsic to the reading material itself. They are taking part in a decision-making process — deciding whether something is of value and how it is to be used — and that is a powerful motivation.

Fifth, now present your material and start the evaluation process immediately.

EVALUATING NEW MATERIAL

Jot down notes as they occur to you. Take ten minutes at the end of the day to put your notes into usable form. Later it will be helpful to be able to remember that a pupil wrote in the booklet rather than on the answer sheet or that a student helper did a particularly effective job with Lesson X.

And what will you be looking for? Remember your criteria for selection; you can never really lay those aside. You will be piling up evidence as to whether the material is doing what you hoped it would do.

Have your pupils play an active role in the evaluation process. Ask them to alert you to stumbling blocks. Find out in what ways the new material is better than that previously used, in what ways it is less desirable. Could you have skipped some parts?

There are pitfalls. Often a teacher gets such extraordinary results with new material and methods that the school goes overboard and extends the program throughout the school, only to find that results do not continue to be so highly successful. The new panacea has turned out to be just another unexceptional program. Here is the famous "Hawthorne effect" at work.

I suspect that this explains some of the remarkably uneven results of many of our new, most promising developments. The language laboratories, some teachers say, are not keeping each child working at his own pace; many are finding time to write on the walls of the booths. In programed material — where no child cheats, because he is supposed to be competing only with himself — some have zoomed through an entire program with no comprehension in order to keep up with others.

POINTS TO REMEMBER

Know the skills you wish to teach.
Select material based on your criteria.

Don't overextend yourself.

Evaluate as you go along; include everyone concerned in the evaluation process.

Try new material out on a small group if possible.

Try out material first as the author intended it to be used; make changes gradually.

Select the portions that prove effective; discard the rest — adapt, then adopt.

* * *

IN GRADES NINE THROUGH FOURTEEN

DANIEL K. HESS

*

IT IS the purpose of this paper to select several of the new instructional materials in the field of reading and discuss briefly their use in grades nine through fourteen. It should be recognized, however, that selection does not necessarily mean endorsement by this writer.

Prior to using new instructional materials, one must understand the make-up of the grade levels for which these materials are intended.

NINTH GRADE

Consider first the ninth grader. The junior-high school population is highly diversified, not only in abilities and achievements, but also in emotional, social, and physical development. The reading tasks required of a junior-high school student increase in number and variety as he moves into the secondary-school curriculum. He has more ground to cover in current science and social studies textbooks as well as greatly expanded background reading. More facts, more abstract concepts, and more complex ideas involving higher readability levels require increased competency in reading skills.[1]

At present, the reading teacher is certainly not faced with a lack of materials. There seems to be no real problem for the resourceful. The difficulty lies in selecting materials that are sound and meet a definite need in a particular program — sifting out the gadgets and gimmicks and evaluating the rest.

To illustrate, we may consider boxes and kits of multilevel programed material, which have received widespread acceptance. One such program published by Science Research Associates embodies a new approach to teaching English in grades seven through twelve — a curriculum which was developed at the University of Illinois laboratory high school, headed by Dr. James Mc-Crimmon. It is based on two assump-

[1] Gertrude Whipple, *Appraisal of the City Schools Reading Program* (Detroit: Detroit Public Schools, 1963), p. 21.

tions: that English is not a collection of vaguely related subject units but a single discipline which is unified in the communication process; and that the sequence of lessons from grades seven through twelve spirals out from basic concepts learned in grades seven through nine. The curriculum is language-centered. Teaching procedures are almost entirely inductive. No anthology is used as such, although significant emphasis is placed on the use of paperback novels and collections of short stories. During the ninth grade, work on interpretation is approached from two points of view: developmental reading and the interpretation of literature. The work on developmental reading consists of vocabulary development, reading for comprehension and speed, and practice in making inferences from what is read. This part of the program is followed by a timed reading sequence using essays ranging in length from six hundred to six thousand words.

The general approach to literature in all grades is through analysis of the structure of the work, with "structure" understood in its most comprehensive sense to include all the elements in a work that affect response. These elements include vocabulary, grammatical structure, stanza or paragraph structure, the selection and omission of material, the emphasis given to particular material, the point of view, the author's attitude toward his subject and audience, the affective elements (such as rhyme, meter, style, and tone), the relation of the parts to the whole, the theme, and the purpose as deduced from all of these observations. The

progression up through the twelfth grade is from simple to complex, structures — for example, from *The Yearling* to *The Sound and the Fury*, followed by *Hamlet* and ending with *The Love Song of J. Alfred Prufrock*.

There are other new reading materials not in kits which can be used for supplementary reading by teachers in the subject areas as well as teachers of reading. *Words: A Programmed Course in Vocabulary Development* (Science Research Associates) is designed to aid the student increase his vocabulary. *The Right Word* (Houghton Mifflin) is somewhat difficult and is more appropriate for precocious ninth graders or for high-school students. Its purpose is to encourage the student to explore the meaning of words and the uses of the classics. Students must have a fair background to cope with this workbook.

A significant change has occurred in the *Adventures in Literature* series (Harcourt, Brace and World), which has now added a *Better Reading* book—programed instruction in reading and literature to accompany each text.

Another useful kit is the *EDL Study Skills Library* (Educational Developmental Laboratories). The following description is from the Teacher's Guide accompanying the kit (p.4).

The STUDY SKILLS LIBRARY is a new approach to the teaching of essential study skills and the improvement of reading in the content areas. Designed for use by the classroom or subject-area teacher, reading specialist, or librarian, it can help students to bridge the gap between the reading done in the developmental reading program and the reading skills required in the content areas.

. . . .

The program is individualized and largely auto-instructional so that the student is able to work at his own pace and level in order to accomplish maximum growth in the least possible time. Through a step-by-step program, students learn those skills which enable them to read competently and critically in the content areas: to select, understand, judge, and use the important ideas found in their texts and in reference material.

. . . .

The STUDY SKILLS LIBRARY is based on a subject-level approach: each box represents one reading level in science, social studies, or reference skills, with a total of three boxes for each level. Each subject-level box contains ten lessons of comparable difficulty . . . .

. . . Six major study skill areas are considered: *following directions, interpretation, evaluation, organization, retention* and *reference* (locating information). Following directions is given continuous emphasis in all study skill lessons. *Retention* is an outgrowth of the application of the other skills. Each of the four major areas is broken into the specific skills listed on the facing page.

Perhaps one of the most unique materials to have been put forward for teaching the reading of newspapers is *The Newspaper in the Classroom* from the Copley Newspapers, Department of Education. It is an instructional aid which can be used to supplement teaching in most subject areas. It provides some material which will attract interests, and its use encourages critical and analytical reading.

SENIOR HIGH

The senior high school plays an important part in the sequential development of reading competencies. The large majority of high school students will receive no further formal education. Those who do go on to college, vocational or other schools will receive little additional instruction in reading. The senior high school reading instructional program must culminate for many pupils in such a way as to make them independent readers. Students who go on for advanced training should be well equipped in the basic study skills, and they should be able to employ their reading skills and abilities to meet the demands of the college subjects.[2]

A good developmental reading program on the high-school level gives attention to word study and comprehension, abilities, expanding interests and tastes, increasing reading fluency, and adjustment of abilities to fit the demands of the content fields. In order to accomplish this, high-school teachers have sought a variety of reading materials — and there is much competition for the attention of the classroom teacher by the publisher. Basic textbooks are more and more frequently accompanied by supplementary audiovisual materials, such as the Purdue High School Reading Films, the EDL Controlled Reader, and the SRA Reading Accelerator. The caution one should remember here is that these audiovisual materials and instruments not be used as a substitute for good teaching but rather as motiva-

[2] Guy L. Bond and Stanley B. Kegler, "Reading Instruction in the Senior High School," in *Development in and through Reading*, Sixtieth Yearbook of the National Society for the Study of Education, Part I (Chicago: University of Chicago Press, 1961), p. 320.

tional and supplemental to the basic program.

Corrective reading programs in many high schools have been given an added boost by series entitled *Vanguard* and *Prospectives* (Scott, Foresman). The *Be a Better Reader* series (Prentice-Hall) has introduced special work in remedial reading in the areas of literature, math, science, and history; there are six books in the series ranging from grades seven through twelve.

Advanced Skills in Reading (Macmillan) may be used independently at the high-school level since it presents all the significant reading skills in a mature treatment. According to the Preface to Book 3, "The main objectives of this book are focused upon the complex of skills needed by any student for the comprehension and study of high school texts and reference materials. The book is intended to help the student apply himself efficiently and confidently to various kinds of reading techniques."

COLLEGE

The college reader has still other problems. "An entering college Freshman at once is aware of greater freedom than he enjoyed in high school. He is given assignments without being told what to look for. His homework is not checked regularly. Course syllabi are without limiting specifications. . . . In the classroom, he takes notes when and how he wants to, and outside of class he reads and studies as he chooses." [3]

Quite often the colleges and universities have set up courses for reading improvement, although little is done to teach reading in the subject areas. The character of most college reading programs is either mechanical-aid, textbook, or individual counseling.[4] Frequently the course combines the student's own textbook and how-to-do-it books, such as Smith's *Read Faster, and Get More from Your Reading* (Prentice-Hall), or reading workbooks. One such workbook to appear recently is Heilman's *Improve Your Reading Ability* (Charles E. Merrill). The purpose of this workbook is to teach the reader how to read better and faster. It includes one hundred exercises which provide drill in such areas as phrase reading, rapid visual perception, skimming for critical reading, and vocabulary development.

[3] Phillip Shaw, "Reading in College," in *Development in and through Reading*, Sixtieth Yearbook of the National Society for the Study of Education, Part I (Chicago: University of Chicago Press, 1961), p. 336.

[4] *Ibid.*, p. 349.

IN CORRECTIVE AND REMEDIAL CLASSES

GUS P. PLESSAS

∗

SELECTING suitable reading material is vital to the successful treatment of retarded readers. Inappropriate materials easily reinforce their feelings of inadequacy and failure. What, then, are essential considerations in selecting materials for the retarded reader?

First, reading materials must not be too hard, especially at the initial stage of instruction. For retarded readers, difficult material often serves as a painful reminder of their previous unsuccessful efforts. Books should be chosen that are at the students' instructional levels. If at least 95 per cent of the vocabulary is familiar, much of the content will be understood. For this purpose, a student's reading skills may be assessed by informal inventory procedures as well as by standardized achievement tests. The use of inventory techniques avoids trial-and-error judgments and is likely to ensure a successful match between material and learner.

Second, whenever possible, reading material should be high in interest. Although interest alone cannot compensate for undeveloped reading skills, it is a primary source of motivation and has a strong influence on attitudes toward reading. Interest affects comprehension and memory. When students read interesting stories, they achieve greater understanding and retain more of what they have read than when they read uninteresting stories. Heightened interest supports learning and remembering, particularly when the reading material is related to a reader's experiences.[1]

Early in each school year, the reading interests of each class member should be explored. This can be done by inventories or questionnaires, observation, listing of favorite stories, and rating titles.[2] With this information, a teacher can select reading material with reasonable confidence that it will appeal to each student.

Third, if instructional material is to be effective, the rate of increase in difficulty, the length of selections, and the developmental sequence of reading skills should be carefully considered.[3] One major weakness of certain purportedly high-interest, low-vocabulary books, is to be found in the introduction of new words. Some of these introduce new words too rapidly. Poor readers who have severe problems in word recognition do not progress eas-

[1] Ruth Strang, *Diagnostic Teaching of Reading* (New York: McGraw-Hill Book Co., 1964), p. 11.

[2] *Ibid.*, pp. 103–13.

[3] Helen M. Robinson, "Corrective and Remedial Instruction," in *Development in and through Reading*, Sixtieth Yearbook of the National Society for the Study of Education, Part I (Chicago: University of Chicago Press, 1961), p. 368.

ily when each lesson presents too many new words. Even though at the start a book may have been judged at a student's instructional level, there is no assurance that his rate of reading development will parallel the rate of increase in difficulty of the new material.

A closely related consideration is the length of each reading selection. For initial instruction, a long selection is seldom appropriate, especially for the development of certain reading skills or abilities. A long selection may be desirable for supplementary reading if a learner has confidence in his reading ability. The purpose of each reading assignment as well as the shorter attention span of the retarded reader should influence the length of material.

Another consideration is that instructional materials should provide a systematic development of skills and should include sufficient variety to correct specific weaknesses. Despite publishers' claims, many practice materials are not adequate. That is, a single volume or workbook is likely to be insufficient to develop a specific reading skill. Most materials introduce too many skills to give ample attention to the reinforcement of each skill.

USE OF INSTRUCTIONAL MATERIAL

Retarded readers seldom have exactly the same deficiencies and often also perform at different reading levels. Therefore, no single textbook or practice book is adequate for all members of a class. Even in a small group of disabled readers, a wide assortment of materials that vary in readability and interest will be required.

Unfortunately, time and again, working on phonic workbooks passes for remedial reading. Retarded readers are constantly drilled in letter-sound activities with seemingly little regard for their precise needs. Without discrimination, they are required to follow the same prescription page after page. What is really accomplished? How efficient is this procedure? A classroom teacher may say that these boys and girls have phonic deficiencies in word attack. This observation, however valid, is inadequate. The discovery that a student has trouble in phonics or in word recognition in no way identifies the precise fault or particular need.

The weakness or need should be made perfectly clear. In reading, the chief areas to evaluate are word recognition, word meaning, comprehension and interpretation, and speed. When a problem is identified only in terms of a general area, the assessment lacks adequate specificity, since each area subsumes a host of distinct but related skills. Word recognition includes, for example, sight recognition, context clues, and word analysis, which in turn are comprised of phonic and structural analysis skills. In a further breakdown, phonics is composed of auditory and visual associations of letters in words. These letter-sound associations involve such elements as blends, digraphs, short vowels and long vowels, to name a few. What then does it mean to say that a pupil has difficulty with word recognition or even in phonics? Difficulty with what in particular?

Consider the area of comprehension. In the intermediate and upper grades, some boys and girls fail to respond successfully to many questions on the literal meanings of various passages. This failure indicates a weakness in understanding stated ideas. Results of standardized tests may perhaps confirm this observation. What is needed, therefore, is improvement in this particular area of reading, provided that the students have adequate word perception skills. A logical approach would be to use material that stresses development of comprehension skills; however, this teaching pattern would be only a partial solution. To be effective, the instructional material should first meet a precise need before attempting to deal with a general weakness. In this illustration, we do not know the specific comprehension faults of the readers. Some of the students may be confusing important details with main ideas. Others may be unable to recall a sequence of ideas satisfactorily. Each instance requires a different kind of corrective work. Even though all the retarded readers may have comprehension difficulties, the materials employed for each one should vary according to the type of disability.

For this reason, to have retarded readers engage in daily oral reading is of questionable value whatever materials are used. In many classrooms, low groups are assigned basal readers with stories that often involve immature interests and characters that are younger than the class members. Seated in a circle with book in hand, each retarded reader is supposed to take a turn reading aloud. In this approach, corrective instruction is viewed as correcting errors in pronunciation. Actually, many errors in oral reading are merely manifestations of a weakness in word attack. Telling children which words have been mispronounced or are unknown is no substitute for instruction to correct the specific causes of mispronunciation.

A vital program should include materials that vary not only in the fault they are designed to correct but also in the type of activity to reinforce learning. With different types of material, interest will be maintained and improvement will be secured. Retarded readers are easily bored by performing the same task again and again without variation in material and yet they need much more practice than average readers. Every instructional session should involve at least several distinct sorts of corrective or remedial activities, each aimed at the improvement of a specific reading skill. Games, practice materials, laboratory kits, supplementary books, devices prepared by the teacher, and audiovisual aids are examples of instructional tools that have a place if used intelligently.

Although emphasis should be on the correction of weaknesses, a balanced program of reading activities is important. Teaching materials should include meaningful practice in all areas of reading. Deficiencies in skills that are essential to instant success should receive special but not sole attention. Thus, retarded readers who have rate problems, for instance, should not be given materials to increase speed to the exclusion of work on word perception and comprehension development.

NEW TYPES OF INSTRUCTIONAL MATERIALS

Let us now consider various types of teaching materials. Certain trends in new materials are discernible.

1. For the first time, special readers in the form of an ordinary basal reading series have appeared. Organized on a developmental scheme, these books are designed to accommodate students who read below grade level. Unlike regular basal readers, however, they are geared to the learning pace of retarded readers, although the sequence of skills and the developmental procedures are basically the same. The *Open Highways Books* (Scott, Foresman) follow this new trend.

2. Closely allied to the trend described above is the development of work-type readers or text workbooks for older students or adults who have serious reading handicaps. One such series of teaching materials is the *Reader's Digest Adult Readers* (Reader's Digest Services). In this series, the stories are short but of mature interest. Readability of the first four books in the series is reported at the upper first- and second-grade levels. Another series in this category is the *Turner-Livingston Reading Series* (Follett). The content of the six worktexts is centered on problems of adolescents, but the reading level is that of the middle grades.

3. A trend that started several years ago and has since expanded is the development of multilevel materials in kit form. Science Research Associates publishes reading laboratory kits of all sorts. Organized by reading levels, these materials include separate selections to develop word analysis, vocabulary, and comprehension skills and also games and reading-rate exercises. For different purposes, but similar in form, is the *EDL Study Skills Library* (Educational Developmental Laboratories). The latter stresses improvement of reading in the content areas. Reading selections are individualized and largely self-instructional; they are designed to teach the student to link developmental reading skills with study skills in dealing with reading materials in the content areas.

An outgrowth of this trend is "packaged" materials. Publishers are presently offering in packaged form a wide assortment of reading aids and practice materials including supplementary readers. One such package is *Webster Classroom Reading Clinic* (Webster). A similar package, the *Macmillan Reading Spectrum* (Macmillan), contains seventy-two booklets that are designed to develop skills in the various reading areas. Each area is developed separately by a series of text-workbooks at different levels of difficulty.

4. Programed materials represent another distinct trend. Independent learning is purported to occur as the student responds to each instructional frame and has an immediate opportunity to check his answers. Examples are *Sullivan's Programmed Reading* (McGraw-Hill) and *Building Reading Power* (Charles E. Merrill).

5. For several years, high-interest level and low-difficulty level books have appeared in impressive array. These materials are popular as supple-

mentary or recreational reading for retarded readers. Typical of the new series of easy-to-read books are *The Wildlife Adventure Series* (Harr Wagner) and *The World of Adventure Series* (Benefic).

6. A trend may be starting in specialized materials for retarded readers who have weakness in sensory functions. The trend is suggested by the appearance of the *Frostig Program for the Development of Visual Perception* (Follett.) . Several research projects are directed at the perceptual aspects of learning, and the knowledge derived from these studies may lead to new materials for use in the treatment of sensory disabilities.

CHAPTER V

INNOVATIONS IN READING INSTRUCTION

*

GEORGE D. SPACHE

*

A FITTING subtitle for this chapter would be "Or How To Promote a New Approach to Teaching Reading," for the chapter outlines the specific steps by which anyone can invent a novel, profitable system of teaching beginning reading. These steps are those followed by the purveyors of many new reading materials, as illustrated by the programs cited in this chapter. Let us consider four principles essential for the preparation of an innovation in reading instruction.

PRINCIPLE ONE — START WITH A CLEAR MIND

In order to devise a really successful new method of teaching reading, we must first clear our minds of all that we now know about the reading process, the strengths and weaknesses of present methods, and the psychology of learning. Second, we must eradicate from our memories any knowledge of previous reading research, particularly that which has occurred during the past seventy-five years. Now we are ready to begin thinking with a clear mind.

Let us start with an analysis of this process called reading. It starts with letters, does it not? These letters are put together to form words, the words are combined into sentences, and sentences make paragraphs. There is good logical progression. Why should our new method not recognize this obvious logic? We will begin our system with the letters and teach each child to read every letter of the alphabet. Then he can read any word in the language because, after all, they are all formed by the same letters. If he learns the names of these letters during the early weeks of school as Leonard Bloomfield and C. L. Barnhart tell us he will,[1] we shall be ready to begin with words. We must remember to use only the capitals, as Charles C. Fries suggests,[2] because they will function so much better in subsequent reading. Our system will now teach any child to spell out any English word.

There is a key word — *spell.* What words shall we teach him to spell first? We had better choose some nice, easy words and stay away from such irregularly spelled words as his name or *mother, father, grandmother, Christmas, boy, girl,* and the like. Does Fries

[1] Bloomfield and Barnhart, *Let's Read* (Detroit: Wayne State University Press, 1961), p.3.
[2] Fries, *Linguistics and Reading* (New York: Holt, Rinehart & Winston, 1963), p. 191.

not tell us that the child should not attempt to learn irregularly spelled words?[3] But, just a minute. Does the irregularity make them hard to spell or hard to read? There is a study that points out that such words are hard to spell but not necessarily hard to read.[4] Perhaps it does not really matter, because it amounts to the same thing. Spelling is the same as reading.

We will teach him to spell words with a common element such as *at*: *cat, hat, fat, dat*. What is a *dat*? It does not matter that this is a nonsense word. He will learn to spell it because it is one of the *at* family. (Careful there, we used a term that used to be popular about fifty years ago. We will have to watch out for such slips.)

If we stay with three- and four-letter combinations of words and nonsense groups, we shall have enough material or enough words for several months. Even if we use vowels just in the middle of the three-letter words, we can teach him many, many words. There will be twenty-one different beginning letters, about twenty different vowel sounds, and twenty-one different ending letters. That will be 21 times 20 times 21, or 8,820 words. What other method can teach over eight thousand words in a few months? Now we are making real progress with the discovery of our new method. The new system is working so well we shall not have to look at Bell's 1797 materials for any more ideas. After all he was

not very successful with this same system.[5]

When we prepare our lists of words with common elements, we must remember not to clutter up the page with pictures. Like Bloomfield, Barnhart, and Fries, we must remember not to let the children go off on their own tangents. The first thing we know they will be using some combination of clues, such as the length of the word or its shape or the picture, to help them read. After all, according to these scientists, reading is basically a spelling process — the recognition of words with similar letters by knowing the names of the letters.

We must be particularly careful of the pernicious tendency of pupils to attend to word form. Did J. C. Daniels and Hunter Diack not point out how false this Gestalt concept is and how much it has contributed to the outright failure of most current methods?[6] Like Barnhart, Bloomfield, and Fries, we must keep the letter combinations in our list of a constant length — say, three or four letters — to combat this tendency.

But have we not simply revived some earlier methods like Bell's of 1797 or the *Gradual Primer's* of 1853 or, even worse, initiated some brand-new-approaches? We are using the same old alphabet as everyone else. Perhaps we need a really new twist — a new alphabet. Now, there is a fresh idea. Let us

---

[3] *Ibid.*, chap. xi.

[4] W. R. Lee, *Spelling Irregularity and Reading Difficulty in English* (London: National Foundation for Educational Research in England and Wales, 1960), No. 2, p. 72.

[5] Ronald Morris, *Success and Failure in Learning To Read* (London: Oldbourne, 1963), p. 29.

[6] Daniels and Diack, *Progress in Reading in the Infant School* (Nottingham: Institute of Education, University of Nottingham, 1960).

see how it would be arranged. Shall we make a new letter for each of the old ones or a new letter for each of the sounds in English? What is it that those people are calling the sounds now? Oh, yes, "phonemes." We must remember that it is not phonics any more; the proper term is "phonemics." Let us try a new alphabet with a letter for each of the sounds. Of course, Edgeworth was not very successful with the idea in 1798, nor was Isaac Pitman in the nineteenth century.[7] But then, they were not very scientific.

If we devise a new letter for each sound and use that symbol no matter how the word is spelled, it would simplify the whole language, would it not? That is why the other methods must be such failures. They do not recognize this simple principle as clearly as John Downing or Sir James Pitman today [8] or as clearly as many innovators of the eighteenth and nineteenth centuries.

Perhaps it would be simpler just to mark the sounds of each letter the way they are marked in a dictionary. Were there not readers like that a long time ago, or was it just recently? [9] Spelling words the way they sound, however, might not help pupils to read words more quickly unless they knew all the marks as well as something about silent letters and how to represent many different sounds by letters. The new phonemic alphabet would be simpler

to learn, provided we can find someone to design the letters and publish some books in it. Perhaps it will not be too difficult to find a publisher, for this idea should be a real money-maker.

PRINCIPLE TWO — MAKE THE APPROACH DRAMATIC AND DIFFERENT

In order to make our new reading method really effective, it must have some dramatic aspect. After all, if we are to convince teachers and pupils that our approach is really effective, we shall have to offer something newer and better than any other method. We shall have to help them see that all other systems are faulty and not suited to their pupils' abilities. As Morris has so cogently advised, we must encourage the future users of our innovative system to believe that it is guaranteed to help all pupils of all types, if we expect to succeed.[10]

We could achieve this needed dramatic effect by advertising. Perhaps our copy should read something like the following quotations from our competitors.

Men . . . women . . . children . . . . Now read more than twice as fast with this easy, fascinating technique . . . .

Most average readers are able to double or triple their reading speeds by faithfully following the ——— program. You learn to read entire sentences in a flash. Read your newspaper columns by simply running your eyes down the center. . . .[11]

You'll find this Automatic Speed-Reading course renders virtually obsolete any pre-

7 Morris, *op. cit.*, p. 39.

8 John A. Downing, *tω bεε or not to be* (London: Pitman Publishing, 1962), p. 19.

9 Edward Fry, "A Diacritical Marking System To Aid Beginning Reading Instruction," *Elementary English*, XLI (May, 1964), 526–29, 537.

10 Morris, *op. cit.*, p. 141.

11 Two quotations from an advertising brochure of the Speed Reading Institute, Oak Park, Illinois.

vious method of reading training. . . . Guaranteed to double your reading speed in just 30 days.[12]

Developed at ———, this simple and joyous approach to early learning has been successfully proved in more than 50,000 homes. . . . Tiny children, two, three, four year olds want to read . . . . Tiny children can learn to read . . . . Tiny children should learn to read . . . . Now, your child can take advantage of these dramatic advances with the ——— Reading Development Program.[13]

Perhaps it would be well to achieve this dramatic effect by carefully planning for the motivation of our system's users. We could first try the method on our own children, as Flesch, Bloomfield, and Barnhart did.[14] That certainly ought to ensure the proper motivation. Or we could hunt around until we find a few teachers who accept it enthusiastically. If these teachers were really excited about the system, as were the teachers selected by Daniels and Diack to try out their method,[15] we should get some very dramatic results.

Then there is that new approach to motivation called "operant conditioning," the system which rewards pigeons with corn. For our pupils, candy might be better. Or, better still, since most of those who really need motivation are boys, we might use marbles. Now, how could we maintain a high pitch of interest with marbles? By giv-

ing a free bag of marbles with each teacher's manual That would not work; some teachers would probably never have played marbles and would not know how to use them for reinforcement. We shall have to devise a cigar box in which the child can put his book while he is reading. The box will have a plunger on the side for him to push as he finishes a page, thus releasing a marble. Now there is a good system of motivation-reinforcement by marbles. But suppose he makes a number of mistakes in reading the lists of words? Should he not have immediate correction before receiving the reinforcing marble? We shall not have to worry about that very much. If I know teachers, they will be making him read most of the pages aloud; and they will probably take the marbles away if he makes many mistakes.

One very effective means of providing motivation for our pupils will be to enlist the interested support of their parents. If we can get them actively involved, our new system will certainly be benefited and strengthened. Following John Downing's example, we will prepare books from which our parents can learn our new alphabet, as well as a manual to help them write it.[16] With constant parental support at home and an intensive program in the classroom, all our pupils should quickly learn the new alphabet.

Perhaps we can get the dramatic effect we need by adding a variety of audiovisual aids to our materials. We could have filmstrips made that duplicated each page of our lists of words. After all, did Glenn McCracken not

[12] From an advertising brochure of the National Reading Institute, Waterford, Connecticut.

[13] Advertisement in *Family Weekly*, December 20, 1964, p. 12.

[14] Rudolf Flesch, *Why Johnny Can't Read* (New York: Harper & Row, 1955), chap. x; Bloomfield and Barnhart, *op. cit.*, p. 3.

[15] Daniels and Diack, *op. cit.*

[16] Downing, *op. cit.*, p. 51.

get very impressive results with film-strips, particularly when he used reading tests that were about ten years old? [17] Then we could add flash cards, records, films, and other good aids. This would certainly give us a completely impressive reading program, like the expanded Richards-Gibson method,[18] even though we might not know the exact value of controlling the use of letters in words. Although all these adjuncts to a basic idea, such as a new alphabet or a limit to the number of letters in words, make it a bit difficult to judge what the essentials are, they do increase the appeal of the system.

The use of color may be another way to add dramatic appeal to our materials. Nellie Dale used it in 1899,[19] and the latest application, *Words in Color*,[20] is making quite a splash. Just think, we could use a different color for each of the forty or so phonemes, or we could print three-letter words in three colors, four-letter words in four colors, and so on. Perhaps if we varied the colors and the letters and used alternating capital and lower-case letters as one innovator does,[21] there would be even more appeal. This system would also make it difficult for pupils to acquire that bad habit of recognizing some words by over-all shape or the shapes of the letters. Of course, all the old research indicates that the use of color contributes nothing, but we shall just ignore those earlier studies.

We have now assured certain dramatically different facets for our new reading program. There remains only the need for a really new vocabulary to put this system out in front. What brand-new terms that very few teachers know can we use? We can call the sounds of the letters "phonemes," and we can call the letters "graphemes." These have a good Greek sound. Then the order in which we present the graphemes will be a "programed sequence." Our cigar box of marbles will be an "auto-instructional device." That's a good group of new terms to start with.

We have not done anything about the sentences and the stories. Oh, well, the stories do not matter too much; they are just sentences strung together. But we must plan varied sentences, since the Strickland study showed us that first graders use almost all kinds of sentences: simple, complex, compound, statements, requests, questions, and so on.[22] Let us see whether we can write the first story, using many different kinds of sentences and our regularly spelled words.

Let us start with a sentence like that used by Gattegno in *Words in Color*, which his pupils can read after five or six weeks.

[17] McCracken, "The New Castle Reading Experiment — A Terminal Report," *Elementary English*, XXX (January, 1953), 13–21.

[18] I. A. Richards and Christine Gibson, *First Steps in Reading English* (New York: Washington Square Press, 1959).

[19] Morris, *op. cit.*, p. 45.

[20] C. Gattegno, *Words in Color* (Chicago: Learning Materials, Inc., 1962).

[21] *Izzy Sight Vocabulary Cards* (Medina, Ohio: Antof Educational Supplies).

[22] Ruth G. Strickland, *The Language of Elementary School Children: Its Relationships to the Language of Reading Textbooks and the Quality of Reading of Selected Children*, ("School of Education Bulletin," No. 38; Bloomington: Indiana University, 1962), chap. ii.

pat met on a mat a man as fat as tim.

And now a question:

what pat met on a mat a man as fat as tim?

That is good. Now for a request.

put pat, the man as fat as tim, on a mat.

That is a good complex sentence, too. And now for a quotation. We shall have to write it like a line in a play, because we cannot use those irregulars "said" or "asked."

pat: tim met a man on a mat as fat as dan.

Now for a compound sentence.

pat had a mat and tim had a cat.

That should be a good beginning story. It is certainly different from those in the old basal readers. We really are emphasizing structural patterns here; Carl A. Lefevre ought to be very pleased with our stories.[23]

It may be that there is no good reason to expect pupils to be able to read sentences as complex as those they use or listen to. Some studies have shown that it is not until children are at least twelve to fourteen years of age that they can begin to read language structures as advanced and complex as those common to their speech or listening experiences. On the other hand, perhaps there is something to the opinion of students of linguistics that we are retarding pupils in language development by using sentence patterns in ear-

ly reading that are simpler than those the pupil can comprehend or use in speech. Let us go on with our stories in varied sentence patterns anyway. They are much more interesting and dramatic when varied than when simple to read.

PRINCIPLE THREE — GIVE THE
METHOD A CAREFUL TRIAL

The next big step is to give our method a careful, scientific trial. Of course, we have already shown its values with our own children, as Bloomfield and Flesch did. Now we have to find a classroom in which our system will show its superiority. There's Mrs. Jones's class downtown. She is always enthusiastic about any new method. We shall try it there and get another teacher in the same building to use a phonics workbook. That is the way the Bloomfield-Barnhart materials were studied,[24] and this test is sure to prove how superior our "linguistically-oriented programed sequence" with its "auto-instructional device" is to those systems that call themselves "phonetics."

We must remember not to burden Mrs. Jones with the keeping of careful records, such as the amount of time she spends teaching reading each day. Nobody else reports the amount of class time spent on reading. And if she wants to spend all day teaching her pupils the new alphabet, as some teachers using ITA do, that is no one's business but hers. Nor will we ask her to give readiness or intelligence tests to her children, or to report on their socioeco-

23 Lefevre, *Linguistics and the Teaching of Reading* (New York: McGraw-Hill Book Co., 1964), chap. v.

24 Bloomfield and Barnhart, *op. cit.*, p. 12.

nomic status or any of those fancy research details. We need not match children or classes; all we need is an enthusiastic teacher, and the program will take care of all other problems.

As Charles C. Fries has warned us, we must remember to instruct Mrs. Jones not to be distracted in her teaching by noting that some children spontaneously use a variety of clues to word recognition.[25] She must remember to keep them concentrating on learning words only by our alphabet. The children must be warned against deducing word meanings from picture clues and familiar sentence patterns. The sentences are for reading, not for using as context clues. She must also remember not to waste any time on readiness training. After all, as the linguists tell us, any child who can talk is ready to read.[26]

We shall devise our own reading tests, which will be printed in the new alphabet for two reasons: (1) the results will prove that children do learn to read with this new alphabet, and (2) no one can disprove our results, for it will be impossible to tell what the children's performances really mean. We do not have to worry whether our pupils will be able to read in the normal alphabet, for by the time we really get our system and our publisher friends working, most books will be published in the new alphabet. After all, this is the type of scientific trial that helped the ITA alphabet get started. If it worked for them, it will work for us.

25 Fries, *op. cit.*, p. 199.

26 Bloomfield, *op. cit.*, p. 3; Fries, *op. cit.*, p. 112.

PRINCIPLE FOUR — PUBLISH
YOUR RESULTS

Let us review the scientific data that we will report. We will compare the mean score in our word-recognition test, printed in our alphabet, with the mean score of the other class. But if the other group's test is printed in the usual letters, how will we compare the two mean scores? Oh, well, it will be obvious which class learned more words. We do not need any tests of the statistical significance of the results; they are too complicated for most teachers to understand anyway.

What kinds of results may we expect? In the first place, the emphasis upon letter sounds will make our pupils stronger in that type of word-analysis skill. They should be better in reading words than the phonics group. If we can judge from Richard H. Bloomer's study, they will also be superior in reading sentences but not in reading paragraphs.[27] Let us just omit the latter type of test; after all, we shall have enough information with the other tests.

What other results will we probably find? Our pupils certainly ought to know the alphabet better than the other pupils. We shall give a test on the alphabet; it should give good results. We should give a spelling test, too. Our pupils ought to be somewhat better in spelling, particularly if we make our own test of the regularly spelled words with which they are already familiar.

We should certainly point out how

27 Bloomer, "Reading Methodology: Some Alternative Organizational Principles," *Reading Teacher*, XIV (January, 1961), 167–71.

desirable our system will be for retarded readers. The dramatic change
from traditional orthography to our
alphabet will provide precisely the lift
toward success that most retarded readers need. Our "programed sequence"
by means of an "auto-instructional device" will be the greatest contribution
to remedial reading yet invented.

Since most follow-up studies of earlier innovations resembling ours were
not very successful in finding any long-
range gains in word recognition, spelling, or comprehension, we had best not
employ such tests. Furthermore, we
had better not make a study of the
breadth and variety of reading done
by our pupils since there will not be
much class time for recreational reading and there are not many recreational books published in our alphabet.

EPILOGUE

This chapter has treated a number
of innovations in reading instruction
with a satirical tone because it appears to the writer that there is no other way of treating these pseudoserious
attempts to discover new approaches to
our old problems. As Jeanne Chall has
observed, many of these innovations
and their feeble supporting studies
seem, first, to be completely unrelated
to the knowledge we have acquired in
the field of reading, and second, to
have been devised not only in a vacuum but also as an attempt to prove
the author's prejudiced beliefs about a
particular approach or system. Each
innovator has declaimed his own definition of the reading process, as well
as his own aims and goals for the instructional process, and has then proceeded to invent a system that paralleled his unique view.

In addition to an obviously unscien-
tific approach, some innovators ignore
all that is known about careful research design, the control of experimental variables, and statistical evaluation. In these circumstances this writer can draw no defensible conclusions
from many recent developments other
than that the authors apparently
thought they were trying something
new. Is it shocking, then, that I find it
so difficult to regard these magnificent
delusions with solemnity?

CHAPTER VI

EXPERIMENTAL PROCEDURES IN READING

*

INITIAL TEACHING ALPHABET (ITA)

SADAKO TENGAN

*

THE forty-four letter Initial Teach-Alphabet, known formerly as the Augmented Roman Alphabet, was designed by Sir James Pitman. Twenty-four of the traditional symbols are retained (exceptions, *q* and *x*) and twenty new symbols are added, as close to the traditional configuration as possible, to make for a single sound-symbol relationship (or phoneme). Enlarged letters (majescules) are substituted for capitals, thus eliminating additional letters. Double letters are retained as in original spelling, for example, littl. There is not the total phonemic consistency which one attributes to the International Phonetic Alphabet, but there is a general consistency. ITA was not designed to be a phonetic alphabet but a medium for beginning reading. That it has a high phonemic consistency is certainly an advantage over the traditional medium.

One of ITA's major contributions is in the learning of vowel sounds, an area of word analysis in which the beginning reader encounters much difficulty. In a regular sequence, the study of vowels is begun in the second grade; but because of the consistency of ITA,

the teaching of vowels can be begun as early as the teaching of consonant sounds.

In ITA, the long vowels, æ, ee, ie, œ, ue, are so designed that the silent *e* is attached to the vowel to form one symbol. The conventional vowels take on the short sounds, and new symbols, a combination of two vowels, represent other sounds.

Let us take a few words in pre-primers using the symbol *o* and see how ITA works for the young reader. Consider the words, *go, look, come, on,* and *you.* These five basic words each contain a distinct sound value of the letter *o*: ō, ŏo, ŭ, ŏ, and ōō, respectively. Then there are words such as *work* and *one,* which also add to the already inconsistent pattern of sound-symbol relationships. With ITA, all the above words can be spelled with their appropriate symbols: *gœ, lwk, cum, on, yω, wurk,* and *wun.*

To carry this further, let us examine words with a single sound, the long *o.* As he progresses through preprimers and primers, the child encounters *oh, go, coat, don't, home, know.* In ITA

61

this sound is represented by the same symbol, œ: œ, gœ, cœt, dœn't, hœm, and nœ.

In the consonant complex, words with *kn, gh, ph, ld, gn*, and other confusing combinations are eliminated. All these are replaced with an appropriate consonant symbol.

Other basic words, such as, *get, will, run, did, funny*, and *jump*, remain the same. This adds to the similarity of ITA configuration and traditional orthography (TO).

AN EXPLORATION

In September of 1963, the University of Chicago Laboratory Schools initiated the ITA project in one first-grade class. This undertaking, strictly speaking, has been an exploration rather than a research project.

From three kindergarten classes, twenty-five children were selected. The criterion for selection was obvious: they were all beginning readers, with the exception of a few who were reading at preprimer levels. We felt that these children would not be handicapped by inclusion in the project.

Parents were informed as fully as possible about the nature of the project. The film *The 40 Sounds of English, Initial Teaching Alphabet* (John A. Bransby Productions, New York) was shown and was followed by a discussion. The film did much to help alleviate some anxieties. Questions were raised about outside reading in TO, transfer to TO, and spelling problems but not about whether the children would succeed in learning to read through such a program.

Because of the scarcity of ITA books in this country, outside reading was indeed a problem. In addition, reading materials in TO were readily available at home, and it was impractical to ask parents to put them away. One mother did transliterate TO books for our meager library.

Parents needed some assurance that transfer to TO would not be a special problem. Transfer was to be within the school year for most, and the others were to transfer over the summer. For a very few, the second year might be necessary for transfer.

Transfer in spelling would probably take more time, as it would involve some undoing of established visual and kinesthetic patterns reinforced by a long period of reading and writing in ITA. To facilitate this transfer, the children were to be promoted to second grade en masse.

The real working problems arose when school started with a scarcity of library books to fill the need for browsing and reading at the beginning level. Then, too, the *Early To Read Series* (Initial Teaching Alphabet Publications, New York) was not ready, with the exception of Book 1, a phonic workbook. There were enough of the Janet and John readers (James Nisbet, London) and a few library books from England to get us started.

On the first day the children came into the room and started calling off the alphabets which were on display, "*a, b, c. . . .* Hey! That's not an *a*! That's the new alphabet." They were prepared for something new. This newness, coupled with general anxiety over reading, presented a new dimension in the emotional phase of learning to read.

THE READING PROGRAM

Since almost all of the children were beginning readers, we began with the English readers, which came in two series: one using the look-say approach and the other using the phonic method. The look-say series was used simultaneously with Book 1 of the *Early To Read Series*, thus facilitating a reading program combining look-say and phonics.

With the *Early To Read Series*, it was found that quite a few children were sounding out each word much too carefully, including basic words. The workbook was discontinued temporarily in order to encourage a reasonable fluency in reading and to facilitate a smoother flow of ideas in the stories. By this time, each child was in an individualized program, and as soon as a child began having difficulty with a word, he was told the word.

There was also a creative writing program to add to the children's reading vocabulary. Each child was given an alphabetized box with forty-two indices (*r* and *ʒ* being omitted). Words that could be used for stories were written on slips and filed alphabetically. Phonics was worked into the program as the children became comfortable with story-writing.

The children enjoyed this aspect of the program, and their stories generally began to grow longer and were more interestingly written. Ideas seemed to flow more smoothly. As the children became more adept at word analysis, spelling no longer constantly interrupted their trains of thought.

In February and March, the more capable students began transferring easily at third- and fourth-grade levels. These children read with fluency and understanding, and readily attacked unfamiliar words. From this point and on up to June, the levels of transfer gradually dropped. Without a sufficient number of trade books and other reading materials to satisfy the need to browse and read outside their textbooks, the children read from their readers out of necessity. The result was transfer for some who were unprepared for it.

The children who made the transfer were given a special library corner for browsing and reading in addition to school library privileges. The special library contained books ranging in ability levels from the easy-to-read to third- and fourth-grade. As these books found their way to the pupils' desks, other children in the program got hold of them and soon some were reading comfortably from them.

As expected, transfer in spelling took awhile. The children were making a decided effort to spell in the "other alphabet." Individual help was given during creative writing, and workbooks in TO were provided for further practice in writing. But much of the transfer was worked out during the following year.

The second group was a decidedly different one. First, the children had been exposed to ITA in kindergarten through its readiness program, and some had already been using the Janet and John readers. Second, since they came from the middle group (chronologically) of kindergarteners, the children were older and more mature in many respects. Third, there were more books in ITA. Fourth, children and teacher were more comfortable with ITA.

From the beginning, the reading was individualized. The range extended from one child who had transferred over the summer to the beginners. The program was not as phonically oriented in the beginning as it had been in the first year. More importance was placed on building sight vocabulary. Creative writing was again emphasized. The phonic workbooks were used, and in addition, each child was given a box of tiles for a game similar to Scrabble.

Needless to say, these children transferred earlier than the first group. It was hoped that three children who had not transferred by the end of the year would transfer during the summer. In general, these children made a better transfer in spelling, with a number spelling comfortably in TO very quickly.

CONCLUDING STATEMENT

The following observations can be made at the conclusion of the second year of exploration of ITA as a medium for beginning reading: (1) Children and adults readily learn the alphabets; (2) transfer to traditional orthography is smooth, provided that the child is ready for it; (3) ITA seems to encourage a freer expression of ideas in creative writing; (4) children are more aware of sound-symbol relationships; (5) ITA greatly facilitates word analysis; (6) transfer in spelling occurs later than transfer in reading; (7) ITA seems to give children that sense of confidence so essential during the early stages of reading.

Because the ITA project at the Laboratory Schools was an exploratory one, there are no data to be reported here. The Initial Teaching Alphabet cannot be declared a panacea for all reading problems. It is for those involved in carefully designed research projects to answer the gnawing question, "Is the Initial Teaching Alphabet a good medium for all beginning readers?"

* * *

PROGRAMED READING MATERIALS
SAMUEL WEINTRAUB

*

THE ORIGINS of the concept of programed instruction, and of most commercial programs developed therefrom, are directly traceable to B. F. Skinner of Harvard. Programed instruction was born in the animal laboratory and is based on operant conditioning as a means of learning. The basic learning premise is immediate reinforcement of a correct response to a stimulus situation. Reinforcement may come in the form of a buzzer, a green light, a piece of candy, the exposure of the correct answer, or in a number of other ways. Although another form of programing does exist and reference will be made to it later, it is fair to state that most current programs are essentially Skinnerian, or linear, in nature and based on what is fundamentally stimulus-response learning.

In linear programing, the learner is led through a series of steps to the ultimate achievement of the desired terminal behavior. Each step is reinforced by knowledge of results. The correct response is elicited in order that it may be rewarded and thus learned. Although the means of response emission is irrelevant, a basic assumption has been that some kind of response is necessary. Because of the need for errorless responses, a need which is based upon the concept of reinforcement of correct responses, linear programers have constructed their sequences in very small steps; that is, the amount of information presented to the student in each step, or frame, tends to be minute.

SOME QUESTIONS

At this point some questions relevant to the philosophy behind programed instruction as well as some doubts raised by research with specific linear programs are in order. First, a linear program asks the learner to work for a value that we might question — the right answer. In a program there is only one correct response or certainly only a limited number. Is this the goal of learning and of education — to come up with the right answer? This is the value currently being instilled.

Second, the claim for individualized instruction needs to be questioned. Linear programs individualize in one respect only, namely, the rate of progress through a program. All students receive exactly the same program, go through exactly the same procedures, and learn, supposedly, exactly the same things. Thus, it is assumed that everyone comes out equal in knowledge, understanding, and ability at the end of the program. This is a questionable assumption. Inasmuch as a program is written to be errorless, it must be paced at the level of the slowest learner for whom the program is intended. Such procedures have led to dissatisfaction with programs.[1]

A third question to be raised concerns the concept of reinforcement used in linear programing. In Skinner's operant-conditioning theory, reinforcement increases the probability of the repetition of certain responses. Although an animal can be taught to reproduce a response when he is given a pellet of food for doing so, one wonders whether getting the right answer serves the same function for a human learner. In fact, if the research in programed instruction is at all valid, there appears to be evidence that immediate reinforcement may not be an essential

[1] Robert Howard Roth, "Student Reactions to Programed Learning," *Phi Delta Kappan*, XLIV (March, 1963), 278–81.

element in learning from programed materials.

Research evidence collected thus far lays open to question the premises that students must respond overtly, that knowledge of the correctness of a response must be relayed to the student immediately, that steps must be small, that the error rate must be low, or even, indeed, that there must be a sequence to the program. Studies have shown that all these points, most of which constitute the basic tenets of linear programing, need a great deal more investigation.[2]

Some brief reference needs to be accorded a second school of programing — intrinsic programing. Not so extensively used as linear programing, it affords a quite different technique. Norman A. Crowder, the prime developer of the intrinsic programing movement, says the technique is based on one fact: "The student's choice of an answer to a multiple-choice question can be used automatically to direct him to new material; the student who chooses one alternative can automatically be directed to different material than that to which a student choosing a different alternative is directed."[3] Intrinsic programing often appears in what is called a "scrambled book format." The student is presented some material and responds to a multiple-choice question testing the point of what he has just read or heard. On the basis of his answer, he is sent to the next bit of ma-

terial. In the event his answer is correct, the material will be new; in the event he selects one of the wrong answers, he will be sent through a remedial loop to correct his particular incorrect impressions or concepts. It is essentially a diagnostic technique. One can readily see that this type of material is difficult to produce because of the need to devise remedial loops. For this reason most programed materials now on the market are linear in nature, and this paper is concerned almost entirely with them.

EVALUATING PROGRAMED MATERIALS

The Joint Committee on Programed Instruction and Teaching Machines has proposed that programed materials be evaluated on the basis of two characteristics, those which are "internal" and those which are "external."[4] Internal characteristics are the features of a program which can be judged by visual inspection, such as content. What does the program require the student to do, and does this reflect the kind of competence the school wishes to develop?

External features are the more objective aspects of a program. Two measures of external features have been suggested as being particularly useful in evaluating a program's effectiveness: (1) measures of gain in achievement and (2) evaluation by students, teachers, and experts in particu-

2 John F. Feldhusen, "Taps for Teaching Machines," Phi Delta Kappan, XLIV (March, 1963), 265–67.

3 Crowder, "On the Differences between Linear and Intrinsic Programing," Phi Delta Kappan, XLIV (March, 1963), 251.

4 "Criteria for Assessing Programed Instructional Materials," 1962 Interim Report of the Joint Committee on Programed Instruction and Teaching Machines: American Educational Research Association, American Psychological Association, Department of Audiovisual Instruction of the National Education Association, in Audiovisual Instruction, VIII (February, 1963), 84–89.

lar subject matters.[5] School systems must employ some means of evaluation inasmuch as commercial concerns to date have been extremely lax in presenting schools with validation data on their published programs. In examining forty different programs published by fifteen different firms, Hannelore Vanderschmidt discovered twenty-five which presented no validation data whatsoever.[6]

CURRENT READING PROGRAMS

What programs are available in reading? At the primary level, although a number of programs are on the market, possibly the most extensive is the one prepared by Cynthia Buchanan for Sullivan Associates, *Programmed Reading* (McGraw-Hill). The materials emphasize small differences rather than gross differences in presenting letters and words. Heavy amounts of practice are called for in the series. The emphasis is on the letter and the word throughout, although some attempt is made to get at meaning. Only after he is well into the program is the student called upon to read more than a single sentence. Compre-

hension skills are limited to literal interpretation. The program is linear and must be followed exactly. It is, therefore, inflexible and makes no provisions for individual differences except in rate of progress through the program.

In a program developed by Donald E. P. Smith and others, the *Michigan Successive Discrimination Language Program* (Ann Arbor Publishers and Operant Associates), the student does not appear to be given knowledge of the correctness of his responses. One can only assume the teacher is to use the books in a workbook manner and grade the pages himself. The eighth book in the series begins by presenting a story in six pages. The next 211 pages present various programed exercises on the one story. The terminal goal for the student is to be able to read the story he saw at the beginning of the book. The teacher's manual accompanying the reading and listening materials is also programed. The Smith program appears inadequate from the standpoints of programing, learning, and production. The illustrations in the exercises at the back of Book 8 are so small they are almost unrecognizable on occasion. Certainly, some students will learn with this program; but one must be concerned about the side effects of such poor conception and poor execution.

Above the primary level, vocabulary improvement has been most extensively programed, doubtless because programing of vocabulary materials seems fairly simple and because results are almost certain to be positive. An example of a vocabulary program is

[5] Henry C. Ellis, "Judging the Teaching Effectiveness of Programs," in *Trends in Programmed Instruction*, ed. Gabriel D. Ofiesh and Wesley C. Meierhenry (Washington, D.C.: Department of Audiovisual Instruction, National Education Association, and National Society for Programmed Instruction, 1964), pp. 207-9.

[6] Vanderschmidt, "Validation Data for Programmed Texts: A Checklist for Evaluation of Testing," in *Trends in Programmed Instruction*, ed. by Gabriel D. Ofiesh and Wesley C. Meierhenry (Washington, D.C.: Department of Audiovisual Instruction, National Education Association, and National Society for Programmed Instruction, 1964), pp. 210-12.

Word Clues (Educational Developmental Laboratories). This program presents a great many words but gives extremely limited practice on each. Only four frames are devoted to each word. This number may be adequate for review, but it is doubtful that words will be learned with such brief practice. A single paradigm is followed throughout in introducing and giving the meaning of a word. It seems likely that the student using the program will rapidly approach a point of boredom caused by monotony. One can hardly call *Word Clues* either good programing or good learning. Many other programs currently on the market are either fragmentary in nature or subject to the same criticisms as those above.

PROGRAMS FOR WHOM? WHEN?

At this point, some comments based upon the writer's observations of children during a project to develop and try out programed materials for beginning readers appear to be relevant. The comments center on an essential question: Programs for whom? A program is merely a type of material, albeit a somewhat more sophisticated type in certain ways than traditional materials. As with any other type of material, it will not work for everyone. Much more research is needed to discover who can profit from programed materials. Several leads based on very limited evidence gathered while working with young children appear worth following.

Certain children are socially oriented. They need to respond to other people and to have others respond to

them. Other youngsters are shy, retiring, fearful — they do not learn as well in a classroom setting because of their fears. An inanimate machine might not pose nearly the problem for them that facing other people does. These different patterns of behavior began to emerge in the tryout phases of the reading program mentioned above. The patterns prevailed regardless of intelligence. Some very bright children who learned through the program did so in spite of the program because of their social inclinations. It was strongly felt that for these children learning would have been more efficient in a social setting. Children who constantly demanded the attention of the teacher and the peer group appeared to be a group that could benefit from a machine program. For them, the machine seemed a good approach to the beginning stages of learning how to read because it was not distractible. One could cavort in front of it and receive very little attention from the instrument. None of these comments are "truths." They are only hypotheses which will require a good deal of testing before they can be shown to be either valid assumptions or false leads.

When and how are programs most beneficial? As yet we have no firm answers to this question. Again, in our experimental program, some leads appeared, and we can find other cues through classroom reports and observation. At the present time, most programs appear to be best used as supplementary practice. They can be excellent for review and additional practice. They may also be effective in helping a child who has been absent catch up with his classmates. Certainly no program should be adopted throughout an entire school system without some careful trial periods in one or two classrooms.

THE FUTURE OF PROGRAMED READING

One might gain the impression from this article that programing is totally undesirable. This is not so. Programed instruction in the field of reading is still in its infancy, as is the whole field of programing. Present-day programs are, on the whole, rather poor; but it is to be hoped that the programs of tomorrow will be better conceived, more soundly based, and developed from a broader perspective than linear programing. Intrinsic programing holds more promise, but it, too, is limited.

As a supplementary tool of instruction, programed materials have already proved helpful. For the student who has been ill and out of school, for the child who needs additional practice in a particular skill, and for the student who learns best from this type of instruction, programed materials may be one answer. In the meantime, schools must be very careful in the use of a program, in the evaluation of it, and in the selection of those who are to use it.

Perhaps the future will bring an additional consultant to school systems. He will be a programer who is familiar with the strengths and limitations of commercially produced programs and who also is able to help teachers develop their own programs for presenting particular skills to their classes. Perhaps we shall have mechanized reading centers in which students may select from among the many programs available the ones that best suit their needs at the moment. It may be that the reading material of the future will program student interaction with their teachers and peers upon completion of a particular story or segment of the over-all program. In the event that some of these things do come to pass, the teacher will be called upon to teach at a much more creative level. If programs can overcome their current inadequacies, we may find the students will demand much more from us in the way of intellectual and creative teaching. Let us hope so.

* * *

TEACHER TEAMS IN READING

PHILIP M. CARLIN

*

A TEACHING team, according to Judson T. Shaplin, exists when two or more professional teachers, working together, assume joint responsibility for all, or a substantial part, of the instruction of the same group of students.[1] The key words here are

[1] Judson T. Shaplin and Henry F. Olds, Jr. (eds.), *Team Teaching* (New York: Harper & Row, 1964), p. 15.

joint responsibility, for if this requisite is not satisfied there is no team teaching. In departmentalized programs, for example, teachers specialize in a particular area of instruction and assume exclusive responsibility in that area; in team programs, however, each teacher, although specializing in one area, is involved in the planning and development in every area.

Organizationally, team teaching may assume many diverse forms. Thus a team program may involve a highly structured hierarchy with team leaders, senior teachers, regular teachers, student teachers, teacher aides, clerical assistants, and the like, or it may be no more than a loosely connected confederation of associates who all share equally in authority and responsibility.

The former type of structure provides incentives of increased prestige and pay for those teachers who work up the hierarchical ladder. It also makes it possible for them to attain higher positions without having to forsake actual teaching for administration. The co-operative type of team enables teachers in conventional programs to move into team programs with a minimum of dislocation. It also eliminates the possibility of organizational infighting for top positions, a frequent threat to the hierarchical team. Whatever the structure of the team program, however, it is obvious that a true team must have a certain feeling of "togetherness" running through it in planning, teaching, and evaluating. This, not organization, is what makes a team a team.

But we are concerned here chiefly with team teaching and reading. We will not dwell on the myriad organizational plans that team teaching has spawned, nor the intricate scheduling that sometimes takes place. Suffice it to say that most of what has been done in the past few years has been experiment and is subject to many changes.

TEAM TEACHING AND FLEXIBLE GROUPING

As a teacher team meets to plan its program, one of the first considerations that becomes apparent is the need to adapt the size of the group to the content of the course and to the teaching methods. (Incidentally, in the formation of teams, the administrator should be careful not to impose too much of his own thinking concerning the ultimate operation of the team. A team will function best — indeed, it will fulfil one of the most desirable functions of team teaching — when it is allowed considerable leeway in formulating its instructional goals and methods. It is this function that enhances the professional features of team teaching.) Thus, in planning for the instruction of seventy-five to one hundred students, for example, the team will soon see the need for flexible grouping.

Although specially designed school buildings frequently facilitate flexible grouping, such design is not indispensable for grouping or for team teaching. Many existing school buildings have areas that either through minor modifications or simply creative use of school furniture can be adapted to large or small groups. When we think of flexible grouping, we think of large groups, class-sized groups, and small groups. We think of moving groups about, combining them, dividing them, and otherwise changing their size and composition. Teacher teams in reading have been rather late in developing since small groups have commonly been thought to be best for teaching in that area. Reading apparently suffers as class size increases, as achievements and abilities become more heterogeneous, and as the teacher becomes more removed from a close relationship with the learner. But to think that reading cannot be a legitimate area for team teaching because of its necessarily smaller teacher-student ratios is to misunderstand the function of team teaching. Flexible grouping follows the establishment of teacher teams only if the teachers perceive the need for it; and in reading instruction, as in other areas, many opportunities arise to adapt the size and composition of the groups to what is being taught.

A TEACHER TEAM IN READING

Teacher teams usually develop in elementary schools around grade levels or, in non-graded organizations, around levels of achievement. Area specialization usually follows. This progression is not invariable, however, as teams must act according to their own plans if they are to function properly. Let us assume that a co-operative team of three or four teachers is planning the reading instruction of around one hundred students. If the team has not designated a leader in this area, the process of decision-making will usually reveal the one who can best fill this role. At planning sessions, the team will make provision for the daily programs covering at least two weeks so that they will fit into the previously determined plan for the term. (In many smaller school systems that use team teaching, the teams actually determine the curriculum.)

Teachers soon discover that certain types of learning experiences lend themselves to certain types of grouping. For example, oral reading, vocabulary development, word recognition drills, and acquisition of skills in word attack are appropriate activities for small groups. On the other hand, experience-enriching and motivational activities such as dramatizations, choral reading, the introduction of a new skill like dictionary use, or the reading of some selection by a teacher who can perform this type of activity well are all appropriate for large groups.

The team must collect the available materials, consult with the librarian — who should be a specialist member of every reading team — acquire the assistance of any resource personnel who may be available, and think through the advantages and disadvantages of allocating various types of reading activities to various sizes and compositions of groups. The members of the team should then assign themselves functions and responsibilities. For a given large-group session, for example, one of the team might assume the task of directing a choral reading; another might read from a selection calculated to stir the interest of most of the group; or another might use various projection devices to present an exciting activity in vocabulary development. The types of activities available for large-group lessons are frequently limited only by the range of teacher capabilities. Indeed, this method compels a teacher to expand his teaching repertoire. The large-group lesson is teacher-centered, and the teacher cannot "play it by ear" but must have a timed and polished performance similar to that of an actor. Furthermore, the exposure of students to various teaching styles and personalities can have a salutatory effect on learning and attitudes in general. Management problems in large groups are largely nonexistent, mostly because of the experience the learners are undergoing and the extra amount of teacher preparation that has been done.

Large-group lessons do not need to exclude small-group activities. There may perhaps be one member of the team who does exceptionally well with small groups in either remedial or enrichment activities and who may easily be called upon to take over some of these activities. Work in small groups may very well be conducted at the same time that a large-group lesson is underway. It may be that a few students are so retarded in reading that they may not be able to benefit from the large-group lesson. What better time, then, to give them intensive experience in small groups than when the large group is engaged? At the other end of the scale, able learners who may occasionally find what is going on in the large group less than stimulating can be kept interested by individual enrichment activity in small groups.

CONCLUDING STATEMENT

What really makes a team a viable, productive structure for the teaching of reading is the effect it has upon teachers and teaching proficiencies. Such aspects of team teaching as peer supervision and the improvement of instruction by mutual observation are vital outcomes. The exchange of ideas and the greatly expanded resources in material and personnel which team teaching makes available enhance the total instructional situation.

$$* \quad * \quad *$$

THE LANGUAGE-EXPERIENCE APPROACH

ELAINE C. VILSCEK

$$*$$

EDUCATORS have long recognized the importance of integrating each pupil's unique language experiences. In the professional literature, progress in listening, speaking, writing, and reading are often considered as interrelated and interdependent. According to Roach Van Allen, children learn to read by developing an auditory memory through listening and by oral-visual associations that occur as teachers graphically record pupils' experiences. Both at the intermediate- and primary-grade levels, the language and thinking of individual children are utilized to develop basic skills.[1] These underlying principles of the language-experience approach are generally accepted by advocates. Yet there are as many variations and extensions of this approach as there are programs in existence.

In accordance with these underlying principles, workable premises have been formulated during a current research project in reading instruction at the University of Pittsburgh in co-operation with the Pittsburgh Public Schools. In the past year, pupils of varying levels of ability from three levels of the social strata in the city of Pittsburgh have been taught through an "Integrated Experience Approach to Communication."

As viewed by the Pittsburgh project, pupils' experiences within and beyond the periphery of their immediate environments can be appropriately integrated in order to effect maximum language growth. "The Integrated Experience Approach to Communication" can be expressed as follows:

Incidental and Structured, Direct or Vicarious, Integrated Experiences + Motivation + Individualized Instruction = Degree of Success, Desire to Communicate, Transfer in Learning, and Creative Language Development.

[1] Roach Van Allen, "Three Approaches to Teaching Reading," in *Challenge and Experiment in Reading*, International Reading Association Conference Proceedings, ed. J. Allen Figurel (New York: Scholastic Magazines, 1962), VII, 153–56.

IMPLEMENTATION OF THE INTEGRATED-EXPERIENCE APPROACH

A common question asked by teachers is, "How does one begin?" As an initial step toward integrating the varied experiences of children at all elementary-grade levels, teachers should provide pupils with opportunities to share their ideas. Consequently, the instructional foundation at these grade levels is facility in listening and in oral expression.

Particularly at the kindergarten and first-grade levels, the teacher must frequently act as a scribe, recording the orally expressed ideas and experiences of the whole class, small groups, or individual children. This recording should take place in the presence of the children and should retain the natural language patterns to as great an extent as possible. Auditory-visual discriminative abilities, directional-motor abilities, and a basic sight vocabulary are acquired by this technique. Concept development, growth in an awareness of phonics and its application, comprehension abilities, and oral reading skills may also be introduced by this means. Most important for success, throughout this natural process of language growth is the teacher's extension of each pupil's experiential background through timely incidental and structured, direct and vicarious activities.

When the children have acquired a basic sight vocabulary through experience stories, they are ready to make the transition from chart reading to individualized reading in trade books. Children have little or no difficulty making this transition if the trade books utilize a closely related linguistic pattern. On occasion, small groups of children at comparable comprehension levels may read the same story or tradebook for a common learning experience.

At upper primary-grade levels and intermediate-grade levels, some use may still be made of dictated experience stories, charts, and poems. As the pupils become more proficient, they will begin to assume more independent writing responsibilities. Their written stories should be shared with their classmates. To some extent, pupils are able to reinforce skills by using other children's written products as well as their own.

Various other types of instructional materials may be used for developing specific skills in listening, speaking, writing, and reading. In addition to trade books, there are records, tape recorders, picture files, word lists and files prepared by the pupils themselves, selected stories from basal readers, self-directive kits and workbooks, commercially prepared worksheets, magazines, newspapers, and basic or supplementary books in the content areas. Varied instructional materials play an important role in implementing the language-experience approach.

In order to provide appropriate individualized instruction, teachers must continually re-evaluate pupils' experiential backgrounds, language potential, and immediate instructional needs. Some use should be made of standardized and informal evaluative measures. But since these measures have decided limitations, teachers should also depend on their own observations.

Whole-group, small-group, and individual or paired-pupil instruction are equally indispensable as teachers attempt to provide for individual differences and needs. *Whole-group instruction* includes (1) experiences that accomplish a common instructional purpose, (2) the study at all levels of an instructional objective that is dependent upon the use of a common instructional tool such as an experience story, and (3) the pursuit of a specific objective on the vertical learning spiral by means of a common activity but utilizing differing levels of instructional materials.

Small-group instruction includes (1) experiences that accomplish a common instructional purpose for a smaller group than the class, (2) experiences that provide enrichment on a horizontal learning track or reinforcement, and (3) experiences in which attention is given to an individual child's potential mode of learning.

Individual or paired-pupil instruction may include (1) experiences designed to satisfy unique individual instructional needs, (2) experiences that develop pupils' specific aptitudes, and (3) individual pupil-teacher conferences.

Because of the number of possible types of instructional organization, teachers should remember that a flexible, block-time schedule is essential. It is also important to remember to direct adequate attention to each area of the language arts.

DEVELOPMENTAL CURRICULAR GUIDELINES

Adequate implementation of the integrated approach to communication is certainly a task which requires total, unified faculty attention. If an instructional program is to lead to maximum language facility, it must necessarily be very carefully developed. To ensure some measure of methodological success in Pittsburgh, a curriculum that would provide guidelines of stability was devised. The curriculum was based on the assumption that the language arts are theoretically fused by continuous interconnecting channels that facilitate the transfer of learning. Though many language understandings, habits, skills, attitudes, and appreciations can be appropriately interrelated, others are unique to one area of the language arts and were so considered in the Pittsburgh program.

At each grade level, teachers were provided with spiral guides that included charts of expected instructional outcomes as well as fairly complete outlines for the development of six to nine distinct topical interest areas. The latter, called Interest Area Unit Guides, contained suggestions of optional multilevel, multidimensional communication experiences for achieving certain instructional outcomes. Suggestions included whole-class, small-group, and individual activities. Teachers were also encouraged to substitute personally devised plans for accomplishing a timely pupil experience or language objective.

Since selecting trade books and also other types of audio-visual-kinesthetic instructional materials is most time consuming, a complete bibliography for teachers and pupils was also provided with each guide. In addition, the guides contained an appendix of assorted material. The last section of the complete curriculum guide served as a summary of a year in perspective. Teachers were encouraged to evaluate critically their achievements and attitudes. Through this final note of introspection, it was hoped that teachers would become more aware of their own individual role in the implementation of a program.

REACTIONS AND PROBLEMS

One of the most interesting aspects of our work in Pittsburgh was the apparent change in the behavior and attitudes of teachers. When the program was initiated, the teachers expressed doubt about their possible success with the new approach. A number were apprehensive about the reactions of parents. Though considerable amounts of time were spent reassuring teachers and helping them reassure parents, their fears were allayed only as they began to observe the children's success in the program.

Many questions and problems were encountered. Some changes had to be made in previous techniques for reporting pupil progress. The result were the Diagnostic Mastery Checklists of Instructional Outcomes, which proved to be most valuable. Other questions about grouping and the amount of individualized instruction were posed continually. At the outset, we attempted to give teachers help in these areas by informally charting the specific pupil needs that had been revealed by an early application of standardized and informal evaluative instruments. Teachers were given regular opportunities to attend as a total group or as individuals in-service training sessions conducted by staff members from the University of Pittsburgh. Sharing ideas, demonstrating techniques, and resolving problems became prominent aspects of the in-service meetings.

Near the close of the school year, we recorded some of the reactions of teachers to the Integrated Experience Approach to Communication. Most felt that pupil growth in total communication abilities was amazing. They all expressed sincere satisfaction with the heightened desires of their children to write, read, speak, and listen.

OBSERVABLE INSTRUCTIONAL OUTCOMES

The following observations about the language-experience approach seem significant at this point in our experimentation:

1. Growth in aural-oral vocabularies is apparent. There is a sharp contrast between the chart stories dictated early in the program and the stories written later by children themselves.

2. Teachers are more aware of the growth and needs of individual pupils. The very nature of the approach rejects a mechanical application of the program.

3. Teachers have extended their own instructional ingenuity beyond the suggested guidelines. Each teacher has become more flexible in classroom management and has grown in ability to provide higher quality independent work-type activities.

4. Fewer, if any, pupils feel the dejection of failure since each child is naturally sensitized to personal measures of success.

5. Children appear to sense a beauty of language and manifest strong desires to communicate in writing.

* * *

SUPERVISED INDEPENDENT STUDY

MARJORIE ROYER

*

AN EVALUATION of the Perry Central Junior High School developmental reading program demonstrated that many of the reading skills were not being applied in the content areas. It also appeared that reading skills taught in isolation remained largely in isolation. The staff began to search for some methods of making reading and study skills meaningful in terms of the junior-high school curriculum.

A program to meet this need was written by Marjorie Royer, the reading teacher, and George Callon, the principal. Their over-all goal was a natural approach to the teaching of reading in all content areas by means of the problem-solving method. The program was called Supervised Independent Study (S.I.S.) and provided for the teacher to teach, direct, and guide the student in solving problems independently by employing maximum critical thinking. This was to be achieved by teaching the student how to choose and use the best skills, methods, resources, and references for solving a particular problem.

As a student worked on a problem he was to use appropriate reading and writing skills. When there was a breakdown in his comprehension or communication, the teacher would go immediately to his aid and teach him the correct skill. If the student did not respond, he was to be referred to a tutor. When he had mastered the skill, he would return to his original problem.

S.I.S. was tried four times during the school year 1963–64. Each time the project was centered on a natural problem: (1) How can freshmen be taught the use of research skills in the most proficient way? (2) How can freshmen best be taught to read and interpret a new textbook being adopted in the science department? (3) What can be done to enrich a German class in the background and culture of that country? (4) Can some of the criteria used by S.I.S. to help gifted and average students interpret novels be employed by an eighth-grade remedial English class?

S.I.S. PROJECT—SCHOOL YEAR 1964–65

During the school year 1964–65, because of class-schedule conflicts, a class of seventh graders was established with a greater divergence in ability than is the policy of this school. The students were hostile, and keeping discipline became a problem. The Block of Time Program (a program correlating English and social studies in a two-hour and forty-minute block) had previously worked well at Perry Central, but not with this group. Evelyn Lovelace, the classroom teacher, asked several members of the staff to sit in on the class to see if as a group they could come up with some answers to meet the needs of these students and to eliminate the very aggressive group interactions. After observing the class, the guidance staff, Mr. Callon, Mrs. Royer, and Mrs. Lovelace met for a conference. It was decided to try the S.I.S. program. Team teaching was decided upon in order to free the teachers to meet the individual needs of the slower students and to challenge the gifted. Small groups were also to be used, as it was felt that peer approval might best help this class to solve its individual problems. The over-all objective was to establish an artificial problem structure that would help to solve the already existing problem, that of discipline.

The problem chosen was "The Civil War: Its Causes and Effects," since it was the next topic to be studied in social studies. The staff felt that this topic would provide an excellent opportunity to use many of the skills suggested in the English textbook relating to written reports. The S.I.S. program would not introduce all of these skills but rather would explain them when the student could not master them independently. As the student worked, researched, and wrote, it was expected that he would discover that he needed special tools to proceed. The team of teachers would then come forward to assist him.

The *Gates Reading Survey* (Bureau of Publications, Teachers College) was administered as the first step. The team of teachers checked the records in the guidance office for I.Q.'s and achievement reports on all students. By this time the students were aware that something different was happening and were anxious for an explanation. Mrs. Royer gave them the first clue in her introduction of S.I.S. They were informed of the meaning of S.I.S. and to a degree why they had been chosen. They were pleased. Discipline problems began to disappear almost from the first session. Their first assignment was to "write all that you know of the Civil War." This paper was written in class without any books and with no assistance from the team of teachers. The papers ran the gamut from a few sentences to three pages. What the teachers wanted to learn from this assignment was the extent of students' knowledge of the Civil War.

Two days later, Arville Funk, a social studies teacher from Perry East Junior High, was invited to speak and show slides of scenes that had been photographed by Mathew Brady, a famous photographer of the Civil War. Mr. Funk then showed his own slides taken of the same scenes as they were today. Enthusiasm was high. The students asked one question after another.

The second speaker, Donald Royer, research adviser for the Civil Rights Commission for the State of Indiana, presented some pictures on the overhead projector and correlated them with a talk on the "History of the Negro."

Now that motivation had apparently been created, Mrs. Lovelace presented the main topic. Students then chose subtopics of the greatest interest to them: Causes of the Civil War, The Roles of Lincoln and Lee, Cultural Development during the War, Pickett's Charge, The Battle of Shiloh, and The Reconstruction. The team of teachers placed the students in groups according to interest and ability. Leaders who were not too aggressive and who would accept suggestions from others were chosen.

Next the students were taken on a field trip to the city library to become familiar with the kinds of information that could be found in other libraries than their own school library. While they were there, the Dewey Decimal System and the *Reader's Guide* were explained to them by the head librarian. Their greatest learning experience, however, was connected with the card catalog. They were completely overwhelmed to learn that there were at least a thousand titles written on the Civil War.

This group was given exclusive use of the school library for the first two periods of the next four Tuesday mornings. During the first part of the initial session, a film called *Know Your Library* (Coronet) was shown. A question-answer period was led by the librarian.

The second half of this session was led by Mrs. Lovelace, who asked the question, "How can a record be kept of the information you collect from books to be used in your papers?" Most students immediately started listing items, although it was soon clear that all they needed was a form for keeping notes. An overhead projector was used to show them a method. The students were allowed to make up the proper form on a blank transparency. The entire class seemed to feel satisfaction with this endeavor. Those students who grasped the idea of taking notes went on with their projects. Some began to look over material pertinent to their own subgroup's work. Here the librarian directed and suggested. Mrs. Royer talked to other groups who were more advanced on their projects and were now in need of some further direction, and Mrs. Lovelace worked with the slower students who needed a step-by-step review.

The first part of the second Tuesday session was spent in continued research. A filmstrip, *Constructing Reports* (Encyclopedia Britannica Films), was introduced in the second half of the period. The filmstrip started the group thinking about outlines. Again, the slow students needed specific instruction. Before the period was over, however, all groups had listed the points they wanted to include in their outlines, and all were anxious to begin the writing of rough drafts of their papers. They were to return the next Tuesday with their outlines completed, ready to begin on rough drafts.

Between the second and third Tuesday sessions the students decided they would like to make a mural depicting their group topic. Earl Snellenberger, art director of Indiana Central College, had heard of S.I.S. and volunteered his services to teach the group about line, form, space, and color schemes. The mural was worked on during homeroom period and other spare minutes. Students also listened to music of the period, "The Union" and "The Confederacy" (Columbia) .

The next two Tuesday sessions were spent in writing rough drafts. The papers were collected and carefully checked. The teachers wrote suggestions for additions or deletions in the margins. Errors in grammar and spelling were indicated but not corrected. No grade was given. When the papers were returned to the students, excitement began to mount. Competitions emerged. Each leader wanted his group's paper to be the best. Genuine rapport and communication developed among the students in each group. The atmosphere was alive, teeming with interest, work, learning, and communication!

The final papers were graded. Grammar, content, comprehension, expression, and creativity were the main criteria for grading. Growth in reading and writing skills appeared to be excellent.

One member from each group presented the finished paper to the group. The class evaluated the papers indicating weaknesses and strengths. They felt the papers on "The Reconstruction" and "Cultural Development" were the best ones. The teachers concurred.

Mr. Snellenberger revisited the class

after the mural was finished. His evaluation was "far above average."

The concluding step of this project consisted of four evaluations: the student's evaluation of each member of his group; each member's evaluation of S.I.S.; each student's self-evaluation; and a test of skills taught and learned during the period of the project.

CONCLUDING STATEMENT

Though no statistical data is yet available, the teachers who have helped on the five projects of S.I.S. to date have informally observed that students' growth in problem-solving and independent use of writing, reading, and library skills has been significant. Although conclusions must be tentative and all the evidence is not in, many faculty members have adopted the program, or some facets of it, as an integral part of their departmental curriculums.

CHAPTER VII

SPECIFIC TRENDS IN READING

*

INDIVIDUALIZED READING

HARRY W. SARTAIN

*

BRIEFLY described, individualized reading is a procedure by which each student chooses a library book, a literary reader, or possibly a basal book that he would like to read and reads it at his own pace during most of the daily reading time. Instruction is provided through conferences between learner and teacher. Conferences with each individual are scheduled once or twice a week and may last from three to ten minutes. During the conference the teacher discusses the chosen story with the student, listens to his oral reading, and teaches whatever skills are currently needed. He leads the student toward an understanding and an appreciation of the qualities of good literature and tries to interest him in further reading. Occasionally, a teacher may bring small groups together on days when several students need to be taught the same skills. Groups may also be called together to share stories that various members have read.

The major points of difference between proponents of individualized reading and those of basal instruction in groups are listed below. The latter recommend these features for reading programs, whereas the former usually consider them unnecessary or undesirable.

1. A controlled vocabulary for beginning reading.

2. A preliminary introduction of new vocabulary and a discussion of strange concepts to be met in the selection to be read.

3. A predetermined sequence of skills to accompany the stories.

4. Direct reading instruction at least once or twice every day.

5. Division of classes into instructional groups.

6. Deliberate assignment of selections from various types of materials for literary or factual content.

7. Use of the basal reader workbook exercises to reinforce skills.

STRENGTHS AND SHORTCOMINGS
OF THE INDIVIDUALIZED APPROACH

To the experienced teacher, two advantages of the individualized approach seem apparent immediately. First, youngsters may read books and stories in which they are truly interested instead of being required to partake of the same fare as everybody else in the class. Second, the range of individual capabilities in a classroom is recognized and accommodated far more adequately than is possible by a division of the class into only three groups, the common practice in basal instruction.

A third advantage, one that is not frequently mentioned by proponents of individualized reading, is the opportunity given the teacher to observe the perceptual approach through which a child is best able to learn. Some students are more efficient as visual learners, whereas others are more successful using an auditory, a kinesthetic, or a combination method.[1] Individuals who find the visual approach most congenial, for example, may be hindered in the early stages of learning to read by an overemphasis on auditory and kinesthetic techniques for the acquisition of vocabulary and word analysis skills.

The most obvious fault of the individualized approach is its lack of efficiency. Teachers who have difficulty scheduling time for more than three reading groups in the day's reading block are staggered by the suggestion that they plan and conduct thirty different instructional sessions in that time. Obviously, it is not possible to have a conference with every student every day. The individualized reading enthusiasts indicate that two or three conferences can be scheduled for each individual during the week and still allow time for a few group lessons and sharing activities. In practice, however, a team of observers of individualized reading programs in action have found

that some pupils were actually invited to instructional conferences as seldom as once in three weeks.[2]

An inherent weakness in individualized reading, deriving from the seemingly logical belief of proponents that "children should learn skills when they need them to unlock a communication which they wish to receive," is the lack of a systematic skills program.[3] The danger lies in the fact that students may not know when they are not obtaining maximum understanding from a selection or why; that is, they do not have the experience to know what additional skills they could be utilizing. The teacher who has only a few minutes in which to discuss several hours of reading will hardly have time to explore the student's understanding in enough depth to determine which interpretive and evaluative skills he needed but did not have.

STUDIES OF INDIVIDUALIZED READING

One might justifiably ask whether these views are supported by research. Unfortunately, most teachers' conclusions have been based on subjective evidence. Even the studies involving both experimental and control groups have sometimes been loosely planned or inadequately described; therefore, one must read the reports of these stud-

1 Robert E. Mills, "An Evaluation of Techniques for Teaching Word Recognition," *Elementary School Journal*, LVI (January, 1956), 221–25.

2 Mary C. Austin and Coleman Morrison, *The First R: The Harvard Report on Reading in Elementary Schools* (New York: Macmillan Co., 1963), pp. 87–94.

3 Rodney Johnson *et al.*, *A Three-Year Longitudinal Study Comparing Individualized and Basal Reading Programs at the Primary Level: An Interim Report* (Madison: Lakeshore Curriculum Study Council, University of Wisconsin, 1965), p. 9.

ies very critically to reach valid conclusions.[4] Only a few can be mentioned here.

The study that is most damaging to individualized reading is reported by Alton L. Safford, who found that teachers following the individualized approach in a non-experimental situation obtained results far inferior to those of basal group teachers.[5] Experiments by Harold Kaar and by Irving H. Anderson, Byron O. Hughes, and W. Robert Dixon also showed some superiority of achievement through basal group teaching.[6] Two other experiments, by Clare Walker and by Ben A. Bohnhorst and Sophia N. Sellars, revealed no significant differences in achievement despite the increased interest of the students who had done individualized work.[7]

Philip Acinapuro, who attempted careful controls, obtained results favoring individualized reading, but the experiment itself suffered from a lack of libraries in the classrooms of control groups.[8] Sam Duker's findings were effected by the extra time his experimental groups spent on reading study, and Miriam S. Aronow's New York findings may be questioned on the basis of an earlier report suggesting that the teachers using individualized programs were superior to most.[9]

In Minnesota an experiment was designed to permit several teachers to use both methods with the same students in both experimental and control groups. Five second-grade classes were taught by the individualized method for three months, and five others were taught in basal reading groups. At the end of three months, the teachers of these ten classes exchanged methods and used the new method for another three months. One hundred or more different books at various difficulty levels were kept in both the experimental

[4] Harry W. Sartain, "Evaluating Research on Individualized Reading," in *Improvement of Reading through Classroom Practice*, International Reading Association Conference Proceedings, ed. J. Allen Figurel (Newark, Del.: International Reading Association, 1964), IX, 96–98.

[5] Safford, "Evaluation of an Individualized Reading Program," *Reading Teacher*, LX (April, 1960), 266–70.

[6] Kaar, "An Experiment with an Individualized Method of Teaching Reading," *Reading Teacher*, VII (February, 1954), 174–77; Anderson, Hughes, and Dixon, "The Relationship between Reading Achievement and the Method of Teaching Reading," *University of Michigan School of Education Bulletin*, XXVII (April, 1956), 104–8.

[7] Walker, "An Evaluation of Two Programs of Reading in Grades Four, Five, and Six of the Elementary School" (Ph.D dissertation, School of Education, New York University, 1957); Bohnhorst and Sellars, "Individual Reading Instruction vs. Basal Textbook Instruction: Some Tentative Explorations," *Elementary English*, XXXVI (March, 1959, 185–90, 202.

[8] Acinapuro, "A Comparative Study of the Results of Two Instructional Reading Programs — An Individualized and a Three Ability Group Pattern" (unpublished doctoral dissertation, Teachers College, Columbia University, 1959).

[9] Duker, "Research Report: Effects of Introducing an Individualized Reading Approach by Student Teachers," in *Reading in Action*, International Reading Association Conference Proceedings, ed. Nancy Larrick (New York: Scholastic Magazines, 1957), II, 59–62; Aronow, "A Study of the Effect of Individualized Reading on Children's Reading Test Scores," *Reading Teacher*, XV (November, 1961), 86–91; *Individualized Reading Interim Report* (New York: Bureau of Educational Research, Board of Education of the City of New York, 1957).

and control classrooms throughout the study, and children in both programs were encouraged to read extensively. The statistical analysis of data revealed no significant differences in mean gains on standard vocabulary and paragraph-reading tests for the capable students whether they were using the individualized or the basal group method. The less capable students, however, achieved a mean gain in word recognition by the basal group approach that was significantly superior at the .05 level to their achievement during individualized reading.[10]

A more extensive study has recently been completed by a Wisconsin committee under the chairmanship of Rodney Johnson.[11] This was a three-year study, beginning with fourteen experimental and fourteen control classes, from which data on 208 students in basal group reading and 259 students in individualized reading were available at the end of the third year. In addition to the usual achievement test data, information was obtained through sociometric techniques, personal interviews with children, parent questionnaires, and teachers' logbooks. At the end of the first year, children in the individualized reading classes averaged slightly less than two test points higher than children in the basal reading groups on tests of word knowledge, word discrimination, and reading comprehension. These differences, were, however, large enough to be significant at the .01 lev-

el. At the end of the third year, which was also third grade, the differences were even smaller but were still considered great enough to indicate the superiority of the individualized reading method.

Experienced teachers interviewed large samples of children from both the experimental and control classes to test their oral reading skills. Using a form to tally all types of errors, they found no significant differences in oral reading abilities between the two groups. During the first year, children in the individualized programs read more extensively than those in the basal programs, but this tendency was reversed during the third-grade year. No significant differences were found between the two groups in respect to social adjustment, positive attitudes toward themselves, or in parents' attitudes toward the reading program.

It was surprising to note in this study that the superior performance in arithmetic of the children in individualized reading groups as compared with that of the children in the control groups was even greater than the superiority they exhibited in reading achievement. It is difficult to explain why individualized reading should produce superior results in arithmetic computation, and this leads one to wonder whether there were differences in teacher capability in spite of the efforts to control that factor.

TENTATIVE CONCLUSIONS

It is quite amazing to see the different conclusions reached by the proponents and the opponents of individualized reading on the basis of the same

10 Harry W. Sartain, "The Roseville Experiment with Individualized Reading," *Reading Teacher*, XIII (April, 1960), 277–81.

11 Johnson *et al., op. cit.*

experimental studies. A fairly objective evaluation might lead to the following generalizations:

1. Some teachers, especially the more enthusiastic and experienced ones, can teach individualized reading successfully.

2. Many children, especially the more capable ones, make adequate progress in individualized reading programs.

3. The less capable students are less likely to progress satisfactorily in an individualized situation because they are not able to work independently for long periods of time. (However, if the slower children in basal group programs are given textbooks that are decidedly too difficult for them, they will do just as poorly or even worse than in individualized programs.)

4. The personal conference between the student and teacher seems to have great motivational value for the child.

5. Most children read more books in a program of individualized selection and conferences than in a basal program with supplementary books. But this additional amount of reading practice does not necessarily result in proportionately greater attainment of skills, perhaps because the teacher cannot give enough help during the short conferences.[12]

12 Harry W. Sartain, "Research on Individualized Reading," *Education*, LXXXI (May, 1961), 515–20.

* * *

NEW DEVELOPMENTS IN
HIGH-SCHOOL AND COLLEGE READING

EDWARD G. SUMMERS

*

THERE ARE numerous questions to be raised and problems to be met by any high school or college concerned with developing a reading program. Space permits the discussion of only a few of the many.

HIGH-SCHOOL READING

What trends are apparent in the organization of secondary reading instruction? The plans and experiences of others often provide valuable guidelines for action. Although no school system should adopt another school's program as a whole, certainly much that is good in one program can be adapted to similar situations. There is a tremendous diversity in methods, schedules, and content of reading programs; in fact, there appear to be as many ways of organizing secondary reading instruction as there are programs in existence.

Margaret J. Early identifies the "all-school developmental program" as being the most desirable type, which induces the special reading class, the substitute English class, instruction within the regular English class, and developmental reading as part of the core course.[1] Edward G. Summers groups classes at the junior-high school level into remedial and corrective programs, programs utilizing some form of grouping, programs conducted in a reading laboratory or workshop, and programs for single classes of students.[2] Elizabeth A. Simpson indicates that reading programs must be tailor-made to meet the needs of each school and lists five requirements for the success of such programs: (1) readiness on the part of the staff to develop the program, (2) administrative enthusiasm and support, (3) active interest on the part of the parents, (4) an adequate budget, and (5) emphasis on the values of reading.[3] With the addition of federal funds under Title III of the National Defense Education Act for the improved organization of reading instruction, dispensed through state departments of education, one can only speculate as to the major trends and shifts in organization that could develop in the near future.

How can the reading needs of secondary students be identified and the *effectiveness of a program be evaluated?* Programs are beginning to broaden their points of view and utilize sources other than standardized tests to determine student needs. A sound program includes standardized tests and informal evaluative measures. Informal inventories are often the only way to probe deeper into individual needs in reading. An excellent new publication called *Informal Reading Inventories*, by Marjorie S. Johnson and Roy Kress, is available as part of the *Reading Aids* series of the International Reading Association. A recent text by Ruth Strang is a comprehensive attempt to orient the teacher toward a diagnostic approach to teaching reading.[4] Shelley Umans describes techniques for developing informal reading analyses and inventories in the subject areas at the secondary level.[5]

Marjorie Seddon Johnson indicates that evaluation of the reading program must be comprehensive and part of the total instructional plan of the school. It is paramount that the objectives of the program be viewed as basic not only to the program being pursued but also to the evaluative procedures.[6]

What are the trends in providing training in reading for secondary school personnel? Probably the most

1 Early, "What Does Research Reveal about Successful Reading Programs?" *What We Know about High School Reading*, National Conference on Research in English (Champaign, Ill.: National Council of Teachers of English, 1957–58), pp. 7–17.

2 Summers, "An Evaluation of Reading Growth and Retention under Two Plans of Organization for Seventh Grade Developmental Reading" (Ph.D. dissertation, University of Minnesota, 1963).

3 Simpson, "Organizing for Reading Instruction in the Secondary School," in *Reading Instruction in Secondary Schools*, ed., Margaret Early ("Perspectives in Reading," No. 2; Newark, Del.: International Reading Association, 1964), pp. 18–19.

4 Strang, *Diagnostic Teaching of Reading* (New York: McGraw-Hill Book Co., 1964).

5 Umans, *New Trends in Reading Instruction* (New York: Bureau of Publications, Teachers College, Columbia University, 1963).

6 Johnson, "Evaluating the Secondary Reading Program," in *Reading Instruction in Secondary Schools*, ed. Margaret Early ("Perspectives in Reading," No. 2; Newark, Del.: International Reading Association, 1964), pp. 117–29.

immediate concern in meeting the reading needs of secondary students is the staffing of schools with teachers who can provide adequate instruction in reading. Numerous studies have evaluated the status of secondary reading instruction in specific locations. Almost invariably such studies point out the need for better training in the teaching of reading.

Mary C. Austin and others sought to determine what training institutions are doing to prepare tomorrow's teachers of reading and to suggest methods of improving training. They recommend that all prospective teachers at the secondary level be required to take a course in the teaching of reading.[7] Nila B. Smith, looking specifically at the preparation of secondary teachers of reading, makes specific suggestions for in-service training of teachers, the preparation of reading consultants and supervisors, and the provision of courses for undergraduates who have indicated that they will become secondary-school teachers.[8] After surveying state certification agencies, Carl H. Haag, Daniel G. Sayles, and Donald E. P. Smith conclude that there is a trend toward certification of teachers of remedial and developmental reading and a need for professional certification standards.

In some states courses in reading at the undergraduate level are a required part of the training of secondary teachers. Pennsylvania, for example, requires that reading be taught to all students in grades seven and eight and that all undergraduate secondary majors take a course in the teaching of reading.[10] In other states, secondary teaching certificates are endorsed to include reading after a minimum training requirement is met. Many states have set up training requirements and certification requirements for reading specialists and supervisors. The area of teacher training is perhaps the most crucial for improving the teaching of reading at the secondary level. Much remains to be done in providing undergraduate training, in-service training, and improved training for specialists and supervisors. The extended Title III of the National Defense Education Act should aid states to improve teacher training in reading through state-supervised workshops and consultative services to schools.

At present only three states have reading supervisors. Institutes under Title XI of the amended National Defense Education Act provide for four years of reading institutes at three levels of training. A total of fifty-three institutes were funded in 1965. Roughly half of these involved improvement of the teaching skills in reading of secondary teachers. The institutes represent a significant opportunity, but

[7] Austin et al., The Torchlighters: Tomorrow's Teachers of Reading (Cambridge, Mass.: Harvard University Graduate School of Education, 1961).

[8] Smith, "The Professional Preparation of High School Teachers of Reading," Reading Teacher, XIV (May, 1961), 326–30.

[9] Haag, Sayles, and Smith, "Certificate Requirements for Reading Specialists," Reading Teacher, XIV (November, 1960), 98–100.

[10] Charles H. Boehm, "A State Superintendent Comments on Some Problems in a State Reading Program," Reading Teacher, XIV (May, 1961), 319–22; Sheldon Madeira, "Pennsylvania's Mandated Reading Program," Journal of Developmental Reading, V (Summer, 1962), 221–26.

much remains to be done in properly using the resources that have been made available and planning for future needs.

The newer developments in secondary reading are based on what appears to be a valid analysis of the situation; namely, that it is no longer necessary to spend time justifying the existence of secondary reading programs and that the crucial questions now revolve around the more practical elements of organizing instruction, identifying student needs, evaluating programs, and securing the necessary personnel. The *why* of secondary programs has become obvious; now we must answer the *what* and *how*.

COLLEGE READING

Developments in college reading programs can best be illustrated by examining papers and research presented in three recent yearbooks of the annual National Reading Conference: *Problems, Programs and Projects in College-Adult Reading; New Developments in Programs and Procedures for College-Adult Reading;* and *New Concepts in College-Adult Reading.* As Esther J. McConihe points out in examining some of the newer approaches in the field, those which are sound become a part of either practice or theory, whereas those which are fads "fade away" in due course.[11]

The study of reading improvement

courses per se and the validation of variables related or unrelated to reading improvement continues. An examination of the annual summaries of research by Emery P. Bliesmer, which appear in the proceedings of the National Reading Conference, reveals scores of programs organized with a wide variety of combinations of grouping, materials, and training procedures. Studies are also being made of the factors influencing or related to the attainment of reading skills, such as intelligence, limited language patterns, legibility of printed materials, cultural features, and others. These are legitimate areas of inquiry, and the trend is toward an increased amount of such research in the future. As noted by John H. Matthews, however, there is a need to go beyond methodological and relational studies to an enrichment of concept and methodology in the study of reading.[12]

Three developments seem particularly fruitful in this regard. The counseling approach to reading improvement is one approach currently appearing more frequently in college programs. Michael P. Joseph and Arthur S. McDonald indicate that "in recent years articulation between university counseling services and reading centers has become increasingly greater and more refined."[13] Concern is be-

---

[11] McConihe, "Current and Experimental Approaches in College-Sponsored Programs," in *New Developments in Programs and Procedures for College-Adult Reading,* Twelfth Yearbook of the National Reading Conference, ed., Ralph C. Staiger and Culbreth Y. Milton (Milwaukee: National Reading Conference, Inc., 1962), p. 3.

[12] Matthews, "The Need for Enrichment of Concept and Methodology in the Study of Reading," in *New Concepts in College-Adult Reading,* Thirteenth Yearbook of the National Reading Conference, ed. Eric L. Thurston and Lawrence E. Hafner (Milwaukee: National Reading Conference, Inc., 1964), pp. 86–95.

[13] Joseph and McDonald, "Psychological Needs and Reading Achievement," *ibid.,* p. 150.

ing shown for variables such as the students' attitude toward reading,[14] psychological needs and reading achievements,[15] and personality traits affecting reading achievement.[16] Special methods of aiding students to improve study habits and test-taking behavior and of strengthening academic motivation are also receiving attention.[17]

As a result, a greater number of programs are being initiated which teach reading within the framework of over-all personal development. Such courses include not only reading proficiency but, as one author stated, the whole phenomenal field of the student. Since they are based on the assumption that motivational and personal problems are often significantly related to achievement, they attempt to influence the student's perception of self and also his perception of his total environment. Such programs do not confine themselves to reading skills alone but include study skills in all areas. Low concentration, lack of attention, and other poor study habits are remediable through a counseling approach that

takes into consideration the total personal development of the student. In reports of reading programs operating on a counseling basis, the major problem appears to be the difficulty of providing the necessary time for personal contact between teacher and student within a group orientation. In addition, the counseling approach requires a wider range of materials, including self-instructional materials; provision for self-diagnosis and correction; and greater staff flexibility. Among the newer approaches to teaching reading, the counseling approach seems to be of considerable significance.

Closely related to the broader conceptions of the counseling approach is the discovery that reading should be considered a *developmental* process not only in theory but also in practice. In examining five problems in college-adult reading which present new challenges, Arthur Heilman states that if we believe adult reading is a developmental process we should re-examine our aloofness to high-school reading since the latter is an area of adult reading.[18] The problem of articulation between levels has received some emphasis since Heilman's report (1962), as evidenced by the increasing frequency of papers in this area.[19] Homer L. Carter

14 Edwin Young, "Diagnosis of Depth Attitudes toward Reading by Use of a Sentence-Completion Test," *ibid.*, pp. 126–34.

15 Joseph and McDonald, *op. cit.*

16 Earl F. Rankin Jr., "Reading Test Performance of Introverts and Extroverts," in *New Developments in Programs and Procedures for College-Adult Reading*, pp. 158–66; Walter Hill, "Personality Traits and Reading Disability: A Critique," in *Problems, Programs and Projects in College-Adult Reading*, Eleventh Yearbook of the National Reading Conference, ed. Emery P. Bliesmer and Ralph C. Staiger (Milwaukee: National Reading Conference, Inc., 1962), pp. 174–79.

17 Stanley Krippner, "Hypnosis and Reading Improvement among University Students," in *New Developments in Programs and Procedures for College-Adult Reading*, pp. 100–111.

18 Heilman, "New Challenges and Old Problems in College-Adult Reading," in *Problems, Programs and Projects in College-Adult Reading*, pp. 206–18.

19 Warren D. Fortenberry, "Reading Readiness for College Freshmen," in *New Concepts in College-Adult Reading*, pp. 51–54; James Schiavone, "The Secondary School's Role in Developing the College Preparatory Reading Program," *ibid.*, pp. 36–42; Esther J. McConihe "Pre-College Training on College Campuses," in *Problems, Programs and Projects in College-Adult Reading*, pp. 96–99.

and Dorothy J. McGinnis consider reading training at the precollege level.[20] In comparing responses of secondary teachers and college students, they found a great deal of congruence between those skills high-school teachers were unprepared to teach and those skills college students claimed they needed but had not been taught during high school. Although there would be little disagreement that reading is a developmental process and that the ability to read is the most crucial variable throughout the educational life of the student, much remains to be done in actually implementing these beliefs — in particular, in developing effective programs which will train teachers in the skills necessary for successful articulation between educational levels in reading.

An interesting development in college-adult reading, which also reflects the broadening concepts and methodology employed in the study of reading, is the exploratory analysis being undertaken to define and develop the concept of creativity. Some authors have indicated that this development will have as great an impact on our thinking in ten years as the study and development of the concept of intelligence has had in previous years. Paul Conrad Berg presents an excellent analysis of the current literature related to the identification and under-

standing of creative thinking.[21] In summary, he states that creative thinking appears to be independent of intelligence yet is as related to achievement as intelligence. Creativity is more personal, less dependent on facts than problem-solving. Although it utilizes critical analysis, creativity goes beyond that stage, producing new ideas rather than concerning itself with previously existing conditions. Creative thinking is sensitive to problems, fluent, both associative and ideational, flexible or adaptable, spontaneous, and original in its ideation. It is also integrative and non-rigid. It would certainly seem that creativity in thinking is a legitimate goal for reading instruction. The concept of reading as the vehicle for creativity at all levels has been postulated for some time. Is it the creative person or the intelligent person, or a person with both qualities, who makes the greater contribution to society? Obviously, it is most likely a person who combines both qualities. The question becomes extremely relevant and vitally important as we continue to define the concept of creativity, recognize its dimensions, examine it as a facet of reading performance, and recognize its effect in the development of the total reader. One of the most important questions of the near future may well be, How do we foster, at all levels, the development of creative thinking through our reading programs?

20 Carter and McGinnis, "Some Suggestions Growing out of an Evaluation of Reading Instruction by Secondary Teachers and Their Students," in *New Concepts in College-Adult Reading*, pp. 43–50.

21 Berg, "Creativity as a Dimension of Reading Performance," in *New Developments in Programs and Procedure for College-Adult Reading*, pp. 143–51.

THE USE OF PAPERBACKS FOR IMPROVING READING

DAVID A. SOHN

*

THE PAPERBACK book is a powerful new medium of communication that has, in the past twenty-five years, exploded over the national scene into every nook and cranny. It is found on the beach, in the library, in the schoolroom, in pockets, on trains, on the bookshelves — almost overwhelming us with its availability. Few realize the enormous list of titles available in paperback. The latest count of paperback titles in print is 34,700, with more coming daily, the monthly rate of publishing ranging from 300 to 600 titles. And 1,000,000 paperbacks are sold, on the average, every working day.

The paperback book is a significant, different medium from that of the hardcover book. It is a hybrid of tremendous energy, capable of involving the reader to a greater extent than the hardcover book. This phenomenon occurs regardless of content.

The Board of Education of the city of New York authorized the Bureau of Educational Research to conduct a study comparing and contrasting the utility of both mass-market paperbacks and hardcover textbooks in high-school literature classes.[1] Twenty-five thousand students, two thousand par-

ents, seventy-eight department chairmen, and forty-five teachers participated in the study. Seventy-five per cent of the student respondents favored using paperbacks instead of hardcover texts; 70 per cent of the English department chairman also favored the paperback over the hardcover versions; 60 per cent of the parents favored the paperback; and when all facets of teacher opinion were considered, there appeared to be more approval than disapproval of paperbacks. Some of the features most frequently mentioned favoring the paperback over the hardcover were that they were lighter to carry, easier to handle, and encouraged more reading because they were so portable.

Hence, it seems likely that the paperback can be and will be used in the total reading program of many school systems. There are four areas where the paperback can play a major role: (1) as a primary textbook, (2) as a reference work, (3) as part of the library program, and (4) as a stimulator of reading.

PRIMARY TEXTBOOK OR REFERENCE

The imaginative teacher has before him a wide world of flexibility in the paperback — a giant anthology of whole works. In class sets, the teacher can use an astounding variety of works if he wishes. For the advanced reader,

[1] Board of Education of the City of New York, *Study of Certain Factors Relevant to the Use of Mass-Market Paperbacks in High School Literature Classes* (New York: Bureau of Educational Research, Board of Education of the City of New York, 1964).

almost any classic, modern or ancient, is available. For the average reader, books of high interest are at the teacher's fingertips. For the growing problem of the reluctant reader, paperbacks can help to "bridge the gap."

For those who prefer to use paperback books primarily in the field of reading and study skills, the latest edition of *Paper-bound Books in Print* lists 25 books directly concerned with teaching reading skills and efficient reading, not including the study of language and semantics. In addition, there are 8 books with titles beginning "How To Study." In the area embracing journalism, communications, and linguistics, there are 145 books. In the area of "Study and Guidance," there are 850 books, including one called *How To Pass High on Reading Tests.* One disquieting, major trend in this area is the emergence of the "easy way to study this or that" type of book. There is also an enormous herd of ponies on the market that, if used properly, could be helpful, but one questions the motives of many of the students who buy them. I am referring to the "notes" type of book or the review commentaries on specific works. How often does a student buy one of these critical commentaries on, say, *Don Quixote* for real guidance in reading the work? It is obvious that the student can gain a glib grasp of a work without reading it from one of these "ponies" for the purpose of fooling the teacher. They are frequently quite well done, conducive to "instant learning" when the student is under pressure. One company has produced 105 titles at $1.25, and two other companies have published over 40.

The paperback holds much promise as a direct teaching textbook. Whole works, or anthologies of whole works, can be brought together by teachers for specific purposes and can replace the hardcover textbook for the same amount of money. There is a trend toward publishing thematic units, genre units, and topical units in total packages of paperbacks for those teachers who do not have the time or patience to form their own.

There are 159 different dictionaries in paperback form listed in *Paper-bound Books in Print*. Some are, to be sure, obscure, such as the *Dictionary of Obsolete English*, the *Dictionary of Clichés*, and the *Zen Dictionary*; yet there are 17 general dictionaries available to students that are useful for word meaning, pronunciation, or usage. There are 15 encyclopedias, 35 atlases (18 of which are general works of the world or the United States), and 4 thesauri. There are several reading lists available in paperback. Here again, there is a trend toward packaging desk-top reference libraries as units. There is little reason for the serious student to lack a wide range of paperback reference materials on his home bookshelf.

THE PAPERBACK AS PART OF
THE LIBRARY PROGRAM

The imaginative librarian sees his library as an active environment, capable of incorporating not only books but other media such as filmstrips, tapes, and recordings. He also recognizes the paperback as a lure for shaping reading habits of children and concentrates more on the short-term availability of a wide range of books than on a museum-like atmosphere of permanence — the nice and tidy, unused, sterile, musty archive that exists all too often in our schools.

There are two major ways in which the paperback can serve the library, the librarian, and the student. Paperbacks can circulate from the central library, or they can be extensions of the main library by making up the libraries in classrooms.

Vincent Richards, assistant director of the Fraser Valley Regional Library, Abbotsford, British Columbia, reported recently on his use of paperbacks in the library system.

In April 1962, the Fraser Valley Regional Library, in British Columbia, bought 15,-300 adult paperbacks and put them into seventeen branches. Nearly three years later the library had discarded more than 14,000 worn-out paperbacks, and had added over 37,000 new ones. It was expected that readers would appreciate paperback books, but the success of the experiment provided many surprises.

Initially, paperbacks were bought for adult readers. It was soon discovered, however, that young people were enthusiastically borrowing these paperbacks in large numbers. Their choice of reading was of a higher standard than that of many adults. In a short time the paperback rack had become a bridge between the junior and adult library. As an added bonus much greater use was made of the regular bookstock.

The younger readers soon pointed out the reasons why they preferred paperbacks; they were: easy to carry and handle, "mod-

ern" and "fun," less formidable and textbooky than hardbounds, attractive and bright covers, "the sort of books we have at home." [2]

For the past three years, the writer has had a large paperback library in his classroom in Middlesex Junior High School, Darien, Connecticut. Curious to determine what the impact of availability would be on student reading behavior, I instituted a library of 350 paperbacks and observed the reactions of my 117 students to it. I purposely avoided any compulsion, in my role as teacher, in regard to the library. I mentioned that the library was there for students to use if they wished to do so. In three months, the average student read three of the books. A year later the average circulation was closer to four books per student. This experiment is described in a book called *Paperbacks in the Schools*. [3]

Now every English teacher in Middlesex Junior High School has such a classroom library. In addition to these libraries, the science teachers and social studies teachers have, in many cases, formed libraries for their classrooms. Next year the teachers of home economics will have such libraries. Gregory Coffin, the superintendent of schools, and the principals and department heads in most cases, feel that this method of stimulating reading in the

[2] Vincent Richards, "Paperbacks in Canada," *School Paperback Journal*, I (May, 1965), 23.

[3] David Sohn, "The Stimulation of Reading through Paperback Books: The Classroom Library," in *Paperbacks in the Schools*, ed. Alexander Butman, Donald Reis, and David Sohn (New York: Bantam Books, 1963), pp. 23–38.

subject fields is well worth the relatively minor expense of setting up the libraries. School librarians eager to have students read should not think of such classroom libraries as competition but, instead, as extensions of their services.

THE PAPERBACK AS A
STIMULATOR OF READING

There are three major ways for stimulating reading in a school situation: the book fair, the book club, and the book store. Each of these forms of providing books for student purchase has a different message for the student. The book fair is festive and dynamic. A frenetic enthusiasm tends to develop. Such a method is a convenient way to encourage book ownership in a short and sweet manner. A book fair is simple to set up with the co-operation of a distributor and quick and rather exciting to behold. Paperback book clubs are very popular in many schools. They appeal to the student's tribal instinct and contribute a sense of belonging, plus the excitement of an occasion every month where he can act as a selective consumer. The book store is a long-term operation, usually not designed to make a great deal of money but instituted for the convenience of the students. It has the advantage of making books continually available to students and is a worthwhile service. Each of these types of activity serves a different purpose, but each has the same goal — the encouragement of book ownership — and each is effective in its singular way.

CONCLUDING STATEMENT

Youth would tell us, perhaps, that we are witnessing the decline and fall of the leisure reading habit in hardcover form. Certainly, at this time, the authors and publishers depend far more on the sale of paperback reprint rights for a new novel than they do on hardcover sales. More and more original works are appearing in paperback form first, by-passing the hardcover tradition. The time may not be far away when reviewers will consider original paperbacks to be proper subjects for review rather than second-class non-books, for the paperback, to quote Vincent Richards, is no "country cousin." It is a different medium, providing reading pleasure for millions. Lifetime reading habits can be formed by flooding the classrooms with good books. It is well worth the cost to give the students the books they want to read. As text, as reference work, as part of a classroom or school library, or as a stimulus to reading in other environments, the paperback serves our common goal — to encourage students to read, and read, and read — and to love it.

CHAPTER VIII

EVALUATION OF INNOVATIONS IN READING INSTRUCTION

*

ARTHUR S. McDONALD

*

Each innovation in reading instruction has published reports of research showing dramatic results. Indeed, several new systems appear to approach the panacea stage in their claims for insuring the success of every child in learning to read well, painlessly, and enjoyably. Since each new method asserts its superiority over all existing systems (including yesterday's innovations), educators face the task of careful evaluation.

In preparing this paper, the writer has assumed that you are not interested in inventing novel systems of teaching reading. (Any who are so inclined are probably already at work following the "principles" suggested by George D. Spache in chapter v!) Therefore, this paper will discuss main principles and problems of evaluating systems of reading instruction.

As a first step, you must have an adequate base of knowledge about the reading process, the psychology of learning, and the strengths and weaknesses of present instructional programs. Further, an up-to-date familiarity with past reading research is essential. And you must have an understanding of the basic principles of research design, methods of controlling critical variables, and statistical evaluation. In any evaluation — whether based on reports of research carried out by someone else or on research which you are conducting — knowledge, experience, and professional competence are limiting factors.

BIASING FORCES IN EXPERIMENTAL DESIGN

A majority of published studies reporting the effectiveness of various reading instructional programs are seriously vitiated by inadequate experimental designs. These designs have failed to take into account forces which invalidate research and experimentation. The most common and pernicious of these forces are discussed below.

1. *Hawthorne effect.* Desmond L. Cook has defined this as "an awareness on the part of the subject of special treatment created by artificial experimental conditions," pointing out that it affects the subject and not the experimenter.[1] Cook found that pupils as young as fourth graders recognize significant departures from normal routine.[2] Thus, even nine-year-olds who

[1] Cook, "The Hawthorne Effect in Educational Research," *Phi Delta Kappan*, XLIV (December, 1962), 118.

[2] Cook, "The Hawthorne Effect and Read-

are subjects of investigation realize their special role and are vulnerable to the Hawthorne effect.

2. *Placebo effect.* This is a special form of the Hawthorne effect which accompanies the use of novel materials, special equipment, secret methods, and so on. In the educational realm, a placebo may be defined as a mechanical or electronic instructional or psychological agent, material, or treatment used with or without some form of ritual but always with the suggestion or implication of its power and helpful effects. Unlike the Hawthorne effect, the placebo effect will not be attained unless the experimenter believes in the placebo.

A "placebo response" is a response of the agent or treatment which cannot be ascribed to the agent or treatment itself but which must be the result of some other aspect of the situation. A placebo effect, then, is the apparent effectiveness of an instructional approach or treatment resulting from the faith of both the subject and the experimenter in the efficacy of the method, aided by its face validity.

It has been shown that the mere act of using placebo agents with the appropriate ritual accentuates their effect. Albert Kurland has reported that tranquilizers are often used in far too small a dosage to have beneficial pharmacologic effects.[3] In fact, it has been

reported in the press that meprobamate (the Miltown of story and jest), long believed to be a tranquilizer, has been removed from the U.S. Pharmacopeia. Research demonstrated that it was not a tranquilizer (according to medical definition) but rather a sedative of less power and effectiveness than the barbiturates. (This comment is not intended to deprecate the medical or pharmacological professions but to illustrate the pervasiveness of placebo responses.)

The type and strength of a placebo effect depends on the circumstances under which the placebo is given and on the method of measuring the outcomes of its use. The nature of the subject and the situation in which the activity is carried out are important determinants of the effect. Vague means of measuring results and heavy reliance on subjective evaluation strongly favor placebo responses.

Thus, placebo responses are particularly likely in reading programs in which the instructors rely heavily on specially prepared books, instructional materials, or special instrumentation (believing themselves in the beneficial effects of the materials). They are also likely in systems which have adopted "new breakthrough methods" which the practitioners believe cannot be measured by existing devices or techniques.

2. *Experimenter bias.* As used here, this term does not apply to unprofessional manipulation of data to produce the results the experimenter wants. Rather it applies to influences from the experimenter of which he is un-

ing Research," in *Improvement of Reading through Classroom Practice*, International Reading Association Conference Proceedings, ed. J. Allen Figurel (Newark, Del.: International Reading Association, 1964), IX, 251.

3 Kurland, "Placebo Effect," in *Drugs and Behavior*, ed. Leonard Uhr and James G. Miller (New York: John Wiley & Sons, 1960), pp. 156–65.

aware. Subjects often know what an experimenter wants them to do, even though he may believe he is being quite objective or neutral in his behavior. Martin T. Orne has shown how powerful a set the realization "this is an experiment" can be for students. He asserts that the student subject sees his task as finding out the true purpose of the experiment in order to respond in a manner which will support the hypotheses being tested. Orne points out that a very important source of cues for the subject is the experimental procedure itself. For instance, if a new kind of test is given before and after some type of instruction, even the dullest pupil is aware that some change is expected. Orne emphasizes that response to the experimental situation (which he calls "demand characteristics") is not merely conscious compliance.[4] Instead, the demand characteristics of the experimental situation help define the role of "good subject." The subject does his best to fit the role in his responses.

Robert Rosenthal has found that data obtained by twenty-four assistants of twelve experimenters, who trained the assistants but did not tell them the results they expected, correlated significantly with the experimenters' expectancy of findings.[5]

Thus, the three forces discussed above — as embodied in the novel and dramatic nature of components of the instructional system, heightened willingness to respond because of knowledge of desired results, teacher-student faith and psychological interaction, suggestibility, feeling of importance ("I've been selected for special treatment"), and so on — affect students' performances in experiments. These three forces appear to account for more than two-thirds of all reports of successful results of innovations in reading instruction. George D. Spache has observed that by dramatic use of novel methods or impressive equipment "it is possible to produce for a brief space of time what appears to be more than normal progress by remedial techniques or methods that are completely contradictory or even irrelevant to the causes of the reading retardation." [6]

Thus, in evaluating results of new systems of teaching reading, it is essential to ascertain whether the investigators used experimental designs which would eliminate or minimize the Hawthorne and placebo effects and experimenter bias. Since these forces are so commonly overlooked — even in complex and sophisticated research — it is probable that the investigator has ignored them if no mention is made of procedures employed to mitigate them. Caution should be used in utilizing findings of research which has overlooked these forces. Outcomes will be spuriously favorable and benefits greatly overstated.

[4] Orne, "On the Social Psychology of the Psychological Experiment, with Particular Reference to Demand Characteristics and Their Implications," *American Psychologist*, XVII (November, 1962), 778.

[5] Rosenthal *et al.*, "The Effect of Experimenters' Bias on the Data Obtained by Their Research Assistants," *American Psychologist*, XVII (June, 1962), 328.

[6] Spache, *Toward Better Reading* (Champaign, Ill.: Garrard Publishing Co., 1963), p. 325.

CAN RESEARCH FINDINGS BE GENERALIZED?

One purpose of educational research is the development of generalizations which can be applied in a wide variety of teaching situations. In evaluating reports of research, you should make certain that the findings are really capable of being generalized so that they may be applied to your situation. For reasons to be discussed later, this is particularly important for evaluating innovations in reading instruction.

Learning is a highly personal activity. Most reports of instructional outcomes describe what happened when teacher T_1 used method M_1 with students SS_1 in classroom climate C_1 (perhaps with additional assistants AA_1). When teacher T_2 uses method M_1 with students SS_2 in classroom climate C_2 (certainly without additional assistants), he may find method M_1 no better than the method he was using before or perhaps even less effective. This latter outcome will be probable if the teacher is constrained to use the new method. On the other hand, should the teacher be convinced of its excellence and should the method lend itself to the operation of the biasing forces, he will probably find the innovation "beneficial."

Harry F. Silberman, for example, found that taped presentations of a program to teach first graders to read trigrams were not as effective as were the "live" presentations by the original experimenter.[7] Donald E. P. Smith and others found that, at the college level, students progressed better with programs adapted to their personality patterns.[8] Reviewing the research on new systems of teaching very young children to read, Joanna P. Williams found that all successful experiments used some form of individualized instruction.[9]

Although pupil behavior shows marked similarities, on the basis of age level, in different sizes of communities, there are significant differences in a number of aspects between urban and rural, industrial and resort, and urban and exurban environments. Such differences limit the generalization of findings obtained in one kind of setting. Class size, type of school, and the training and experience of the teacher are other factors which must be considered in evaluating the appropriateness of an instructional innovation for another setting. Experiments which are carried on solely in campus laboratory schools, private schools, or in college psychology classes have limited possibilities of generalization. The use of assistants — not usually available to the classroom teacher — or the restriction of class size to a fraction of the average also casts doubt on the application of findings to other classrooms across the country.

EVALUATING PROGRESS IN
READING PROGRAMS

Four of the most common procedures used to evaluate progress in reading programs are the following:

[7] Silberman, *Experimental Analysis of a Beginning Reading Skill* (Santa Monica, Calif.: System Development Corp., 1964).

[8] Smith *et al.* "Reading Improvement as a Function of Student Personality and Teaching Method," *Journal of Educational Psychology,* XLVII (January, 1956), 47–59.

[9] Williams, "Reading Research and Instruction," *Review of Educational Research,* XXXV (April, 1965), 147–54.

1. Comparison of pre- and post-test scores on equated forms of standardized reading tests and/or informal tests, and comparison of test performance with the performance expected statistically (for example, "Bobby grew two years in reading during this school year").

2. Use of national average yearly gains on a standardized group reading test as a basis for comparing test gains made in the local reading group.

3. Comparison of test-retest results of the experimental group using a new program with the test-retest performance of a control group.

4. Use of subjective questionnaires and interviews designed to "tap deeper changes and inner growth."

The first two methods are most commonly used in classroom and reading-clinic descriptive reports. The third and fourth are usual in published reports of research and experimental studies. The fourth is quite usual with the "new breakthrough approaches" for which established tests and statistical evaluations are "outdated, inadequate, and straitjacketing."

If properly used, these methods can yield valuable information, but they are subject to several types of error. Educators conducting investigations or reading reports of investigations should be aware of these errors and should note what attempts were made to mitigate them (if any were).

These sources of error include the following:

1. Failure to correct for regression to the mean. On a second testing, persons scoring low on the first test tend to move upward, and vice versa. (After all, if a student misses *all* the questions on the first test, he has probability on his side — he cannot get a lower score and his guesses cannot always be wrong.) Frederick B. Davis has given formulas to correct for this source of error.[10]

2. Treatment of reading grade scores as actual indications of month-by-month growth. Reading grade scores are extrapolated from one grade level to another rather than obtained by longitudinal study. Furthermore, principles of learning would suggest that learning takes place unevenly. Spache has pointed out that experiments using repeated testing indicate that reading growth is not evenly distributed throughout the year.[11]

3. Assumption that standardized reading tests provide reliable and valid measures of all the most important aspects of reading. Albert J. Kingston has recently warned against this assumption and has made suggestions for alternative bases of evaluation.[12]

4. Spurious scores obtained from the use of a single test over a wide range of educational levels. (Although extreme heterogeneity aids reliability, it weakens validity.) Such scores are usually too high for those at the lower levels and too low for those at the upper levels.

5. Experimenter-made tests to measure unique definitions or conceptual models of reading. Such results cannot be compared or generalized with other data; hence, they are not sufficient to evaluate outcomes of instruction. To meet this criterion, these special tests would have to be compared with existing measures of

[10] Davis, "The Assessment of Change," in *Phases of College and Other Adult Reading Programs*, Tenth Yearbook of the National Reading Conference, ed. Emery P. Bliesmer and Albert J. Kingston (Milwaukee: National Reading Conference, Inc., 1961), pp. 93–95.

[11] Spache, *op. cit.*, pp. 325, 359–60.

[12] Kingston, "Is Reading What the Reading Tests Test?" in *The Philosophical and Sociological Bases of Reading*, Fourteenth Yearbook of the National Reading Conference, ed. Eric L. Thurston and Lawrence E. Hafner (Milwaukee: National Reading Conference, Inc., 1965), pp. 106–9.

reading and a method of equating results prepared. An alternative would be to establish, by rigorous research, the defensibility of the new definition of reading and the viability of the conceptual model together with the appropriateness of the new tests for assessing the results of the new program.

6. Use of test questions for checking reading comprehension, which can be answered by many children from background knowledge (that is, without reading the selection).

7. Use of inappropriate norms to interpret test data, failure to allow for inter-form differences in equated forms, or the use of an inappropriate test.

8. Failure to select a really comparable control group and failure to control for essential variables.

9. Reliance on subjective questionnaires with low reliability and validity for evaluation.

10. Failure to use any control groups at all. Experimenters use this approach with startling innovations and defend it on the ground that their specially devised methods of evaluation support the "revolutionary" rationale of the system.

IMPLICATIONS

Adequate evaluation of innovations in reading instruction requires the following:

1. Careful delineation of instructional objectives in operational form. This should include specification of how these objectives are to be measured, that is, what will be the evidence of progress in learning.

2. Specification of the limitations of the system of instruction. (What types of students is this system designed to teach? What kinds of learning problems will remain unaffected by it or show only Hawthorne, placebo, and experimenter-bias reactions? What kinds of student background

are assumed? What is the nature of special training, if any, which the teacher must have?)

3. Evidence that the new program can be applied in daily teaching situations with the same effectiveness as in the experimental situation. This evidence should also indicate whether the experimental teaching personnel added instructional procedures from their previous methods of teaching to the new system so that the evaluator can judge whether he is dealing with a pure system or a combination.

4. Controls for biasing forces. (Cook suggests that placebo treatment be used to control the Hawthorne effect.[13] Use some form of special instrumentation or special instructional material — perhaps stamped "A New Approach to Reading" — at specially scheduled times with all students in the control groups. Teachers of the control groups should believe that they are working with experimental groups, and they should be comparable in ability with those teaching the true experimental groups.

5. Use of more than one kind of measurement in assessing differences in performance between and within groups.

6. Demonstration of the direct relationships of the conclusions and implications to the research findings.

7. Detailed explanation of how the results, conclusions, and implications can be put to practical use by the classroom teacher.

8. Avoidance of any program that suggest that the innovation will work with all children under all conditions and with all teachers.

9. Evidence that the experimenter took measures to safeguard against errors resulting from suggestion and experimenter bias. Cook has observed that awareness of the Hawthorne effect is a helpful beginning,[14] and Donald L. Cleland suggests

13 Cook, *op. cit.*
14 *Ibid.*

randomization.[15] Nash advocates as close an approach to the "double-blind" technique of medicine as practicable be built into the research design.[16] This becomes increasingly important as the innovation departs more and more widely from current reading programs.

10. Sufficient information of a design

and statistical nature that it can be replicated.

If a new system of reading instruction is to be evaluated as producing more than a non-specific Hawthorne or placebo response, its research reports must demonstrate that its effects are stronger, last longer, and are qualitatively different from those produced by biasing forces, or that it affects students in different ways than would be expected from placebo and Hawthorne effects. Unfortunately, research reports on innovations in reading instruction often fail to do these things to an adequate degree.

[15] Cleland, "Needed Improvement in Research Design in Reading," in *Improvement of Reading through Classroom Practice*, International Reading Association Conference Proceedings, ed. J. Allen Figurel (Newark, Del.: International Reading Association, 1964), IX, 244–49.

[16] Harvey Nash, "The Design and Conduct of Experiments on the Psychological Effects of Drugs," in *Drugs and Behavior*, ed. Leonard Uhr and James G. Miller (New York: John Wiley & Sons, 1960), pp. 128–55.

CHAPTER IX

RECENT DEVELOPMENTS IN READING IN SWEDEN

*

EVE MALMQUIST

*

So MUCH has happened recently in Sweden as a result of the great school reform of 1962. This reform, the most far-reaching one we have had in Sweden in more than one hundred years, has touched just about every aspect of educational philosophy and' practice relative to the first nine years of school. We must take a look at the principal aims and scope of this reform in order to understand its implications for the teaching of reading.

The work on the reform began in 1940 when certain governmental committees were appointed to review the entire school system of the country. They were given the guiding postulate that education should reflect not only the changing conditions and needs of a dynamic society and an ever shrinking world but also the increased understanding of the nature of man and of his manifold requirements.

In 1950, after these committees had submitted their proposals, the Swedish Parliament decided, in principle, on an extensive reform of compulsory education. It specified, however, that before such a reform could be embarked upon it would have to be preceded by an experimental period of eight to ten years duration. Finally in 1962, the reform was made law. Hence, for the first time in the school history of Sweden, the Parliament arrived at important decisions regarding the goals and design of the national school system after intensive consultation and through intimate co-operation with research workers from such relevant fields as education and psychology. Although this reform pertains only to the first nine years of school, comparable reforms are in process for all levels of higher education throughout the land — for Gymnasiums, which correspond in the United States to high school plus two years of college, as well as for universities and teacher-training institutions.

BASIC POINTS OF VIEW

First, to provide an equal educational opportunity for everyone, regardless of where he may be living, his sex, and the socioeconomic background of his parents. To implement this, the expenditures have been increased to the point where 15 per cent of the national budget and nearly 30 per cent of all local budgets are designated for education, including free textbooks, transportation, meals, and so on. In this connection we may note that there are practically no parochial, and only very few private, schools in Sweden.

Second, to support the total personality development of the individual child, to help him use his potential resources in order to reach as full a self-realization as is possible. This point of view puts the acquisition of subject matter into a subordinate place, though the learning of skills and of subject matter is still seen as highly important and closely related to the primary concern, the individual personality development of each child. We therefore now, more than before, stress a diagnostic approach and individualization in teaching. Steps to further this have included (*a*) extending the years of schooling from seven to nine years of compulsory education; (*b*) reducing the class size to a maximum of twenty-five in the first three years and to thirty in the remaining six years (at the present time the mean size, for the country as a whole, lies between seventeen and eighteen children per class) ; (*c*) continuing with the practice of having the child start school at the age of seven on a six-day a week basis (this six-day school week is presently being studied, and if the research findings warrant it, there will likely be a change to a five-day school pattern) ; (*d*) providing better opportunities than before for individual tutoring, small group teaching, and teaching in clinics and special classes of various kinds. During 1965, 58 reading clinics and 147 special remedial reading classes were established in Stockholm, servicing 1,650 students. Written into the teaching load of every teacher of the first three grades is a weekly two-hour block of time for tutoring any individual in his class who, in his judgment, needs such help.

Another procedure which has contributed significantly to individualization of teaching is that of dividing the class in half for a certain number of hourly sessions a week for the teaching in the first three grades of reading, writing, and mathematics and in the higher grades of biology, chemistry, physics, English and other languages, including Swedish. In the first grade, for instance, one-half of the class meets with the teacher the first two hours of the day. The second half comes to school for the next two-hour period, during which the first half is free to play or engage in other activities. By this means the teacher has no more than thirteen students at a time, often no more than eight to ten.

Third, to develop the child's ability to work in a smooth and efficient way with others, as a future citizen and as a member of his work and home units, and to provide skills and knowledge for co-operative and harmonious living. Our changing society increasingly requires the capacity to work constructively with others for individual and social fulfilment. Teachers are given training in diagnosing and developing the student's capacity to work first with only one other student at a time and then with two, three, and more students, until the time, in the later grades, when he can work effectively in somewhat larger problem-solving groups, not only in classroom learning situations, but in situations requiring other types of teamwork.

Fourth, to postpone specialization, at all stages, up to the age of twenty and twenty-one in favor of a broader education. This point of view reflects the premise that each individual must be seen primarily as a whole, to be developed to his utmost, and that his professional or vocational contributions are an outgrowth or an expression of this wholeness. It also reflects the thought that swift technological developments and other changes in society quickly render early specialization obsolete. It is expected that individuals may have to be retrained for at least one shift in vocation, during a lifetime which will span the year 2000, and that broad skills and understandings will be needed for this later re-education, retraining, and readjustment.

IMPLICATIONS FOR THE TEACHING OF READING

Because of the noted great differences between and within children in every school class, it is generally held by Swedish teachers and reading specialists that there does not exist any ideal method of teaching reading. Every program for the teaching of reading should contain several methods of instruction, analytical as well as synthetical, from the very beginning. Otherwise, it could not provide for the aim that every individual should be given just the type of assistance he may need when he needs it. In addition, all phases of the language arts, namely, listening, speaking, writing, and reading, are integrated and dealt with concurrently, beginning with the first lesson in formal reading.

Success must be assured. Growth in reading, as in other learning, cannot be hurried without some undesirable,

and even damaging effects on some children. Therefore, we try to make the transition from home to school as easy as possible by having the children go to school for only two hours a day the first two or three weeks of school and in groups of no more than twelve or thirteen children. With these beginning seven-year-olds we are of the opinion that it pays to "waste time," to start very easily, introducing a variety of reading-readiness experiences and using materials, for many children, on a difficulty level far below their capacity level. This "makes haste slowly" policy permeates the teaching of reading, with the emphasis on interest and easily won achievement, since we believe that this skill is central to much of the children's subsequent learning.

Early diagnosis is the keynote. Even before the child enters school he is tested as to over-all readiness. With the new smaller class size and the additional time available for individual tutoring since 1962, the teacher has better opportunities to use a diagnostic approach and to provide learning steps, methods, and procedures suited to the individual learner.

The tendency is to emphasize the kinds of material the individual child enjoys, to stimulate his interest in reading so that he, with interest and amusement, may reach out to, and enjoy, books of his choice, often somewhat below his capacity level. Then, when it is time to begin instruction in the various reading skills, the teacher is urged to use materials systematized as to sequence, so that the child is steadily challenged to raise his level of performance. The guidelines from the

Royal Board of Education stress that the step from one phase to another must not be too big and that there must be a great deal of repetition of every skill, though here, too, the teacher must watch with a careful diagnostic eye, for traces of boredom. When the teacher succeeds in choosing the correct time to introduce correct reading materials, the optimum of constructive influence on the development of the child is reached. The policy is to avoid forcing a child to read materials beyond his present capacity.

Previously, teachers used to ask, "How many pages, or how many books, should I have my students read before the end of the term?" Teachers are now urged to ask, "Where are my various pupils as to reading ability just now? That is where I am going to start with each one, right now." Such a diagnostic approach also requires the teacher to have a clear picture of the particular interests of each individual, discovered through a close observation of his likes and preferred activities, through testing, and through interviews with parents. In this connection we might point out that although previously teachers were encouraged to make contacts with the parents of the children the Royal Board of Education has now made it mandatory by specifically stipulating that the individual teacher has the responsibility of making the first contact with the home. Thus, in order to get a picture of the student's out-of-school activities and pattern of living, the teacher has to communicate with the family of each individual in the class before school starts, or early in the term, and then at frequent intervals during the school year.

When the teacher has been given adequate training to handle these contacts with the home in a skilful and tactful manner, this kind of intercommunication is likely to give him valuable help for his teaching job. It is generally assumed that a teacher of reading, or a teacher of any other subject, cannot function effectively unless he knows a great deal about some of the most influential individuals and groups in the student's life.

To obtain the most from this intimate knowledge of the student, as well as to achieve a satisfactory follow-up, it has long been a practice in Sweden to have the first-grade teacher continue with his class through the third grade. The fourth-grade teacher, similarly, stays with his class for three consecutive years for the essential part of the school day, though teachers in specialized areas such as athletics, art, handicrafts, and music extend the classroom resources by their contributions.

In short, to prevent reading disabilities, both a diagnostic approach and an individualization of teaching are stressed. Further, the concept of reading readiness is applied not only to the beginning stages of reading but, in accordance with the new curriculum, to all reading levels in all subjects. The teacher is expected to ask himself at all points whether the individual is ready, is adequately mature, to grasp the reading, to utilize it, and to incorporate it — in other words, whether he is able to gain both an understanding from the reading and the ability to put this understanding to use. This approach is also applied, in many ways, to the teacher's guidance of the student's development and to his interests and tastes in recreational reading in or out of school.

These ideas are accepted by nearly everyone. They may even sound trite and so obvious that they are not worth restating. To put them into practice, however, is another matter. It will take time to get every Swedish teacher to accept these views completely, in the sense of applying them in their classes.

From the first day at school the child should be helped to view his studies, his experiences, from a kind of research point of view. The intention is to aid him to explore, to investigate, to find out for himself, to promote his individual work through a variety of sources, and then to help him interpret and evaluate. Even at that early age he can readily compare and find similarities and dissimilarities and assess what seems true, false, reliable, predictable, and the like. The child should be encouraged to bring to the surface his reactions, his thoughts, and his feelings, to make his own evaluations on the basis of his findings, and to compare them with the evaluations of others.

As he proceeds through school, it is expected that he will learn to interpret and evaluate more and more critically, developing his capacities to identify propaganda, to evaluate advertisements, to discern the values of literature, to discriminate between good and inferior literature, and, further, in his social and personal life, to evaluate his behavior and goals and to create his philosophy of life and his own standard of values.

It is assumed that learners nowadays need a much broader range of reading skills than before, because in our rapidly changing world they may not long be able to rely on the facts they have learned in school. This represents a shift from an earlier philosophy in which stress was put on teaching as many facts as possible, submitting the learners to rigorous tests, and then grading them on the results of these tests. The climate in which the skills are now taught has also undergone a change. Formal examinations are avoided. Tests are used as a means, within the total educational process, of assessing the growth in achievement and the personality development of the individual child. Monthly grading, as used in many countries, does not exist in Sweden, and there are no formal examinations at the end of the nine-year compulsory period of schooling.

There is still a great need for more adequate training of teachers in the fruitful use of small group instruction. How often have we heard of teachers, accustomed to working only with large groups, embarking upon small group work with children, only to find it ineffective and chaotic, and subsequently, and rightly, returning to their large-group methods. For, without preparatory exercises, and without many kinds of reading skills, children cannot work together, or for that matter, even individually, with success.

Teachers must be urged to proceed slowly and systematically, in order to give students the instruments necessary for co-operative work. At first, games are used to teach children to speak in a soft voice while working together, since loud talking can create a din disturbing to others. The trend is to start with rather detailed instruments. By the fifth grade, most groups have been able to construct their own working plans by themselves; some groups do not achieve this until the seventh grade, and occasionally, a third grade group is able to manage its own planning, without prepared instruments and working plans produced by the teacher.

The effectiveness of group work depends to a large degree on a friendly, congenial relationship between the teacher and the students and among the students themselves. To this must be added adequate reading skills, availability of suitable reading materials, and careful planning. Through systematically arranged games and exercises, the teacher will teach the needed skills. For instance, the students need to be shown how to use indexes in order to gather and organize facts. They need help with key words and headings. They need training with alphabetical games and exercises for dictionary use. They need to be taught how to read diagrams, graphs, and charts of various kinds, how to find the meaning of foreign words and phrases, and how to decipher their pronunciation and accent.

There is in Sweden a need for more ready-made work plans and units and for extensive resource materials, properly catalogued and readily accessible.

Such materials, if they are to be effective, must be available in a range of readability at least as wide as the range of reading ability of the group members; otherwise, as is self-evident, the individual using the materials will not be able to get what he needs in order to make an effective contribution to the projects of his group.

The teacher is urged to provide whatever stimulation he can to strengthen the motivation and to help develop attitudes for teamwork. Even the bulletin board may be useful in this context by directing the students' attention to items of interest for their units. Phonograph records, tapes, television programs, films, newspaper clippings, and so on, and in particular, experiences such as excursions and group activities other than reading should be used to enrich the experiential background for reading.

Broadly speaking, reading skills range from the first step of comprehension and understanding, to the second step of reactions and critical reading, to the third step of evaluation, retention, and application of findings, and lastly, to the step of creative reading. The first three steps deal with the reader's responses to the material. If this can be called "reacting," then creative reading can be described as "acting" or "acting creatively," the highest goal of reading. It is expected that the child will be helped by being engaged to a degree in all four of these steps from his very first lessons in formal reading. Even before learning to read, from the first day in school, the child should be helped to develop his ability to draw inferences, to make generalizations, and also to anticipate coming events.

Students must also be helped to become successful, inquiring readers in specific subject fields such as arithmetic, in which a difficulty with reading, an inability to get at the meaning of the problem, will cause additional problems. The student needs to be taught the meanings of certain key words, how to read directions and explanations, and various means of presenting quantitative facts and relationships so that he can understand the problem to be solved. Similarly in history, a student often needs help in perceiving the meaning of events, dates, and places as well as in following the writer's reasons for reaching his particular conclusions regarding the events. Various subjects, in a variety of content fields, present different problems in reading comprehension. The special type of reading required in a given field must be taught within that field.

There has been a marked change in Sweden in the operational definition of special reading disabilities. In the past, only those individuals who, on the one hand, tested as having normal or above average intelligence and, on the other hand, demonstrated an extremely poor reading ability were considered to have a reading disability that required special remedial work. Not enough emphasis has been placed on those having very high intelligence and reading only at a normal or a little above average level or on those having below average intelligence and reading on an extremely low level. Wherever there is a deviation in a negative direction of more than one sigma between I.Q. and reading ability, the writer would propose that the pupil be given remedial help. This would apply to all school levels up through the university.

Investigations made in Sweden into the rate of reading in the elementary and upper grades have come up with some rather disquieting results. It was found that for a great number of pupils speed remains fixed at whatever rate was attained by the third or fourth grade. Further, this rate did not change regardless of the purpose of the reading or the nature of the reading material. Our students need to be helped to acquire the ability to modify their pace of reading, from very slow reading with high concentration up to rapid scanning. With each passing year this adaptability in reading is becoming more urgently required of students, no matter what their content field. In Sweden, programs of teacher preparation have just recently started to emphasize this concept in reading instruction.

Some decades ago, in Sweden, learning was often thought to be a formal process of acquiring and memorizing facts. Consequently, assignments of a routine character were often made. The students had to acquire certain facts, to be remembered and later put to use. They read with little or no motivation, and progress was measured largely in terms of the ability to retell what the book had said. In contrast, the good teacher today thinks of learning as a dynamic process which gives the student opportunities to satisfy needs, to adjust to new situations, and to solve problems which he is interested in working out and which, at times, call for exploration into written sources. It is in situations such as these that reading becomes effective. It should be considered imperative that the child have as a starting point a clear understanding of his purposes in reading. Otherwise he will not know what type of reading or what reading speed is best suited to the situation. The teacher must be urged to help the student develop a "prereading" habit of thought or meditation to clarify his purpose in reading.

In short, the motive for reading must be identified, acknowledged, and accepted in advance, in order that the reader may cope most efficiently with the materials to be explored. A teacher who accepts this view does not restrict questions about the reading, as if the answers were some kind of secret to be revealed *after* the reading has been completed. Instead, he clarifies, with the students, the goals of the reading *before* they begin. The learner, accepting the goals and having been given clues as to how best to achieve them, then chooses the reading attack which seems the most promising to him.

If the learner, upon graduation, throws his books in the corner and promises himself never to touch those detested things again, we can scarcely say that his teachers have succeeded in their task, regardless of the amount of knowledge he may have obtained. Instead, the teachers' goal should be to create in the student a love for books, an enduring joy in reading, and a pleasure in learning, as revealed in the desire to explore, to analyze, and to evaluate writings of both an educative and an entertaining nature.

The reluctant readers in our classes have often eluded our attention. They can read, but they do not. In order to prevent reading disabilities from developing among these students, it has been urged that special attention be given to them until they reach the place where they can experience the fun and excitement that reading can give and can see its great usefulness in their own world.

Here a diagnostic approach is recommended, including an exploration into the individual's out-of-school life. Possibly his parents or peers do not hold reading in high regard, and he may have accepted their assessment rather than their teacher's enthusiasm. This is especially likely to have happened in cases where the teacher puts emphasis on the mechanical aspects of reading or where the reading materials have encompassed too limited a range of interest. On the basis of this general information, the teacher can diagnose the difficulty and introduce the student to reading and to project groups which reflect his interests. Further, it is hoped that the teacher can help the learner move toward a clarification and acceptance of his own capabilities and special interests, and thus toward a greater degree of self-realization, which may well include a degree of self-liberation from any over-identification with the ideals and points of view of other individuals in his particular world. It is in this pursuit of self-realization that a close cooperation between the classroom teacher and the school librarian, as well as the neighborhood librarian, is urgently advised. Children need help in learning how to choose books of interest and of a suitable degree of difficulty.

Communication and the ability to read in foreign languages takes on special significance in nations as small as Sweden, where it is becoming increasingly imperative to be able to read several languages in order to follow the developments in and to keep in touch with a variety of countries. Therefore, the curriculum of today in Sweden puts a great emphasis on the teaching of foreign languages.

English is begun at the age of ten, French or German at the age of thirteen, and a third language at the age of fifteen. Readings in Danish and Norwegian are engaged in on a small scale from the age of ten and pursued a bit more extensively from the age of thirteen. Consequently, in brief, by the time a student enters the university he will have had nine years of English, six of either French or German, and very often three or four years of a third language, usually French or German, in addition to several years of training in reading some of the literature of Denmark and Norway. Generally speaking, the teaching of these languages involves much practice in everyday oral communication and study skills comparable to those used in learning the mother tongue.

The establishment of the National School for Educational Research was decided upon by the Swedish Parliament in 1958. This research school, which is still the only one of its kind in the country, was founded in the city of Linköping, situated approximately one hundred fifty miles south of Stockholm. The research school was established in response to a variety of needs: (a) the need for a permanent institution where studies could be carried out within ordinary classrooms in a systematic and scientific manner; (b) the need to provide channels for the dissemination of research findings to all of the schools throughout the nation; (c) the need to use the feedback from the schools in a systematic way; and (d) the need to provide for a continuous re-evaluation and revision of the curriculum, instructional materials, methods, and other aspects of ongoing school reform.

At the research school, studies, mostly of a longitudinal nature, are carried out on a number of questions. A recent study dealt with the possibility of preventing reading disabilities by early, preschool diagnosis and by the introduction of special auxiliary teaching measures from the first day of school and throughout the first years. So far, very promising results have been gathered in both the pilot study, from 1958 to 1961, and the large-scale verification inquiry of 1961 to 1964. In both studies significantly better results were noted within the experimental groups receiving additional supportive help. The use of the typewriter as an aid in improving reading ability has also been investigated. Although there is no objective evidence at present, the subjective assessment of the teachers is that it has had a very beneficial effect in remedial work.

Another study is investigating the value of postponing the changeover from manuscript to cursive writing from the first to the third grade. In light of the results from the three-year pilot study, considerable support is given to the value of such a postponement. If the three-year verification period, started in 1964 on a large population, provides similar findings, we will most likely introduce this change throughout all the schools in the country.

In this manner, as educational reform is put into practice, we can anticipate constant remodeling, both of goals and of procedures. At the time of the adoption of the great reform of 1962, the minister of education expressed a view that this must be the last great school reform. From now on, we must engage in constant evaluation and revision, with reforms introduced as needed, creating, as the years go by, a kind of "a rolling school reform," derived from the joint work done with students, teachers, and researchers in education throughout the land.

CONCLUDING STATEMENT

Central to all these changes is the ability to learn to read effectively, not only for survival in the labor market, but far more significantly for self-fulfilment and a balanced view of life. The requirements for reading have entered a dimension referred to earlier as "creative reading," demanding the capacity to reach beyond the printed page to see, detect, and envisage new problems and to make new discoveries in thought and feeling. Modern technology has created answer-making machines. As humans we are par excellence the question-makers. More than ever man must be released to formulate questions, relevant and fruitful, so that he may develop those values and attitudes that will lead him to assume the responsibility of his own social and emotional fulfilment.

The ability to read creatively will become, in the years ahead, one of the most important tools for self-liberation and self-realization. It will provide a lifeline to pull the individual through an oceanful of challenges and wonders, such as we can but vaguely visualize, that are in store for individuals who will live their productive lives in the twenty-first century, the students whom we humbly teach today.

CHAPTER X

LINGUISTICS AND READING INSTRUCTION: CONTRIBUTIONS AND IMPLICATIONS

*

WILLIAM F. MARQUARDT

*

READERS of this chapter will note long before they finish reading it that the title has about the same relationship to the content as a bikini has to its wearer: it doesn't exactly cover the subject. There are at least four reasons why this is so. The first is that the title was provided, and even gray-haired scholars occasionally like to risk being rebellious.

The second is that the title implies that this writer knows a good deal about reading instruction in general as well as about linguistics. Actually, he is a rank newcomer to the reading-teacher fraternity; his own first-hand experience of formal reading instruction dates back to grade school in a little Wisconsin town. But even that experience is suspect because as the first-born of a brood of four — later expanded to seven — of German immigrant parents he was often puzzled by what the teacher or his classmates were saying to him. Consequently, it will be more comfortable to deviate from the title than to stick to it.

The third reason for deviating is that, although much has been said in recent years about the contributions of linguistics to the teaching of reading in general, very little has been said about the role of linguistics in helping teachers understand the problems of that increasingly large proportion of their students who do not speak the standard English of the classroom at home or at play.

The fourth and most important reason for deviating is that, like the well-known preacher who always used the same Bible text and successfully resisted every attempt to sidetrack him from it, the writer has these past fifteen years never really thought or written about anything else than the teaching of reading to non-native speakers of English.

Now, having prepared you to expect a discussion of the contributions of linguistics to teaching a rather special group of learners to read English, I will postpone that discussion for a little while longer. Despite the tremendous attention that has been focused on linguistic science by teachers of reading and on the teaching of reading by linguists in the past three or four years, it has not yet become a waste of time to set forth those statements about the nature of language and its functions which have become more or less axiomatic among linguists. By selecting those axiomatic statements that have a particular relevance for the teaching of reading and putting them in terms that reading teachers find comfortable to use, we should have a clear basis for understanding exactly how linguistic science helps teachers of reading solve their problems.

This mode of beginning the discussion of what linguistics has to offer is encouraged by linguists themselves these days. In recent years linguists have been turning from a nearly exclusive preoccupation with revealing the structural patterns of individual languages according to differing theoretical models to a search for the universal or near universal features of all languages. The most important manifestation of this search to date was the Conference on Language Universals held at Gould House, Dobbs Ferry, New York, in April, 1961. The proceedings of that conference has had a strong impact on the thinking of linguists and scholars in related fields.[1]

At the Gould House conference anthropologists, structural linguists, psychologists, semanticists, and philosophers came together to share views as to what is significant in a language and common to all languages from the standpoint of their own disciplines. Needless to say, the insights about language that such a mixed group of scholars would want to share with one another would also be of value to teachers of reading, especially those concerned with the problems of teaching reading to non-native speakers of English. Unfortunately, however, in the eleven papers presented at the conference, several hundred "universals" were touched upon. Although it could be demonstrated that a large proportion of them are of interest to reading teachers, such a demonstration would probably be too massive and tedious an undertaking for the scope of this chapter.

A more feasible undertaking, and a more modest one, will be to distil from these proceedings and from the writings of other linguists who are concerned with the relevance of their special studies to other disciplines those assumptions about the nature of language, its structure, its acquisition, its use, and its effects that would be of special help to teachers of reading — again, especially to those involved in the teaching of non-native or nonstandard speakers of English. After listing these assumptions in language as non-technical as possible, we will try to show how they relate to the problems of the learner or to techniques that the teacher might adopt.

Before proceeding with the task, however, let us define linguistic science by using Charles C. Fries's often repeated definition, so that you will be able to relate the handful of assumptions chosen for discussion to the content, procedures, and goals of linguistic science. Fries defines linguistic science as

a body of knowledge and understanding concerning the nature and functioning of human language. This knowledge and understanding is built up out of information about the structure, the operation, and the history of a wide range of very diverse hu-

---

[1] Joseph H. Greenberg (ed.), *Universals of Language*, (Cambridge, Mass.: M.I.T. Press, 1963).

man languages. It is built by means of those techniques and procedures that have proved most successful in establishing verifiable generalizations concerning relationships among linguistic phenomena.[2]

SOME ASSUMPTIONS GENERALLY AGREED UPON BY LINGUISTS

The assumptions more or less agreed upon by linguists will be grouped into five categories for the sake of convenience in showing their relevance to teachers of reading: the nature of language, the structure of language, the geography of language, the psychology of language, and the meanings of language.

A word of caution is in order. These statements do not all have equal standing as agreed-upon assumptions. Some are of ancient standing: others were established in the linguistic debates of the latter half of the nineteenth century and in the "structuralist" debates of the first half of the twentieth century; and a few have emerged in the efforts of the past ten years to set up communication across the disciplines of linguistics, psychology, anthropology, mathematics, and information theory. Furthermore, it must be kept in mind that these statements are assumptions. Like all assumptions, they should be tested for their applicability to a given set of conditions — in this case the teaching of reading — before being accepted fully.

  I. Assumptions about the nature of language.
    A. Language is a code of signals by which meaning is communicated from one human being to another.
    B. Language is basically a code of vocal symbols.
    C. The relationship between the symbols of language and their referents is arbitrary.
    D. Writing is a set of visual symbols which represent incompletely the underlying auditory code, leaving out in particular the intonation patterns of speech.
    E. No known natural language is more advanced per se than any other. Each language is capable of expressing any experience apprehended by its users.
 II. Assumptions about the structure of language.
    A. The code of symbols in every language is systematic.
    B. Each language is a unique system and can be described only in terms of its own structure.
    C. Living languages change constantly and systematically, and future changes can often be predicted.
    D. A writing system changes more slowly than the spoken language, and pressure to bring the writing system into line with the spoken form will be resisted by the literate members of the society.
    E. The sentences of a language are either kernel sentences or transformations of these kernel sentences.
    F. In all known languages in which there are declarative sentences with nominal subject and object, the dominant order is almost always one in which the subject precedes the object.[3]
III. Assumptions about the geography of language.

[2] Fries, *Linguistics and Reading* (New York: Holt, Rinehart, & Winston, 1963), p. 92.

[3] This appears as Universal 1 in Joseph H. Greenberg, "Some Universals of Grammar with Particular Reference to the Order of Meaningful Elements," in Greenberg, *op. cit.*, p. 61.

A. Every human being has a language to which he belongs and dialects by which he interacts and achieves identity and co-operation as a member of different subgroups.

B. In every language the spoken forms of interaction between a given group of speakers differ in patterns and conventions from the written forms.

C. The spoken language of a linguistic community will vary greatly depending upon the regional speech characteristics of the speakers, their social or occupational status, and the particular situation in which the speech event takes place.

D. Each language is better suited for expressing the cultural concepts and activities of the speakers than any other language is.

IV. Assumptions about the psychology of language.

A. Language is learned habits.

B. The habits acquired in mastering the mother tongue are deeply rooted and constitute points of interference in the learning of a second language wherever its structure is different from that of the mother tongue.

C. Although language is systematic and follows certain rules, one masters a language best by behaving in it and having his behavior reinforced rather than by learning the rules.

D. As behavior, language is measured by its effectiveness in terms of purpose — its appropriateness to the situation, the user, the audience, and the subject matter.

E. Because languages encode objective experience in different ways, language users tend to perceive experiences in different ways (and to be affected behaviorally)

according to the categories provided by their respective languages.

V. Assumptions about the meanings of language.

A. Sentences do not get meanings from their constituent words; the words get their meanings from the structure of the sentences in which they appear.

B. The ultimate unit in language is not the word, the sentence, or the paragraph; it is the total perception being transmitted, to which the parts are bound.

C. Languages seem to have varying proportions of "transparent" and "opaque" words. (Transparent words are words that are "motivated," that is, whose meanings can be partly grasped from their sound symbolism, or from their morphemic makeup, or from their metaphorical or semantic connections. Examples of phonologically motivated words are *swish*, *boom*, and *splash*; of morphologically motivated words, *armchair*, *thinker*, and *retell*; of semantically motivated words, "the *focus* of an argument" and "the *horns* of a dilemma." Opaque words are words whose meanings cannot be guessed from their forms.)[4]

The list of assumptions could have been increased tenfold by adding the universals of phonology, of language change, of morphology, of grammar, of semantic structure, of semology, of ethnolinguistics, and of psycholinguistics, all of which are identified and discussed in *Universals of Language*. (On-

[4] This assumption and subsequent explanation are discussed as Semantic Universal 1 in Stephen Ullmann, "Semantic Universals," in Greenberg, *op. cit.*, pp. 175–76.

ly two have been taken directly from that book, though all of them are implicit in its discussions.) Similarly, these statements could have been reduced to half their number through a more rigorous selection and through carefully combining several statements into one. There are so many painstakingly acquired insights about the nature and function of language that the reading teacher could use with profit that it is difficult to designate any one list of them as more essential than another. Now that we have before us a substantial list of "givens" about language provided us by linguistic science, let us see what implications teachers of reading can derive from them. Although most of them will have significance for the teacher of the average student of reading in our public schools, the intention is to point out their implications for the teaching of non-native or non-standard speakers of English.

TEACHING NON-NATIVE AND NON-STANDARD SPEAKERS OF ENGLISH

Although the non-native and non-standard speakers of English have many common problems in learning to read and write English and though there is increasing evidence that the techniques that have been used with some success with non-native speakers can also be used effectively with non-standard speakers, there is a fundamental difference between the two groups. The difference is mainly a psychological one. The non-native learner is considered both by himself and by the native American a cultural and linguistic outsider trying to acquire enough proficiency in communicating in a second language and culture to enjoy the many opportunities of all kinds available in the English-speaking world. He and everybody else assumes that he can remain loyal to both his native culture and his acquired culture and that his bilingualism will make him a more efficient worker and a better man. The non-standard speaker, however, perhaps one of the millions of adolescents or adults among our migrating families who have come to our large cities from depressed rural or mining areas in quest of the better life, is made to feel that although he belongs to the culture and language community of the people around him, much of what he says and does is unacceptable to them. He is told by his teachers that he must learn, like Eliza Doolittle in George Bernard Shaw's *Pygmalion*, to talk and act like his social betters — the middle-class speakers of standard English — and must erase his earlier practices from his behavior. Needless to say, unless we can make the non-standard speaker feel that he too should remain loyal to his mother tongue and culture and should become multidialectal only in order to be able to communicate across dialects, he will be harder to motivate to learn to read standard English than the non-native speaker.

There is one other observation that should be made about the differences between the non-native speaker and the non-standard speaker. Teachers of reading have generally not grasped the implications of the changing role of English throughout the world in the postwar years. English is fast becoming a vehicle of international, interlingual, and intercultural communication such as the world has never seen. This means that there will be an increasing variety of written forms of English, and an even greater variety of spoken forms underlying them, as writers from the non-English-speaking cultures vie with those from the English-speaking cultures for attention. Anyone wishing a foretaste of the variety that will be increasingly appearing can find it in a pamphlet of articles reprinted from the *Times Literary Supplement* (London) entitled *A Language in Common*.[5]

Non-native learners of English are generally more aware of what is at stake in their learning to read English than many non-standard speakers of English. Making the latter group aware is one of the problems and challenges of the teacher.

IMPLICATIONS FOR READING TEACHERS

Now that we have recognized the characteristics of the learners we are concerned about, let us see what implications the linguists' assumptions about language have for the reading teacher of non-native or non-standard speakers of English.

The assumptions in the first category — those about the nature of language — are not likely to be startling revelations to teachers who have worked with non-native or non-standard learners. They should recognize, however, the need for proficiency in the vocal code underlying the writ-

ten words as a basis for progress in reading. Since the written language is a symbolization of the primary symbolization — the spoken language code — the learner should be taught to read (and write) at the outset only the structures and words that he can understand and produce in spoken form. The teacher should inculcate in his learners awareness of the fulness and richness of the signaling power of the intonation patterns of speech as compared with the sparseness of the signals on the printed page. Carl Lefevre devotes special attention to the intonation patterns of English and their corresponding written forms and suggests techniques by which teachers can help learners develop rhythm and speed in reading through drills in the intonation patterns that characterize the sentence sequences found in reading.[6] The teacher of non-native or non-standard speakers of English will find in this text many valuable suggestions, as will the teacher of average American students.

A final implication of this category of assumptions is that the teacher must not be led, by ethnocentricity or awareness of the enormous utility of standard English in world communication, to show disrespect for the student's native language or his native non-standard dialect. If the teacher can come to understand that the student's language or dialect has all the structural machinery he needs to communicate any concept he has grasped, he will probably not reveal an attitude that may stand

[5] Published by Oxford University Press in 1962.

[6] Lefevre, *Linguistics and the Teaching of Reading* (New York: McGraw-Hill Book Co., 1964), pp. 43–75.

in the way of his establishing rapport with his students. The teacher should also be aware of the reason his students may attach meanings to English words that do not correspond precisely to the meanings attached by native Americans — they may be attaching meanings of closely equivalent words in their own language. A Puerto Rican student who has promised to assist at some event may show up and do nothing with a clear conscience because one of the more common meanings of the word *asistir* in his language is "to attend, to be present at." Since words and their referents are in arbitrary relationship, the range of meanings attached to a word in the student's language will not be the same as its equivalent has in English.

The basic assumptions about the structure of language have somewhat more to suggest to the teacher of non-native or non-standard speakers of English than do those about the nature of language. Since English is a unique system of linguistic symbols in different patterns from any other language, these patterns must be identified and described inductively rather than through terms and definitions traditionally derived from Latin grammar.

The concept taken from transformation grammar that all sentences are either kernel sentences or transformations of kernel sentences offers the teacher of reading a procedure by which his non-native or non-standard students can learn to transform the predominantly kernel sentences of their everyday speech to longer and more complicated sentences. Later in their reading they can be taught to get at the meaning of a sentence by finding the kernels embedded in it. Before long they should be transforming such kernel sentences as "The hound bit Jack" and "Jack kicked the hound" into the following: "Jack was bitten by the hound." "Did the hound bite Jack?" "The hound didn't bite Jack." "Whom/Who did the hound bite?" "Why did the hound bite Jack?" "The hound was kicked by Jack." "Did Jack kick the hound?" "Jack didn't kick the hound." "What did Jack kick?" "Why did Jack kick the hound?" And "Bitten, Jack kicked the hound."

The assumptions that language change is regular and partially predictable and that the writing system changes more slowly than the spoken language are useful for the reading teacher in several ways. They help him see why the correspondences between units of speech (phonemes) and units of writing (graphemes) are so irregular and how an understanding of the grapheme-phoneme correspondences and the complexities of their patterns can help him design ways of teaching the learner to decode spellings into their spoken equivalents and meanings or to encode spoken words into spellings. Studies of English spelling-to-sound correspondences like that recently completed by Ruth H. Weir and Richard L. Venezky of Stanford University under a U. S. Office of Education grant, "Formulation of Grapheme-Phoneme Correspondence Rules to Aid in the Teaching of Reading," will give teachers of reading more precise direction in this area than phonics or Bloomfieldian linguistics have done up to now.

The last of the assumptions listed about structure — that in languages with nominal subject and object in declarative sentences the subject generally precedes the object — is one of the "universals of grammar" (Universal 1) identified by Joseph H. Greenberg. The relevance for the reading teacher of this type of universal is illustrated by Walter P. Allen's finding that "the ratio of variations from the actor-action-goal (subject-predicate-object) sentence pattern" is one of the most important factors in the prediction of the degree of difficulty a non-native speaker will have in reading a passage of English. The other factors identified by Allen are ". . . the number of words per sentence, the ratio of different hard words (words not in Dale's list of 769 easy words) , the ratio of personal pronouns, the ratio of dependent clauses, the number of auxiliary verbs, the ratio of two-word verbs . . . and the amount of dialog." [7]

The third category of assumptions made by linguists — those related to the geography of language — is of special interest to the teacher of non-standard speakers of English, though it will also give orientation to the teacher of non-native speakers. The assumption that a person's language behavior is related to his environment, his goals, and the situations in which he is pursuing his goals should help a reading teacher see that it is better to adjust the reading materials, especially in the beginning stages, to the student's language habits and cultural background than his language and culture to the reading materials. In reading materials involving cultural situations familiar to the learner, the learner's speech patterns will also be appropriate, more so, in fact than the widely accepted patterns of standard English.

The teacher should also recognize, however, that the spoken forms of language differ in patterns and conventions from the written forms. In a recent article included in a symposium on linguistics and reading, the writer pointed out that children have already acquired a complicated system of communicative behavior by the time they are taught to read. The signals involved in this behavior have become habits through the application, albeit unconsciously, of small-step reinforcement procedures by parents and peers. As a coherent system, these habits tend to interfere with the learning of the somewhat different system involved in reading.[8] How different the language habits involved in reading are from those involved in conversation was pointed out in an article by David Abercrombie.[9] The present writer suggested to reading teachers that they lead the learner through small steps with continuous reinforcement from mastery of the signals of conversational English to mastery of the signals of "spoken prose" and then on to mastery

[7] Allen, *Selecting Reading Materials for Foreign Students: A Technique for Selecting Reading Materials Which Provide Cultural Background for Learning English* (Washington, D.C.: English Language Services, Inc., 1955), pp. 33–34.

[8] William F. Marquardt, "Language Interference in Reading," *Reading Teacher*, XVIII (December, 1964), 214–218.

[9] Abercrombie, "Conversation and Spoken Prose," *English Language Teaching*, XVIII (October, 1963), 10–16.

of "other meaningful behavior related to reading."

The assumption, in the fourth category of listed assumptions, that language is habits and that the system of habits acquired in mastering the mother tongue will interfere with the learning of the sound system, the writing system, the syntactical patterns, the lexicon-meaning correspondences, and the verbal-cultural correspondences of English should help the teacher identify the reading problems of his non-native and non-standard speaker-students that result from interference of previous habits. For example, the problems of learning to decode the printed page effortlessly will be different for learners whose native writing systems use ideographs (as in Chinese), a syllabry (as in Amharic), right-to-left sequence (as in Arabic), or top-to-bottom sequence (as in Japanese).

The assumption that language is mastered best through reinforced behavior in the language rather than through studying the rules of its system also has implications for the reading teacher. It suggests that drill involving reinforceable responses to meaningful stimuli is an effective way of giving the learner control of patterns first in spoken English and then in written.

The assumption that language should be evaluated in terms of its appropriateness for a particular purpose is a reminder that the spontaneous retort by Johnny to the boy across the aisle that the teacher happened to hear and did not consider good English had better not be corrected, unless with an alternate expression more appropriate in a slightly different set of circumstances. Similarly, the learner needs to have demonstrated to him the different intonation patterns and words of public printed messages and private communication by speech or the familiar letter.

The final assumption in this category — a cautious wording of the so-called Whorfian hypothesis that language molds thought — is also a reminder to the reading teacher that both his non-native and his non-standard speakers of English have ways of perceiving experience that the teacher will not be aware of unless he is familiar with the categories of their mother tongues or dialects. Thus he should be constantly on the lookout for language forms in the reading materials that they will be prevented from understanding completely by the mold imposed on their minds by their native languages. For example, the teacher should know why a Japanese student tends to be ill-at-ease when trying to cope with the single form *you* in English for addressing a person — his own language has half a dozen equivalents, each with its appropriate use.

The final category of assumptions — those concerned with meaning — is the area in which the linguist is most cautious. It is the area in which he has had many of his hypotheses regarding structure disproved. It is an area, however, in which, with the help of psychologists, anthropologists, sociologists, and information-theory specialists, he seems to be on the threshold of discoveries possibly of great value to the reading teacher.

The assumptions listed in this category, however, especially the first two, tend to urge the reading teacher to be cautious rather than to look for a breakthrough — to train his students to arrive at meanings through careful discrimination of observable phenomena and to make inferences only from a total view of the language event (linguistic context, paralinguistic context, cultural context, and situational context). The assumption concerning "transparent" and "opaque" words suggests how teachers of reading might exploit to the maximum the associative clues to the meanings of words.

NEED FOR CONTINUOUS COMMUNICATION

You can see from this somewhat impressionistic review of the assumptions about language that linguists of varied interests have agreed upon that there is a considerable body of widely accepted insights that the reading teacher can put to use. These points of consensus will multiply as the frontiers of inquiry and debate move forward and as linguists continue to identify points of agreement in their divergent views. The reading teacher of learners that do not belong to the main stream of English language and culture will find these points of agreement increasingly useful as he helps the members of this group become effective communicators in a world of accelerating diversity and change. Linguists need the help of reading teachers, too. If teachers can show linguists that the assumptions they developed in their past isolation from practical concerns are demonstrably invalid, at least with respect to the teaching of reading, linguists will be forever in their debt.

CHAPTER XI

SPECIFIC ASPECTS OF LINGUISTICS RELATED TO READING

*

A BEGINNING READING PROGRAM BASED UPON LINGUISTIC PRINCIPLES

ROSEMARY G. WILSON

*

THE READING program discussed in this paper was begun in an effort to try out an approach to beginning reading that was based upon the best information which we have about our language and about the nature of the reading process itself. The program was also designed to be preventive, an effort to find the best approach to reading during the all-important first year of school and thus to provide a firm foundation upon which to build a good developmental program in the succeeding years.

Of all the ideas that have come to the fore during the last few years of re-examination of existing reading systems, that which applied some of the basic principles of structural linguistics to the teaching of reading seemed the most promising. Fortunately, by the time we were ready for experimentation, the writer had read an advance copy of Charles C. Fries's book, *Linguistics and Reading*.[1] Having had little to guide me up to this time but the material in Bloomfield and Barnhart's *Let's Read*, I was very pleased to find

[1] Published by Holt, Rinehart, & Winston, Inc., in 1963.

in Fries's book not only a thorough and scholarly treatment of past practices in the teaching of reading and linguistics but also a comprehensive program of methods and materials based upon sound linguistic principles. His suggestions, combined with the early introduction of writing, form the basis for the program which has been in use for the past three years in more than one hundred first and second year classes in the schools of Philadelphia.

BASIC PRINCIPLES

"Learning to read is not learning to *know* something. It is learning to *do* something." These words, which comprise the opening sentences of the Teacher's Manual of a "Basic Reading Series Developed upon Linguistic Principles," by Charles and Agnes Fries, Rosemary Wilson, and Mildred Rudolph, also serve to introduce a detailed statement of the principles basic to this approach to reading. The following digest of these principles will serve to provide some background for an understanding of the program:

1. Learning to read begins with and

builds upon the language control (both receptive and expressive) already achieved by the pupils.

2. The vocabulary presented in the materials of this reading series is within the linguistic experience of the pupils and represents the three major spelling patterns of English.

3. Mastery of the alphabet by learning the special shape that identifies each letter and separates it from other letters is essential and constitutes an important prereading activity.

4. Complete elimination of pictures from the readers forces the pupil to *read* for meaning and eliminates the distracting element which pictures often present.

5. Use of the technique of minimum contrast is essential, with attention centered upon contrasts between words rather than upon similarities.

6. Introduction of a limited number of words with a high-frequency structure permits the writing of normal sentence patterns.

7. Writing in the form of sentences and, later, stories utilizing the reservoir of pattern and sight words in the readers is introduced early.

8. Emphasis in story content is upon humor and experiences which will have meaning and appeal to children.

9. Practice books with simple pictures are useful to check comprehension.

INSTRUCTIONAL MATERIALS

To implement that phase of the prereading program in which discrimination of the letters of the alphabet was taught, it was necessary for us to design and publish our own material in the form of a book entitled *My Alphabet Book*. In a foreword entitled "Why Teach the Alphabet?" we expressed our purposes as follows:

This alphabet book is designed to initi-

ate your program of reading instruction in the way which leads most directly into the reading process itself. It provides (with the supplementary activities suggested) the most meaningful kind of pre-reading or readiness activity for children of all levels of intellectual, physical, and social maturity. It was designed with the following purposes in mind:

1. To teach children the names of the letters of the alphabet.
2. To have children acquire mastery and instant recognition of both capital and lower case letters of the alphabet.
3. To afford the best kind of material for training in visual discrimination.
4. To provide many oppportunities for practice in left to right progression.
5. To teach the sequence of letters in the alphabet.
6. To provide children with a valuable referrent for future use in word recognition and word attack.
7. To lay the groundwork for an understanding of the alphabetic principle upon which our written language is based.

For a detailed description of the alphabet and its relationship to reading, the reader may refer to chapter v of Fries's book. To obtain a point of view concerning the teaching of the alphabet different from that expressed by a linguist, the reader may consult the chapter by Donald D. Durrell and Alice K. Nicholson in the Sixtieth Yearbook of the National Society for the Study of Education [2] and the chapter by Durrell in the recently published U. S. Office of Education booklet entitled *Teaching Young Children To*

2 Durrell and Nicholson, "Preschool and Kindergarten Experience," in *Development in and through Reading* (Chicago: University of Chicago Press, 1961), p. 266.

Read.[3] A salient comment quoted in the second-mentioned publication is the following: "To try to have children make use of phonics without letting them learn the names of letter forms is like trying to teach them arithmetic without letting them learn the names of number symbols."[4]

In addition to a book on the letters of the alphabet, the reading series consists of eight readers and eight practice books which accompany the readers. The vocabulary of the readers has been selected as follows.

1. Readers 1–5: words of first major spelling pattern, that is, "one syllable words with the general shape of consonant-vowel-consonant"; words of first spelling pattern with consonant digraphs and clusters added in initial and final positions; and contractions and various types of inflectional endings.

2. Reader 6: words "that use the final letter *e* to differentiate them from words of the previous pattern, for example, cap-cap*e*, mat-mat*e*, pin-pin*e*."

3. Readers 7 and 8: words with spelling characterized by vowel clusters, for example, b*ea*t, m*ea*t, s*ea*t or m*ai*n, p*ai*n, r*ai*n.

In addition, a few words of a high-frequency structure or function are introduced from the beginning as "sight" in contrast to "pattern" words.

Words at the appropriate levels are used from the very beginning in sentences representing normal speech patterns and, even more important for meaning, in sequences of sentences. To quote again from the Teacher's Manual — "*My First Reader*, therefore, contains only some forty words, but these forty words are used in more than two hundred and sixty sentences, through which the use of reading to get meaning is developed from the very opening lesson." For example, we progress from a typical sentence such as "The cat is on Dan's lap" in *My First Reader* to "Dan is sick and has to be in bed" in *My Third Reader* to the compound subject and predicate of "Tim and Jim went running by and stopped next to Mr. Dennis" in *My Fifth Reader*.

To summarize, the following specific suggestions are given to the teacher:

1. Teach the alphabet during the readiness or prereading stage. Instant recognition and discrimination of letters are essential. Identification should be by letter name only.

2. Introduce words in pattern by reading and then spelling them. Emphasize minimum contrastive features such as difference in initial or ending consonant or difference in medial vowel.

3. Present sight words without spelling them.

4. Use new words immediately in the context of oral and written sentences. Write sentences on the board and have them read aloud.

5. Proceed from individual sentences to related story materials in the readers, directing the initial silent reading through prior questioning.

6. Work toward normal stress and intonation without offering a model or pattern.

7. Encourage a pupil who is experiencing difficulty with a word to spell it. If necessary, assist him by writing other words from the same pattern. Then have

3 Durrell, "Learning Factors in Beginning Reading," in *Teaching Young Children To Read* (U.S. Office of Education, Bulletin No. 19; Washington, D. C.: Government Printing Office), pp. 71–77.

4 M. Lucille Harrison, "Getting Them Ready To Read," *National Education Journal*, XL (February, 1951), 108.

the pupil read and spell the words he knows before respelling the word he did not recognize.

8. Anticipate temporarily slower progress when words with a new matrix are introduced.

9. Reinforce visual-auditory images by having pupils write all new words, preferably at the board. Later, have pupils write dictated or original sentences utilizing these words.

CONCLUDING STATEMENT

In conclusion, it would be well to emphasize that any approach to reading which wishes to lay claim to the term "linguistic" must include a strong oral and written language program. The oral language phase constitutes an important component of the readiness and prereading program and should be continued after formal reading instruction is begun. The task of extending the vocabulary of children by means of varied activities and also of improving their ability to express themselves effectively and acceptably is endless. The linguist has much to offer the classroom teacher in this area from his research into the nature of language — its structure, its dialects, and its relationship to the cultural background of the child.

The linguist's contribution to the development of writing skills has already been recognized at the high-school level in the areas of grammar and usage. Much remains to be done, however, in applying some of these ideas and techniques in modified form to the elementary level. In our own reading program, we have emphasized the writing of original sentences and, eventually, stories at a very early stage. We now need to go farther in working out a sequence, from the "linguistic" point of view, for the teaching of sentence structure and grammar. When completed, this sequence should be a breakthrough in this area of the language arts program as linguistic readers have been in the reading program. It is our fervent hope that such new approaches to the teaching of speaking, reading, and writing will result in children who enjoy their language in all its phases, who are secure in their mastery of its skills and take delight in their ability to understand and interpret the beauty and subtlety of its words and ideas.

* * *

GRAMMAR AND READING

JANET A. EMIG

*

AFTER BEING for many decades — indeed, for many centuries — the dimmest word in the curriculum, *grammar* has become within the past decade one of the most electric. Grammar is the center of the most current research concerning the language development of the child. The topic dominates entire issues of professional journals in education, psychology, and linguistics. It is the theme of endless workshops and professional conferences. In secondary-school English, and more and more in elementary-school English, how and what to teach in grammar are crucial curricular issues. Those of us for whom the word *grammar* still chiefly evokes Miss Cadwallader, her pince-nez, and a vast rooted diagram that we had to turn our notebook paper sideways to accommodate understandably wonder what the excitement is all about.

KNOWLEDGE OF GRAMMAR BY STUDENTS

The use of *grammar* in the introduction, especially in the last sentence, hints at an important first concern: the difference between the definition of grammar as most of us think of it and the current use of the term by students of language. Let us underscore the difference with two brief quotations. The first is an excerpt from an essay by the linguist Martin Joos:

. . . It (learning the grammatical system of the native language) is complete — and the books are closed on it! — at about eight years of age. It is not normal to learn any more grammar beyond that age.[1]

The second is from a review of the literature in the field by the psychologists Susan M. Ervin and Wick R. Miller:

What material is available suggests that by the age of four most children have learned the fundamental structural features of their language and many of the details.[2]

Clearly, if grammar is something we learn naturally by the time we are four and complete learning by the time we are eight, it is quite different from anything connoting Miss Cadwallader and forests of diagrams.

How do such students of language as Joos, Ervin, and Miller define grammar? Most of them regard grammar as composed of three parts: phonology, morphology, and syntax. Phonology is concerned with the sounds of a language, especially the phonemes or minimally distinctive sound features of a language. For example, the features that make *tin*, *tan*, and *ton* different forms, although they are all three letters long and all begin with *t* and end with *n*, are the distinctive sound differentials or phonemes $/ i /$, $/ a /$, and $/ o /$. When he is still very small, the child learns by practice and imitation the phonemic repertoire of his own language, gradually eliminating all those not in the native range. He does so thorough a job, in fact, that if he should attempt to learn a new language as an adult he will seldom be able to achieve an accurate replication of the phonemes of the new language, even though as a small child he probably produced these phonemes many times.

The second part of grammar, morphology, is considered by most students of language simultaneously with

[1] Joos, "Language and the School Child," *Language and Learning*, A Special Issue of the Harvard Educational Review, XXXIV (Spring, 1964), 205.

[2] Ervin and Miller, "Language Development," in *Child Psychology*, Sixty-Second Yearbook of the National Society for the Study of Education, Part I (Chicago: University of Chicago Press, 1963), p. 125.

syntax, the third part; but for the purposes of definition, let us keep them separate. Morphology is concerned with the forms of language. The psycholinguist John B. Carroll defines a form as "any linguistic unit with definite (though possibly varying) phonemic content." [3] These forms are of two types: bound and free. Bound forms are those which never occur alone. Examples are prefixes and suffixes: *re, il,* and *im* as the first element in the unit — *re*turn, *il*legal, *im*proper; *less, ment,* and *tion* as the last — care*less*, state*ment*, atten*tion*. Free forms occur alone; they are what we colloquially call words.

Syntax is concerned with the arrangement of these forms, both bound and free, into orders that a native-born speaker of a language would find acceptable — acceptable, that is, from the structural point of view. Semantically, these sequences can be nonsense. "The dry rain fell up" is a perfectly legitimate English sentence from a syntactical point of view; "the fell up rain dry" is not.

What knowledge, then, of the phonology, morphology, and syntax of English does the child possess by the time he is four or, to make it more relevant to our interests, by the time he enters school? (An important aside before beginning this description: Research on the child's development of language in the past and, in too many cases, at present is informal, unsystematic, and based on very scant data. It is not at all uncommon for these data

[3] Carroll, *Language and Thought* (Englewood Cliffs, N. J.: Prentice-Hall, Inc., 1964), p. 18.

to have an *N* of 1 or 2, frequently the linguist's own children!)

As suggested earlier, the normal child by the time he enters school knows and can produce the sounds of his native language in their full phonemic variety — the count varies from linguist to linguist, but a minimum number is twenty-three. According to many authorities, he knows at least seventy-five hundred morphemes, which he has placed in their appropriate structural categories: either in the four major form-classes — noun, verb, adjective, adverb — or in the function classes — conjunctions and prepositions.

But it is in the realm of syntax that his accomplishments are most striking. He knows that the order of forms is a key element in his native language. He knows, for example, that, given the elements *ran, tall, boy, swiftly, the,* the only basic orderings that form acceptable English are either "the tall boy ran swiftly" or "swiftly ran the tall boy."

He knows that, next to the ordering of forms, markers tell him the form-classes to which individual forms belong and signal the appearance of members of certain other form-classes. These markers are, like other forms, bound and free. In the illustrations given above, for example, the student knows that the bound form *ly* of *swiftly* marks it as an adverb and that the adverb is located in any utterance near an adjective or a verb. He knows that the free form *the* — with *a* and *an,* called determiners — heralds a noun and that it does not normally ap-

pear immediately before verbs or ad-
verbs. He knows what students of language call the twelve basic sentence
patterns. And he can combine these
patterns to form sentences of great variety, length, or compactness.

Hence, it becomes obvious that the
grammatical sophistication of the
child entering school is extraordinary.
In fact, research on the linguistic development of the child suggests that we
have underestimated the grammatical
knowledge of the child on entering
school as grossly as we once did the
size of his vocabulary. And it is this
quite new appreciation of the child's
basic mastery of the structure of his
language that is a major reason for current excitement about grammar.

Throughout this description, we
have used the verb *know* about the
child and his grammar; we do not of
course mean conscious, explicit knowledge. Rather, we mean an intuitive
working knowledge of the language, an
ability to manipulate the patterns of
English, but not to verbalize the concept of structure.

GRAMMAR AND COMPREHENSION

Of what value is this strong and
wide working knowledge when the
child starts to read? It is, simply, the
most powerful resource the teacher of
reading can tap to aid the student's
reading comprehension. This resource
can be used in two ways, often simultaneously: in the direct building of vocabulary through the systematic teaching of certain bound forms and in indirect teaching by means of context
cues that certain structural features of
the language provide. A systematic

teaching of prefixes and suffixes gives
the child an enormous increase in his
functional vocabulary. He can learn
that by using certain bound forms he
can, in a sense, get not only four words
but four form-classes for one. By
changing the *y* of the noun *beauty* to
ify, *iful*, and *ifully*, for example, he
can gain a verb, an adjective, and an
adverb.

The second way in which the child's
background can be tapped is through
indirect teaching using markers, both
bound forms and such free forms as
the, *a*, and *an*, that signal certain form-
classes. And these, again, the student,
at least implicitly, knows. He would
never, for example, use *the* immediately before a verb, except for a play-
ful effect. Through instruction he can
become aware he does not and perhaps
be led to discover the reason: that certain form-classes are regularly identified by certain fixed means.

These markers also help convey the
notion that certain forms — the ones
they signal — are more crucial for comprehension than the markers themselves. The importance of markers for
this function is substantiated in a
study conducted by Vincent Louthan.
Through the use of the cloze technique (the deletion of every *nth* word),
he found that for a sample of 236 seventh grade students the systematic deletion of determiners "produced a significant gain in comprehension." [4] One
reason he offers for what initially
seems the opposite of the result one
would expect is that

4 Louthan, "Some Systematic Grammatical
Deletions and Their Effects on Reading Comprehension," *English Journal*, LIV (April,
1965), 297.

the removal of function words, the syntax and morphology of which already signal the grammatical relationships in a sentence, probably tends to focus the attention of the reader on the larger units of meaning of the passage being read.[5]

Perhaps some modified but systematic use of the cloze technique could be used in the teaching of reading to make explicit to the child the importance of structural cues (a) for establishing the form-class of certain words and (b) for conveying which elements

5 *Ibid.*, p. 298.

in the sentence or paragraph are the bearers of the greatest meaning and are therefore most vital for comprehension.

CONCLUDING STATEMENT

The essence of good teaching has always been to build upon what the pupil knows. The student's extraordinarily powerful knowledge of his own grammar provides more than a base — it probably represents a launching pad to a stronger and deeper comprehension of whatever he reads.

✳   ✳   ✳

SYNTAX AND MEANING

SUMNER IVES

✳

ALTHOUGH THE development of descriptive linguistics was well started by the end of the last century, its results did not begin to spread outside the rather small circle of linguistic scholarship until after World War II. At the present time, there are several approaches to grammatical description; but underlying these differences in purpose and theory, there is substantial agreement on a great many factual details.

Any modern discussion of syntax properly begins by taking the sentence or the clause as its basic unit of analysis. But there are no standard or uniquely correct definitions of the sentence, for definitions result from a total description and these descriptions differ in approach and emphasis. Bas-

ing our definition on syntactic parts and arrangements, we may describe a sentence as any one of certain patterns containing a finite verb form or phrase, having grammatically related ingredients, being relatively self-sufficient, and occurring as a unit in a sequence of similar units. This sequence is an utterance or linguistic communication. A clause is a unit having essentially the same ingredients and conforming to essentially the same patterns but not necessarily grammatically independent of other units. This definition is appropriate to analyses of written English and of extended utterances, such as this paper, an essay, or a story in materials prepared for beginning instruction in reading.

It is immediately obvious that the

pattern, or arrangement of parts, in an English sentence is one factor contributing to its meaning as a whole and, in some instances, the meanings of individual parts. We can illustrate total meaning differences by the classic "man bites dog," which is news, and "dog bites man," which is not. One of the ways by which the pattern affects the meaning of a part can be illustrated by using the verb *freeze* in a set of sentences with different predicate structures. In "the meat froze rapidly," the verb is intransitive; in "she froze the meat," it is transitive; and in "the meat froze solid," it is linking. On a different level, there are such distinctions in meaning as that between the use of *fairly* in "judge the contest fairly" and in "a fairly large pile." On a still lower level, there are various marker words, which have already been described by Emig in the preceding paper.

This kind of discrimination by context occurs even within words. For instance, the noun *arrival* consists of the verb *arrive* plus the suffix *al*; but if *al* is added to a noun, as in *fictional*, the result is an adjective. Any decision as to the part of speech of a word in English must at least consider its context — that is, its syntactic relationship to other words — and its composition — that is, the identity of both the base and the affix.

SENTENCE PATTERNS

The definition of the sequence sentence, or sentence in connected discourse, specifies one kind of word as an essential ingredient. Sentences of this type must have a tense-showing, or finite, form of a verb or verb phrase. The kind of sentence — whether statement, question, or command — is indicated near the beginning by a syntactic device. The punctuation at the end merely confirms this syntactic marking. Except for a very few inversions, a statement is marked by the occurrence of the subject before the verb; a question is marked by the occurrence of the subject inside the verb phrase, unless the verb is a single-word form of *to be*; and a command is marked by the omission of a subject. Thus, we have the statement "you are taking a test"; the question "are you taking a test?" and the command "you take the test," in which *you* is not the subject but the person addressed.

When considering the various patterns of sentences within each of these kinds, it is best to deal with the verb *to be* separately, for it is unique both in number of forms and in range of syntactic patterns. No other verb, for example, can have a prepositional phrase or an adverb as a complement — as in "the car is in the ditch," which differs from "the car was found in the ditch"; and "the book is here," which differs from "he left the book here." When analyzing sentences in which the essential verb is other than the verb *to be*, one notes a close relationship between the kind of meaning the verb has and the kind of complement structure that follows it.

Any verb that has two complements not in parallel structure is a transitive verb in that sentence, as in "cook him some dinner" and "cook it well done" as distinct from "Mary cooks well," which has no complements but has an adverb modifying the verb. Some verbs take either a noun complement or an adjective complement. For instance, "he became president" and "he became unruly."

Still other verbs are transitive with a following noun, or equivalent, and linking with a following adjective. Thus, "he smelled the cabbage at once" and "it smelled bad." A great many verbs are transitive with a following noun, or equivalent, and intransitive without one. Thus, "he drives a Buick" and "he drives well."

Another class of verbs may be transitive, intransitive, or linking, depending on the class of the word or construction that follows. Such a word is *freeze*, mentioned earlier. Other common verbs in this class are *work*, *turn*, and *grow*.

Finally, there is a class of verbs which may be followed by a noun or an adverb, although they are not really transitive, for they do not appear in passive voice. Such a verb is *cost*, as in "it costs a quarter" and "it costs too much." Akin to this class is another, illustrated by *weigh*, which is like *cost* in "it weighs two pounds" and a regular transitive in "he weighed all the packages."

Such diversity in verb class, depending on grammatical context, illustrates the very close relationship between syntax and meaning. In fact, some of the best modern grammarians refuse to draw a sharp line between grammar and semantics, and the direction of work in linguistics is toward greater and greater consideration of meaning classes, since distinctions in meaning are reflected in syntactic possibilities.

The potential occurrences mentioned above underlie the lists of basic sentence patterns which are appearing in recent revisions of elementary- and secondary-school textbooks. The crucial point is that, in nearly every instance, the kind of meaning is a reflection of the complement structure or lack of complement structure in the predicate. Within the limits imposed by its general meaning, the immediate meaning of a particular verb is signalled by the syntactic frame in which it occurs.

INCLUDED PATTERNS

If appropriate changes in case are made, the items which can occur as subjects are the same as those which can occur as objects of verbs, and a list of these items would include those which can occur as objects of prepositions or as complements of inherently linking verbs, including *to be*. Among these are nouns, pronouns, demonstratives, indefinites like *some* and *many*, verb forms ending with *ing*, verb forms introduced by *to*, and clauses introduced by certain words, all of which have other duties. Potentially the most complicated of these is what is usually called a noun cluster. A somewhat generalized model partially showing the range of possibilities is given below.

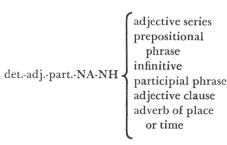

det.-adj.-part.-NA-NH ⎰ adjective series
prepositional
    phrase
infinitive
participial phrase
adjective clause
adverb of place
    or time

The first slot, that for a determiner, can be filled by an article, the possessive form of a noun or pronoun, a demonstrative, an indefinite, or a word for a cardinal number. In some instances, words may occur before the determiner, as in "very nearly all the apples." The next slot, that for an adjective, may have one or more adjectives in it, and these may be cumulative or parallel. Adjectives, of course, may be modified by words like *very* and *rather*, which are usually called intensifiers or qualifiers. The next slot may be filled by a participle, which may be modified by an adverb, as in "rapidly advancing troops." The final slot before the noun head, may be filled by a noun adjunct, or modifying noun, as in "school duties." It is, of course, very unlikely that all these slots will be filled in any actual noun cluster, although some of those writing for academic journals seem to try to do so.

The items preceding a noun head are usually called prepositive modifiers, and those following the head are called postpositive modifiers. Let us simply run down the list of postpositives, giving examples. First, "an old man, ragged, dirty, and hungry"; second, "the man in the car"; third, "a man to be watched"; fourth, "the man riding a mule" and "the man elected last night"; fifth, "the man who was here"; and sixth, "the man outside" and "the test tomorrow." Although any prepositive modifier is necessarily restrictive, postpositive modifiers, at least most kinds, may be either restrictive or non-restrictive.

A sentence cannot be understood unless the syntactic patterns in it are perceived and the grammatical relationships of its words are understood, although this recognition is usually subliminal. When we reread a sentence because its meaning is not clear, we are intuitively performing a kind of grammatical analysis so as to discover the proper groupings and associations. The reading of difficult prose probably could be made easier by a reasonable amount of training in syntax. Certainly, guidance in extending linguistic resources and command should be based on an understanding of major syntactic patterns.

The final point for discussion in this concise summary is the finite verb and verb phrase. Aside from *to be* and certain irregular verbs, each verb has three and only three single-word finite forms: the present form with *s*, which goes with third person singular subjects, the present form without *s*, and the past form. The auxiliaries *have* and *do* and the occasional auxiliaries *go*, *get*, and *keep* have the same three forms. The modal auxiliaries are sometimes regarded as having tense — for example, *may*, present; *might*, past; and so on — but they have largely developed independent meanings. Other modal auxiliaries are *shall, should, will, would can, could,* and *must. Ought* differs from the rest in that it must be followed by *to*, which is usually joined to it in pronunciation, as in "he ought to leave at once." There are a few other items which introduce verb phrases, such as *dare* and *used to*, but all conform to the generalizations below.

Every finite verb in English is one

of three forms given above; every finite verb phrase begins with a modal auxiliary, with some other auxiliary in one of these three forms, or with one of the present or past finite forms of *to be*, which is then an auxiliary. All the phrasal constructions can be very simply described with formulas. Those in the perfect group, for instance, contain a form of *have* plus the past participle. Every discourse sentence must have a finite verb form or phrase; every dependent clause must have such a form, or it must contain enough of a basic sentence pattern for such a form to be supplied intuitively by the reader. Moreover, the necessary recognition of the basic sentence pattern depends on the recognition of the finite form and the proper association of other major parts with it. No one can read an English sentence by recognizing words alone, only be recognizing them in a syntactic frame.

CONCLUDING STATEMENT

Everyone knows that the grammatical structure of English, or of any other language, is extremely complex. In fact, there is no fully satisfactory description of this complexity, although there are numerous approaches. Yet, within the complexity, there is a relatively simple core. Much of the core can be taught very early in the school program, and the teaching of syntax and the teaching of reading can be mutually supporting activities.

CHAPTER XII

RECENT DEVELOPMENTS IN READING INSTRUCTION IN THE CONTENT AREAS

*

BROTHER LEONARD COURTNEY

*

THE IMPACT of reading research on the content fields in the twenty years since A. Sterl Artley made his study of general versus content-area comprehension[1] seems, at first glance, to be slight. There has been progress, perhaps more by publishers and curriculum planners than by content teachers themselves; but it would appear that curriculum and content have far outstripped the insistent admonitions and suggestions of reading experts that reading instruction and content development be integrated.

If we take the limited view and measure our success only by the number of content teachers — in math, science, social studies, both elementary and secondary — who are dutifully scrutinizing textual material, making lists of difficult words, improving conceptual background, seeking phonic deficiency in the spelling and pronunciation mishaps of their pupils, and emphasizing comprehension skills, we shall have to conclude that the reading experts have not been too influen-

[1] Artley, "A Study of Certain Relationships Existing between General Reading Comprehension and Reading Comprehension in a Specific Subject-Matter Area," *Journal of Educational Research*, XXXVII (February, 1944), 464–73.

tial. If, on the other hand, we realize that there can be no good teaching divorced from competent reading instruction, that students cannot learn what they cannot understand — and there is much superb content teaching going on — we may take some satisfaction in knowing that the reading expert's influence has been more subtle and perhaps more profound than could be hoped.

GOOD TEACHING — GOOD READING INSTRUCTION

I have spent much of the past year visiting schools and classrooms. Although committed to parochial secondary education, I have visited many other schools to supplement my own inexperience, elementary and secondary, public and parochial. In all, I estimate that I have been in more than 300 classrooms in the past year. Twenty years an English teacher and only more recently a fledgling reading specialist, I was vitally interested during these visitations in the degree and kind of reading instruction in the classroom, in both English and the other content areas.

I observed some outrageous teaching in which ineffective, evidently unhappy, and miscast teachers were positively harmful to their students. I witnessed much mediocre teaching in which the teacher seemed to limp through his stint of duty in aimless fashion but in which some learning probably occurred. I did not see abundant evidence that content teachers were consciously employing the techniques of reading instruction recommended for improved content mastery. For the most part, however, I concluded that content teaching is generally good, frequently excellent. Furthermore, there was much evidence that the principles of reading instruction indirectly comprised an important part of the techniques of most of these teachers, though they might be the first to scoff at any possible debt to the reading field.

Some examples of these good teaching techniques may substantiate my argument.

1. Unannounced, I visited a fourth-grade geography class, in which the teacher conducted a model "directed reading activity" as she initiated a unit on the New England states. She built background concepts, discussed difficult words with the children, and asked a host of questions to provoke interest and excite good reading. She made maps, charts, and pictures a normal part of the reading activity. After fifteen minutes of lively interchange as she moved through the pages to be studied, she closed with the remark that "you'll want to read the rest of this more carefully by yourself." Remember, this lady was teaching geography, not reading.

2. A sixth-grade history class was studying the Renaissance. Scurrying through glossaries and class dictionaries, the children reached an understanding of the term itself. The teacher placed the several major points of the unit in outline form on the blackboard. After discussion to relate these ideas to their previous topic, the children began to read the new material — but not all from the same text. Four different texts were used in the classroom during the time of silent study, ranging from simple large-print textbooks to one several grade levels above them, each student using materials tailored to his reading ability. After fifteen to twenty minutes of private reading during which the teacher moved about assisting individuals and occasionally calling the entire group's attention to a new or different word or concept, the class together developed the skeletal outline already on the board — each gaining from the reading of the others although none had been taxed beyond his ability in reading.

3. Early last year, I visited a departmentalized junior high school to observe the introduction of the "new" math series in the seventh grade. It was impressive to note the several techniques employed by the teacher, all consonant with principles of reading instruction. Previously, the teacher told me, she had assessed the varying arithmetic backgrounds of her pupils, noting what transfer students had learned the previous year and appraising the retention of basic principles by all the students. On this day, she was introducing the pupils to the new text for the first time. Using standard pro-

cedures, she acquainted them with the format, sequence, and student aids, culminating with the glossary of new terminology contained at the end of this particular arithmetic series. Commonly known terms were noted; words with meanings special to arithmetic were pointed out. Then returning to the opening chapter, a highly verbal discussion of some properties and procedures, she demonstrated how the glossary was to be used in daily study and gave hints and clues to efficient reading and study of the text itself. Certainly none of this is new or startling, but it deserves commendation.

4. The English teacher is, of course, expected to be more committed to reading instruction than other content teachers. The very nature of the material studied, verbal and literate, lends itself naturally to all of the accepted reading techniques. Not all English teachers, it is true, are equally familiar with reading principles or equally impressed by their intimate bearing on the subject matter. Perhaps the two examples which follow are unfair because of the special competence and dedication of the teachers involved. However, it should also be kept in mind that these were regularly scheduled English classes, not special reading classes.

a) This particular ninth-grade honors English class was under an experienced teacher — well versed in reading and knowledgeable in integrating study skills with content work. The students had copies of linear diagrams of paragraphs, all taken from popular sources, newspapers, magazines, and myths; using an overhead projector, the teacher displayed the full paragraphs on a screen and led the students through the reading and analysis of each one so that they might appreciate the internal relationships which united the paragraph: main ideas and details in simple illustration, similar details accruing into sequence, cause and effect, comparison and contrast, generalization and conclusion. When the class had jointly agreed on structure, they were given another paper on which each paragraph was reduced to its basic outline for further study. You will note the teaching-learning scope: variations on paragraph structure, reading for the author's organization and intent, improvement in personal writing through organization, and outlining techniques.

b) The next example is deserving of more detailed description than can be afforded here; certainly, this was the most exciting, creative experience I witnessed during the year. The teacher of this particular ninth-grade below-average English class was dissatisfied with the conventional commercial materials for basic teaching of the language arts; so he constructed his own materials — for written composition sequence, word recognition, vocabulary growth and dictionary work, following directions, and organizational skills. He also constructed composite units which combined all of these skills. The material developed, if not complete, was ample for a semester's work; it was fresh, highly imaginative, and intriguing to the students because it exploited their own hobbies and interests while requiring a great variety of sense activity: visual, tactile, manipulative, and so forth. It is impossible here to describe all of these wonderful materials; but a description of one of the composite units will suffice to demonstrate their explosive potential. First, there is a brief narrative, colloquial and familiar, on "The Gasoline Engine"; two additional sheets give instructions for cutting out and mounting a two-dimensional combustion engine. Next, having consulted the dictionary for unfamiliar words, the students are required to draw a picture "to show you really know what the word means." For example, "Draw some item found in your home which is in the shape of a *cylinder*." Spelling is next with words taken from the gas-engine story, each illustrated through some common item but with essential letters missing. Meaning is then expanded by requiring the pupils to draw a picture showing other meanings of particular words, meanings different from those met in the story. For example, an "eccentric" wheel is drawn; the children must draw an "eccentric" man. Finally, the students are asked on another paper to divide the words into syllables by "making a box for each syllable." This is but one of the many interesting and challenging units of material developed by John Cooper of Maine Township West High School, Park Ridge, Illinois, to make reading and English relevant in the lives of a group of less-gifted ninth-graders.

5. In a tenth-grade biology class, the teacher calmly but effectively aided his students in blending text with charts and diagrams for an understanding of molecular structure. Together they moved from text to diagrams and back, noting how each supplemented the other.

6. A twelfth-grade social studies class was preparing to go to the library for initial work on their research projects. All preliminary planning had been done, and now teacher and class reviewed the physical arrangement of the library, where certain needed books and references were to be found and how they were to be used. On the teacher's desk were assorted standard reference works which were used by the students to illustrate how each could contribute information with maximum economy of effort. This briefing session was intended to permit the class to move expeditiously into and about the library with minimal interference to the study and work already in progress there. In violent contrast to this efficient work, I recall visiting one second-year teacher who was initiating his ninth-graders to the mysteries of the library. The entire class was in the library, from which the librarian had fled in dismay. The pupils milled around the room, aimlessly looking through books, copying titles, shuffling through pages, talking, or doing their own home exercises, except for the few small groups under the direction of the harried teacher.

It is true that these are isolated cases, hardly representative of the full spectrum of American content teaching. In the instances cited, however, none of us would deny that good content teaching was taking place and that an abundance of reading principles and techniques were being employed. We would hope to see these principles and techniques widely applied in all content teaching. That they are already being applied in a great number of classrooms is a tribute to the wise and insistent pleading of reading authorities over the past decade; that they are not universally used by all teachers is deplorable and cause for continuing concern.

READING INSTRUCTION AND THE "NEW" CURRICULUMS

In arguing that competent instruction in any area necessarily implies good reading instruction, we must not ignore the important contributions to better reading resulting from the revolutionary changes which have been taking place in all areas of the curriculum, elementary and secondary. There has been a veritable revolution in school curriculums at all levels. When Arthur I. Gates wrote his superb article on reading in the content areas in 1960,[2] Zacharias had already streamlined and updated physics content and instruction; since then an avalanche of curricular revision has taken place in all areas. BSCS, PSSC, Chem Bond, and Chem Study have shifted emphasis in science from accumulation of information, memory work, and simple confirmation of known phenomena in the laboratory to *inquiry* in the classroom and *investigation* in the lab. SMSG has jolted arithmetic and mathematics from the mechanical memori-

2 Gates, "The Nature and Function of Reading in the Content Areas," in *New Frontiers in Reading*, International Reading Association Conference Proceedings, ed. J. Allen Figurel (Newark, Del.: International Reading Association, 1960), V, 149–53.

zation and computation of an earlier day to the excitement of discovering basic principles, the solution of verbal problems, the social practicality of content, and the mental processes used by the student in judging, estimating, and justifying solutions.

In all, the sciences and mathematics have taken the lead in toughening content and extending efficient reading procedures for learning; the other curriculum areas are only a step behind. Nor have these efforts been confined to the secondary school. Already, the influences of changes are filtering downward, unsettling the junior–high school curriculum and reaching deep into the elementary grades in science, arithmetic, and language. The new curriculums make great demands on the student and attempt to give him more in content than was formerly the case. The new material is attractive and practical, catching the students' interest; but the reading requirements are more complex and subtle than ever before, extending into critical and imaginative reading, the thinking-reading skills.

There are many compensatory factors apart from interest alone, however, and many of these owe a tangential debt to the literature on reading instruction. Curiosity is excited, mental processes both stimulated and developed by the habits of inquiry and investigation instilled through constant practice. The textbooks are models of format; every type of study aid is incorporated: the use of color, graphs and charts, headings and subheadings, surveys and recapitulations. All of this, of course, is evidence of increased awareness and application of the theories of learning and of child and adolescent psychology.

These thrilling advancements are not without practical implications for teaching, both in content areas and in reading.

1. The very weight and complexity of content make imperative the need for improved reading skills, from the basic to the more refined, if the students are to master the material. This naturally signifies that the content teacher must be even more attentive to the reading needs and differences of his students and that teaching of the basic skills — vocabulary, comprehension, locational and study skills — as well as critical and analytical reading skills, must be intensified.

2. The encompassing ambition of the new curriculums contains the threat of widening the gap between the gifted and the slow student. Even though the new materials and methodology venture to provide for a wide range of students, the heavy demands of content and of eager, well-prepared teachers leave little room for the plodder or the inept reader. Of course, some of this gap is reduced by the mass of special material being prepared specifically for the less gifted, but the reading burden must be alleviated somewhere, preferably in the content class itself.

3. As a corollary to No. 2 and especially for secondary-school science and mathematics, we must acknowledge that screening and selection have intensified with the new curriculums, since they are primarily intended to prepare the college-bound student. As Ivor Kraft has pointed out, American education is faced with the likely threat of a wider discrepancy between the academic "haves" and "have nots." [3] There is another factor here we must admit. Science and mathematics teachers are often particularly alert intellectually. They may have faced less difficulty in their own academic work and as a consequence may be either ignorant of or indifferent to the reading difficulties common to most students. Since they are inclined to maximize content, their students are screened severely and the inefficient quickly dropped out.

4. The new teacher today is unusually well trained in his content field and has little time or interest for learning how to incorporate the principles and techniques of reading instruction into his content teaching. National Science Foundation and National Defense Education Act grants are available in every curricular field, and successful applicants are steeped in subject-matter content and methodology. Moreover, there is a trend toward more general education, more subject-matter and less technique and methodology courses in undergraduate preparation. Because of all these factors, background in reading instruction suffers.

5. Though not curricular, another problem facing reading instruction is the matter of scheduling. The new procedures such as the Trump plan, which permits team-teaching and flexible scheduling of classes, and "modu-

[3] Kraft, "The Coming Crisis in Secondary Education," *Bulletin of the National Association of Secondary School Principals*, XLIX (February, 1965), 5–42.

lar" scheduling, which allows the teacher to contract for the amount of time he considers necessary for his work, although of great advantage to the able student, may be an additional handicap for the weak student or the poor reader; classes may be larger, less regular, and less personal. These new plans, too, demand accommodation and adjustment to the instructional reading needs of students.

6. Finally — and let's face it! — our special reading classes and programs are not meeting the needs of students under the new curriculums. We have no clear theory of reading. Reading classes and programs are isolated from the curricular fields without any definite affiliation or any strong administrative or academic fiat, a non-credit enclave a step above physical education or driver training. This indictment should not be taken to reflect on the caliber or dedication of reading teachers. They undoubtedly would elect a stronger, more definite role and function in the school if they had the opportunity. But we are torn among ourselves, not sure what this thing called reading really is, but unwilling to admit it even to ourselves. We could clip a page or a chapter from the manifestoes of the curriculum areas — BSCS, PSSC, SMSG, and the others — and try to sit down and hammer out through sheer pragmatism a common theory, a common core of skill approaches, a common set of procedures and techniques. We could get rid of gadgets and exercise books, use the very textbooks the students themselves are laboring through, and sit in on the math, science, social studies, and English classes to learn where the difficulties are so that we could work proudly and efficaciously with students baffled by their content demands. Or we could, as will be suggested later in this chapter, ally ourselves with the content teachers, imparting to them our own intimate familiarity with reading as it affects the subject-matter fields.

OTHER RECENT DEVELOPMENTS

There are several other developments toward a liaison of reading and the content areas: (1) the growth of imaginative new materials in reading for the entire spectrum of student ability, (2) the current emphasis on study skills as applied to content reading, (3) the increased emphasis on purposeful reading in the subject-matter fields, and (4) the continued plea for administrative leadership in extending reading into the total school program.

Materials. Good teachers have always attempted to break the lock-step of dependency on a single text and to differentiate material as far as possible according to the needs and abilities of their pupils. Interesting and suitable trade books have always abounded. In the fifties, publishers began to produce attractively packaged, easy-to-use, multilevel materials all too readily accepted by many as a panacea for all reading ills. In recent years, there has been a flurry of similar and competitive materials. All of these materials are valuable and if used intelligently and imaginatively may be exceptional supplementary material. Unfortunately, they do tend to encourage dependency and mechanical usage while diluting the initiative of the teacher.

The past five years, however, has seen the emergence of a new era of materials for improvement of reading in the content areas. Many of these materials are designed to meet the needs of culturally different children in the primary grades and of slow learners in the intermediate and junior-high grades. Almost every school publisher today lists collections of supplementary materials for the content areas, particularly English and social studies.

Most of the textbooks emanating from various curriculum committees are attractively designed and amply supplied with study aids; although utilizing many fundamental reading concepts, they also delve intensively into profounder facets of reading comprehension.

Despite the abundance of provocative, attractive material, too few teachers are making use of it. One of the more distressing elements of current teaching is the prevalence of textbook- and teacher-dominated instruction. Reading personnel, consultants, and librarians can do much toward encouraging selection and use of these new reading materials.

Study skills. The gamut of study skills represents a formidable load for any single content teacher. It would seem advisable to find some manner of allocating responsibility for their practice to particular areas of the instructional program, especially in the secondary school and in the departmentalized junior high. Perhaps through administrative intervention or departmental agreement, certain area teach-ers could concentrate on the reading and study skills more relevant to their own content work. The following distribution seems feasible. (1) English classes could concentrate on word analysis techniques, where necessary; vocabulary development; organization of reading materials, both perceived and produced through outlining; summarizing; and precis writing. (2) The social studies could emphasize the locational, reference, and research skills, as well as patterned study methods like SQ3R. (3) Arithmetic and mathematics have a natural opportunity for analytic reading in the highly verbalized "new math" textbooks. (4) Science could specialize in problem-solving and critical reading. (5) The foreign languages might consider the importance of idiom and rhythm in spoken language.

Purposeful reading. This is not actually a recent development but a continuing need. Establishing purpose in reading has always been recognized as one of the basic comprehension skills, but there appears to be increased urgency at present for student self-direction and independence in learning. The skill is not peculiarly abstract or difficult, but guidance is essential for habituation. This guidance is essentially the content teacher's obligation, for he alone can know the kinds of purposes a student should establish before and during study of a particular selection.

Unfortunately, there has been only meager research on this topic although considerable expository and hortatory writing. William G. Perry, Jr., found that only 1 per cent of the entering

Harvard freshmen were able to establish purposes for themselves.[4] Their responses to detail questions, however, were "impressive." Helen K. Smith, in a more recent study, found that poor readers were far less able than good readers to adjust their reading to their purposes.[5] She suggests the need for well-planned assignments and for probing, rather than the traditional factual, questions as essential determinants of student independence. She also notes that few of her subjects had any real guidance from teachers in this respect.

The importance of questioning in guiding students' evaluative and purposeful reading is a subsidiary development closely affiliated to purposeful reading in the content fields. Unfortunately, too many teachers' behavior in the classroom is governed by the quantity of the subject matter to be covered, not the quality with which it should be mastered. Certainly, in English, particularly literature, and the social studies, "why" questions alone will lead students to necessary self-probing and reflection. So, too, in the sciences, questioning is the beginning of inquiry. If students are to gain independence in purposeful reading, they must develop the characteristic of insightful self-questioning, for which the teacher may be the only available model.

Administrative leadership. If ad-

ministrators, superintendents, and principals would assume vigorous leadership in making reading instruction a total school effort, the entire range of skills, reading and study, would have an integral place in every classroom. Only administrative decision and direction can convince content teachers of their personal obligation to select and develop those reading skills most appropriate to their instructional needs. Only such direction can persuade them that their content will not suffer but will be enhanced — that reading is every teacher's responsibility and obligation. And only such leadership can initiate the in-service training programs that will provide content teachers with a basic knowledge of reading principles.

In recent years the literature in the reading field has described a variety of administrative efforts to establish reading practice as classroom policy. Some of these have been school- or district-wide plans; the majority, however, have been specific and fragmentary, concerned with in-service training, cooperation among departments for integration of reading and content instruction, or experimentation with grouping practices and ungraded scheduling. Reading experts are insistent, however, that no effective attack on reading where it really counts, that is, in the classroom, is possible until it becomes a matter of administrative policy.

Enlightened leadership could attenuate the problem considerably by making reading a meaningful component of the total instructional program. Briefly, here is a description of the ef-

4 Perry, "Students' Use and Misuse of Reading Skills: A Report to the Faculty," *Harvard Educational Review*, XXIX (Summer, 1959), 193–200.

5 Smith, "The Responses of Good and Poor Readers When Asked To Read for Different Purposes" (Ph.D. dissertation, University of Chicago, 1965).

fort being made by one such administrator, Earle Wiltse, of the Maine Township High Schools, Park Ridge, Illinois. There are three major aspects to the program. First, there is a special reading program under the direction of competent personnel which initiates all ninth-grade students in those reading skills considered essential for academic growth and successful living. Second, particular effort is made by the English teachers to incorporate reading and study skills into the language-arts curriculum; and special attention is given slower students. Third, all subject-matter teachers are expected to instruct their students in those reading skills specifically relevant to their content area.

Other unique features of this all-school reading effort include (1) a reading strategy committee, composed of representatives from instructional, personnel, and administrative areas, which provides leadership throughout the three schools of the district for the program, and individual building committees with members from each content-area department which implement the recommendations of the central committee; (2) an honorary reading society which lends distinction to reading accomplishment and promotes reading activities among the students; (3) stalls in the several schools staffed by students and well stocked with interesting and stimulating paperback books.

Evidence that the administrative policy toward reading is respected and at least partially effective throughout the district schools is plentiful. (1) Subject-matter fields have prepared vocabulary and reading lists for the students, and curriculum guides include suggestions for sequential skills development. (2) Groups, clubs, and libraries print special materials to promote reading among the students; book displays from various subject-matter fields further this intention. (3) The reading teacher at one of the schools works with content teachers in the classroom, demonstrating better techniques for reading instruction. (4) The librarian selects books of high interest and small vocabulary to stimulate the reading of students in the below-average English classes. (5) There is some provision for special assistance to the more retarded students and those desirous of developing specialized college reading skills.

It is vital that the administrator balance the present-day emphasis on subject-matter competence with sustained in-service instruction in reading techniques as they may be applied to content areas. Such programs must not be on reading *qua* reading but must have specific relevance to the content areas — perhaps first as general disciplines but eventually as individual classes and levels in the content areas. This program would include demonstration lessons, prepared instructional materials, observation, and practice, the content teachers themselves sharing in the preparation of materials with reading teachers as consultants.

We often seem to waste our trained reading personnel. Reading teachers are too well qualified to spend all of their time with a small number of students. Even under the most ambitious schedule, a reading teacher can meet no more than one hundred fifty students a day. The training and talent of these teachers can best be exploited by making them consultants to content teachers, but not on an incidental basis. The consultant — call him what you will — must sit in the classroom, observe the lesson and the teacher's technique, become familiar with the content and how best to tailor reading skills to its structure and purpose, and from all of this derive a set of principles and techniques which fit this teacher, this content, and these students. If reading instruction is adequately melded with content, there will be no need for special reading instruction.

CONCLUDING STATEMENT

Perhaps some readers may be disappointed that nothing has been said of programed learning, flexibility in reading, new techniques for vocabulary enrichment, and other innovations which have some peripheral link with the content areas. Programed learning is still bogged down in technical and mechanical difficulties; in years to come, there may be truly significant developments, but thus far efforts are experimental. Reading flexibility is nothing new; it is only a redefinition of a skill accepted for generations by knowledgeable reading people, a restatement necessary to counteract the deleterious popular appeal for speed. The others are mere detailed techniques with an attractiveness frequently bestowed by the brilliance of a particular teacher but are not yet adequately tested or accepted.

The instances, principles, and developments which have been the core of this chapter have not been universal. In many cases, they are isolated; frequently, they are only ideals. Without exception, however, they are mandatory if adequate reading instruction is to reach more students at the time they most need it — will best heed it — in the content-area classroom. All of us recognize that the vast majority of our teachers ignore the reading principles which have been advocated incessantly over the past many years. If, however, we exert ourselves imaginatively and creatively to develop good content-area teaching, proper reading instruction will naturally ensue.

CHAPTER XIII

DEVELOPING COMPETENCE IN READING

*

IN LITERATURE

WILLIAM A. JENKINS

*

IN FAR too many classrooms love of reading and literature has long since flown through the window. Rather than an affair with peaks of emotion and thrills of new discovery, what ensues between student and book is the daily breadwinning routine of recognizing and analyzing words and stretching a meager budget of context clues until the life of the reader becomes deprived, or at least disadvantaged. The reader, like the partner in any union, can get from reading only what he takes to it. His competence must include reading of a type that is different from that required for science material, mathematics problems, and social studies discussions. He must go beyond facts and think and imagine and wonder about the people and places and things and conditions that an author includes.

Thus, as he reads, his competence can be measured by how well he is able to fill in the gaps which the author has deliberately left for him to fill; arriving at the conclusions that the author has artfully avoided; and in Gestalt fashion, make suggested closures,

by adding one and one and getting two and a half and by removing rough edges which by design have been allowed to pass the literary inspector. The competent reader is equal to the task shifted to him by the artist. He answers the call to duty of the bugler-with-words. He shoulders his gun and gladly serves to ferret out the elusive symbol, shadowy nuance, and camouflaged meaning. His encounter is strictly a personal one. His Legion of Merit is self-awarded.

THE PURPOSES OF LITERATURE

Competence in the reading of literature is probably best assessed in terms of purposes. What ought literature to do for a reader? If it achieves this goal, competence may be assumed. If it fails to achieve it, competence is lacking. Literature, first of all, can enrich one's personal living. If a reader is not a better, fuller, nobler person for having read, his competence is of questionable maturity or the materials he has read are not really belles-lettres. Literature, in quantity, should give one insight into the whole range of man's experiences and ideals. No insight, no competence. Literature traverses time and space. If the reader finds that there are no boundaries for him, that he is transported with greater speed than that of the most powerful rockets, that he can do what the long-fabled but still not invented time machine can do, that the 186,000 miles per second of the speed of light is a snail's pace when compared with his acceleration, we can deem him able.

His competence should include the well-tuned ear that perceives and appreciates the author's cleverly couched hemidemisemiquaver amid the cacophony of belching tubas and wheedling oboes. The imagery of the poet, be it pale or brightly hued, does not escape his gaze. He can identify himself with a character or characters and feel their ease or their discomfort. He puts his hands to the loom with the poet or novelist and weaves with them the threads of ambition or jealousy or love or greed. His heart and mind reach to hold, to examine, to judge, and to reject. He distinguishes between the grains of truth of life and the glamorous, faddish, and false chaff of nonlife. The competent reader of literature appreciates what is and what, by intent, is not. Finally, reading as a self-feeding entity has as its purpose the creation of standards of choice. When one has read and appreciated and enjoyed a book, when he has literally devoured it, in schmoo-like fashion two more will take its place. And like the schmoo, a book can meet almost all of man's needs, and in addition it never can be gotten rid of once it has been encountered.

THE SKILLS OF READING LITERATURE

Competence connotes skill. Skills are our chief concern here, moreover, since they provide the most valid measure of competence. First of all, a student must know what an author is saying and how he is saying it. This skill, of course, is related to basic reading competence, but it goes beyond it since in basic reading instruction we are not truly concerned with elements of style or the various types of literature. When one knows what an author is saying, one may respond emotionally, for the appeal of literature is both to mind and to heart. Literary analysis, including a knowledge of the elements of style, is the key to understanding how an author is saying what he is saying. Specifically, this is the skill of ordering one's emotions to pick out what is relevant in one's emotional responses to affective writing.

Skills, understandings, and appreciations of literature are intertwined. There are appreciative skills just as there are skills of understanding. The appreciative skills include the ability to evaluate what is said, the ability to judge the validity of a piece of literature, the ability to draw conclusions from what is said, the ability to interpret characters, the ability to understand the basic and the minor themes, the ability to understand suspense, the ability to understand dialogue, the ability to appreciate humor, the ability to recognize mood, and the ability to appreciate rhyme and rhythm.

An understanding of character development is a major element of competence. Although it is true that characters in children's literature seldom have more than transparent or translucent motives, and although the plots of much children's fiction tend to be simple or episodic, the principles still apply. A student must be able to react to the behavior and values of story characters, react to their portrayal, react to characters in action, react to the characters' thoughts and remarks.

Literary analysis includes the identification and evaluation of elements of style used by an author: figurative, picturesque, and idiomatic language, colloquialisms, slang, and dialect. Refrain, repetition, and rhythm are elements primarily of poetry, but they are also instrumental in creating the affective overtones of a piece of prose. Choice of words, sentence structure and length, and punctuation are elements of style as well as elements of literary analysis.

THE VARIETIES OF COMPETENCE

Competence in literature can be differentiated, too, according to the type of selection which is being read. With short stories, for example, the first thing one has to do is to decide quickly on the author's purpose. As the incidents flash by, the reader should be able to react to the emotional atmosphere. The rapidity with which the characterization and plot unfold before him should pose no problem to the competent reader. The reading of novels requires competence on a lower level of difficulty because a novel is frequently simply a rapid sequence of exciting events. In such cases one reads simply to follow the thread of the story as it unravels and is unraveled. In some novels, however, the author's purpose is to interpret a segment of life and its problems. Plot becomes incidental. The task, then, is that of arriving at deductions, generalizations, and applications which the author implies but does not specifically make. When the novelist's purpose is merely to show change in a hero's character, the book consists largely of analysis, explanation, and description and contains very little conversation. The task differs in the last two instances because reading must proceed more slowly to be effective.

As a form of literature, the essay primarily places the author's views, ideas, and thoughts on paper. The key here is individuality, and as the reader succeeds in understanding the uniqueness of the writer as a human being and of his point of view, whether serious or humorous, whether brief or rambling, this literary form is mastered.

Poetry presents a problem of still a different sort, because the task is to sense the poet's purpose for writing the poem, to enter into this purpose with him, to free one's imagination, to prepare one's self to see and feel and hear things new or presented in an unusual way, and to fill in the gaps which have been created by the necessity for concise, affective language. How a poem achieves what it means is truly as vital as the subjective conclusion of what it means. Remembering that poems are closely related to music, the competent reader looks for the rhythm and the music of words which may be found there. If a poem is mainly descriptive, the ability to see vivid images is the essence of competence. An amusing poem depends on unusual twists of language as well as unusual images, calling for competence of still a different sort. Finally, there are the highly emotional poems which express man's most basic and deepest feelings, such as hate, love, grief, regret, or death. Here the task is that of recognizing, understanding, and reacting to the highly emotionally charged words which the poet uses.

As illustrated in this paper, the competent reader of literature may be defined in several ways. A competent reader of literature might be defined in terms of the clues he is able to find in the literature he reads. He recognizes them and interprets them with little or no effort. Like the good detective, he seldom retraces his steps, for a clue once met has meaning. A competent reader of literature may also be defined in terms of perceptions. He perceives the subtleties of character development, the suggestion of plot movement, the author's choice of values — both the deliberate and the unconscious.

A competent reader of literature is the writer's equal and peer. Both employ an active mind, for example, in the relating of details. He is interpretive rather than literal in his reading. Thus, he does not take exaggeration at face value, since he understands its purpose. He creates and criticizes as he reads, paying special attention to sincerity and validity.

Finally, the competent reader of literature, very simply, is the person who has mastered the ability to respond emotionally to new experiences, to let his mind be excited by plot, characters, and conflicts of the human heart and to shadings of good and evil. This ability truly sets apart the competent reader of literature, whatever his age.

CONCLUDING STATEMENT

A final thought on the matter of competence concerns freedom. More than any specific approach, wide reading, free reading, coupled with the teacher's and librarian's enthusiasm can lead to greater competence. For this reason, an important step in developing competence must be simply to develop the reading habit, the public library habit. Competence begins with imagination. Imagination is tempered by intellect. Both are nurtured by love, enthusiasm, and freedom. And then we will end where we began — with imagination.

IN SCIENCE

GEORGE G. MALLINSON

*

SINCE this writer participated in the Annual Conference on Reading at the University of Chicago in 1960,[1] there have been many tumultuous and confusing crosscurrents in science teaching. From the furor, two important questions have arisen: "Is there any justification for being concerned with competence in reading in science courses?" and "If there is justification, on what is it based?" Until 1955 neither of these questions would have been posed. The literature of science education contained many reports of research in science vocabulary and other problems related to reading in science. Most of these studies emerged from the milestone work of Francis D. Curtis in 1938, in which the findings of more than one hundred studies of vocabulary were synthesized.[2] This study and many others served as the bases for the production of science textbooks from the elementary through the college level, as well as for other kinds of scientific publications. The studies also provided guidelines for teaching scientific vocabulary and developing understandings of scientific concepts.

Since 1955, however, reading and vocabulary studies have all but disappeared from the literature of science education. In fact, the attitudes expressed about science teaching by a number of scientists and science educators prompted the writer to publish a paper entitled "Will Books Become Obsolete?"[3] In brief, there have been some marked innovations in the philosophy of science teaching and science learning that concern competence in reading science and that need exploration. Many of these innovations suggest that subject matter can be all but ignored in the science classroom and that the "processes" of science and laboratory activity should be almost the only concern. If true, the role of reading in science loses all significance. This raises another question, "But does it?"

SCIENCE TEACHING AND THE READING ANOMALY

A survey of recent conditions affecting science education reveals many contradictions in the relationships between reading competence and science learning. Among the more significant conditions are these:

1. The information explosion in the sciences has been publicized on numerous occasions through nearly every

[1] "Methods and Materials for Teaching Reading in Science," in *Sequential Development of Reading Abilities*, ed. Helen M. Robinson ("Supplementary Educational Monographs," No. 90; Chicago: University of Chicago Press, 1960), pp. 145–49.

[2] Curtis, *Investigations of Vocabulary in Textbooks of Science for Secondary Schools* (Boston: Ginn & Co., 1938).

[3] *School Science and Mathematics*, LXIV (May, 1964), 404–8.

medium of communication. Prior to 1940 it was estimated that scientific knowledge was doubling in volume every fifty years. Thus the volume of scientific knowledge that had been accumulated between the dawn of history and 1940 would be replicated by 1990. By 1950 the estimated period of doubling had been reduced to ten years; currently the estimate is between five and seven years. Although no one could possibly read even a small fraction of the expanding output, there is no reason for assuming that the task of reading in science would be reduced.

2. Several analyses have been made, one at Case Institute of Technology, Cleveland, Ohio, of the job activities of scientists. These analyses indicate that on the average, scientists spend about fourteen hours of a forty-hour work week reading materials written by, or writing materials to be read by, persons who are not their occupational peers. They spend an additional twelve hours reading materials written by, or writing materials to be read by, those who are their occupational peers. During the remaining fourteen hours, they behave like the stereotypes of scientists. The results of these job analyses would certainly support the need for communication ability, both in terms of production (writing) and in terms of consumption (reading).

Here, however, the contradictions and anomalies arise. Prior to about 1955, when science education supposedly lay in the domain of the teachers' colleges, the professional educator was castigated roundly and regularly by the scientific community for his lack of concern with the subject-matter content of science and his preoccupation with skills and processes. With the advent of the Course Content Improvement Program of the National Science Foundation, the scientific community became involved in developing science programs below the college level, and the shoes changed feet! The statements of philosophy emerging from scientists suggested that subject matter was relatively unimportant, whereas the processes of science and critical thinking were the only facets with which science education should be concerned. Obviously, this does not hold true for all scientists, but the reports of most committees and commissions of scientists engrossed in science education would seem to support this viewpoint. Meanwhile, the educator may now be found supporting the role of subject matter. If the educator were formerly correct and the scientist currently correct, the role in teaching of published science material, which deals essentially with content, would seem to be relatively non-existent. This statement carries the philosophy to its ultimate pole, but it is interesting speculation. There must be some ground that is common between the two groups, or if not, at least some ground for compromise. At least, this writer has some suggestions, hopefully pertinent, to make.

SOLVING THE READING ANOMALY
IN SCIENCE

It is assumed that one major aim of science teaching is to develop dimensions of intellectual performance in the student. The laboratory must be more than an environment for the expenditure of calorics through physical manipulation of hardware and participation in isolated experiences. It must develop meanings and perceptions of the experiences the student has, and these can be attained only through a background of knowledge. Obviously, students cannot be put through the cultural heritage of all scientific effort, and consequently the development of meanings and perceptions must rest with his ability to read foundational materials and understand the printed word. The implications of this statement are well summarized by Henry P. Smith:

Words are an important portion of the culture of a people. But words are far more than mere symbols to be used in communication. They are also tools for thinking. For higher-level thinking, words act as a shorthand in that certain words contain the distilled essence of numerous experiences. Thus, though we often hear it said that a picture can replace a thousand words, it may be more important that certain of our words stand for a thousand of life's pictures.[4]

An objective consideration, however, of the innovations in philosophy and the explosion of scientific information indicates that some new approaches are needed in developing reading competence in science. Some are suggested here:

1. There must be a clear recognition that although the foundations of science are continually maturing, there is a base of principles that remains fairly constant. Consequently, reading

[4] Smith, "The Perceptual Determinants of Effective Reading with Some Social Implications," *University of Kansas Bulletin of Education*, XIX (May, 1965), 82–83.

has never been challenged as the most effective way to accumulate the distillation of pertinent experiences against which the process of science become meaningful. The role of the book, therefore, is established.

2. The concept of a fixed scientific vocabulary must be revised. There are, of course, many terms that will undoubtedly remain in the scientific vocabulary, for example, *matter* and *energy*. New terms, however, will continue to become common at a rate far more rapid than anything imagined previously, and scientific vocabularies must be adjusted chronically to include them. The term *thermonuclear fusion* that appears in many fourth- and fifth-grade science books is ample evidence of this point.

3. A major study is needed of the relationships between the oral vocabulary and the written vocabulary. Without question, both educational and commercial television provide continual reinforcement of scientific terminology that did not exist even a decade ago. It may be that some synthesis of oral and written vocabulary may be necessary to encompass the symbols needed in developing understandings in science.

4. Although technical terms should not be used where non-technical terms suffice, the former should not be avoided because they are unusual. Five-year-olds seem capable of rattling off the term "supercalifragilisticexpialidocious" and using it meaningfully, assuming it has a meaning. In the same vein, many scientific terms now avoided could be used in the regular scientific vocabulary.

CONCLUDING STATEMENT

The development of competence in reading in science will not hinge on vocabulary selection and the development of standard symbols for scientific meanings, as may have been the practice in the past. The field of science is too dynamic, and many terms become obsolete relatively rapidly. It will be accomplished only through new techniques for channeling the modern vocabulary of science into experiences for students from which they can develop the appropriate perceptions.

* * *

IN SOCIAL STUDIES

ALICE FLICKINGER

*

WE WHO teach in the social studies have generally been users, rather than producers, of that skill called reading. There is comfort for us in William S. Gray's reasonable and explicit statement of our responsibility: to provide conditions in our classes under which students can use their acquired reading skills for worthwhile goals — in other words, to make good reading useful in our classes. And Gray points out further that we must give special instruction in reading when we confront students with material beyond their reading level or material with difficulties peculiar to the social studies field.[1]

We know that this is our job as concerns reading in our content area. We all *know* much more than we *do*. How to make maximum use of a textbook, how to use literature for enrichment, how to teach map reading — these are vital skills, but they will not be discussed in this paper. If some of us need a refresher in these matters, we could well turn to two booklets, both publications from the National Council for the Social Studies, which are particularly valuable in this regard.[2] What we will consider in this paper is the revolutionary movement in social studies — the *new* social studies if you like titles — and what it means for reading.

CHANGES IN CURRICULUM

In the last five years the whole field of the social studies has known a new

[1] Gray, "Theme of the Conference," in *Improving Reading in Content Fields*, ed. William S. Gray ("Supplementary Educational Monographs," No. 62; Chicago: University of Chicago Press, 1947), p. 4.

[2] Leo Fay, Thomas Horn, and Constance McCullough, *Improved Reading in the Elementary Social Studies*, National Council for the Social Studies, Bulletin No. 33, (Washington, D.C.: National Education Association, 1961); Ralph C. Preston, J. Wesley Schneyer, and Frane J. Thyng, *Guiding the Social Studies Reading of High School Students*, National Council for the Social Studies, Bulletin No. 34 (Washington, D.C.: National Education Association, 1962).

activity. Those who think of this as only another "revision" are mistaking a great wind for a little breeze, for not in our lifetimes has there been such a challenge to tradition, to common practice. Traditional content — still used in the majority of our schools — is under fire. History and geography as the basis for most of the program have been found wanting. The expository and descriptive materials are being rejected. Textbooks and supplements that present generalizations and support such generalization by detail are being severely criticized. A challenge is also being directed toward common procedures — toward reading in groups, discussing, reacting, remembering and toward testing. This is not revision — this is attack; this is revolution.

In the summer of 1965 there were some forty projects of national significance, many of them supported by federal funds, whose purposes were revolutionary. Scholars, writers, curriculum specialists, and teachers are deeply involved. The revolution has the strength of deep dissatisfaction, serious purpose, skilled workers, and much money. This is the background of the new social studies.

It is difficult to describe a movement so segmented, one so young and presenting so many faces. Several illustrations follow.

At the University of Minnesota a study center worked on an articulated social studies program for kindergarten through grade fourteen. The staff developed a tentative curricular framework. Its content and sequence is very new.

At Ohio State University a group worked on an economic curriculum for secondary schools.

At Northwestern University a center developed materials for a new approach to the study of American society. The traditional United States history offerings at grades five, eight, and eleven or twelve will be influenced.

There are many other projects of more than local interest. The progress reports of these working groups show wide variety, and there are conflicting proposals. It is possible, however, to see some common direction.

Almost all planning has begun with an attempt to find out what social studies really is. Scholars in the various social sciences have been asked to sift out what is important from their scholarship. Studies have generally begun by accepting the advice of such scholars. The next task is usually that of arranging a sequence. Then follows the most challenging work — providing experiences and materials through which students can understand the concepts of the social sciences.

Another common element in the centers for study is support of the inductive method of learning. The familiar expository approach is questioned and frequently condemned. There is less explaining, more pondering. The textbook is often rejected. No matter what name is used — discovery method, inductive learning—the methods are roughly similar. Whenever possible, students are presented with data — with raw material — and encouraged to generalize from it.

One class that was studying the Soviet Union, for example, had a set of primary sources available. Their assignment: "Assume that these documents are the only pieces of information you have; from them, explain why the Bolsheviks came to power in 1917." Other directions followed. The documents are proclamations from provisional governments, speeches by Lenin, resolutions by political groups, and public statements from leaders.

Such assignments are significant because of the changes they imply for reading. The materials for learning are taking on new forms, often a bewildering complexity: films, tapes, primary readings, games, sort cards, charts, and transparencies for overhead projectors. The descriptive term used is "a multimedial approach to learning."

Further, old conceptions of readiness are being attacked. Bruner's thesis that young children think as older students think, if presented with appropriate materials, is being seriously explored. The development of the globe concept is planned for the kindergartens of Cleveland. The tracing of the European background of the American Revolution is proposed for seventh graders by a group in Harvard. At Northwestern, materials on the American economy are being prepared for grade five. All of these are based on a new concept of what a child can understand.

The new social studies includes understandings from many disciplines; it arranges a sequential program out of this basic material; it stresses the building of generalizations out of the observations and experiences of the students themselves; and it explores the possibility of young children's working with big and basic ideas.

If you would care to know more particulars of the work back of the new social studies, there are two excellent and current surveys. The April, 1965, issue of *Social Education* (published by the National Council for the Social Studies) is a review of the major work in process. A booklet, *The Proper Study of Mankind*, published in March, 1965, by the National Association of Secondary School Principals, is a handbook for social studies curriculum work.

CHANGES IN READING

Now, what does this mean for reading in the social studies? First, it presents special problems to teachers who have been guiding reading in familiar fields. History and geography comprise the background of most teachers, but even history and geography are changing rapidly under present scholarship. We are already out of date in the areas we thought we knew and are not prepared for other social sciences. The guiding of reading is best done by teachers who feel secure. We face a period of great unease. Many of the new projects have prepared admirable guides for the use of teachers and students. The Newton, Massachusetts, schools have one called "How to Study a Region." Northwestern's project has "A Handbook for Social Enquiry." From Malcolm Collier's group comes "Introduction to the Study of Human History." And Ohio State University has prepared "Structure of Economics." We will be provided with increasing help and we sorely need it.

And another point closely related to reading is that much of the material is being produced for trial use, lacking the familiar organization, vocabulary control, clear print, and page layout of established instructional materials. Already, in many schools, there are notebooks of thermofax pages and stenciled sheets. The technical advances in duplication have opened doors to fine resources. When involved in frontier thinking, students will often face frontier conditions in reading.

In addition to the difficulties of experimental materials — a trouble that may well be temporary — the proposed methods of learning present other problems in reading. The multimedia through which students come to understandings — all this wealth of carefully selected material — require quick adaptability to many kinds of reading. This learning situation gives the widest opportunity to use reading skills for worthwhile goals, as Gray recommended. It also holds the possibility of greatly confusing the student. The new social studies requires a student reader to ask himself certain questions:

First, *What am I doing?* He will have more help than in the past when he was justified in leaning heavily on a text. The problems of the newer social studies demand much more than passive following.

Second, *What is this I am reading?* Here, again, the material has an identity more vivid than that of most of the traditional readings.

Third, *What does the author say?* This is the old basic question for all reading.

And fourth, *How is what I am reading related to what I am doing?* This is the crux of the new social studies method — to make application of data.

CONCLUDING STATEMENT

It is not possible to see the definite shape of the social studies in the schools ten years from now. All beginnings are shadowy. But of one thing we can be certain — great changes have begun. And what has begun will change reading in social studies.

* * *

IN MATHEMATICS

MAX S. BELL

*

MANY OF the problems students have in reading mathematics stem not from inability to read but from the material itself. Dull, uninspired writing will not lead to good reading, and material that has ambiguous, inexact, or wrong explanations should best not be read at all. Hence, the first requirement for developing greater competence in reading in mathematics is the selection or preparation of materials that are interesting and worth reading. Some of the materials representative of the so-called new mathematics are of this sort, and we can hope for more.

The best of the new mathematics materials differ from most materials previously available in the following ways:

1. First, and foremost, the new material is more mathematical. Even at lower school levels, it exhibits a style of exposition and calls for a kind of inquiry that those trained in mathematics immediately recognize.

2. Since it is more mathematical, it is more exact and accurate.

3. It relies more heavily on mathematical symbolism, especially in the upper grades.

4. The best of these new materials are interesting and lively to read. There is consistent emphasis on "discovery" of relationships, patterns, and general principles. A student's natural curiosity and love of games are exploited.

5. Prehigh-school mathematics books no longer cover just arithmetic and its applications; hence, students must cope with and interrelate a wider range of ideas.

6. At all grade levels, the amount of expository material to be read by the student is greatly increased.

METHODS HELPFUL IN
READING MATHEMATICS

Reading in mathematics is different than reading in other disciplines, though not necessarily more difficult. One must proceed at a much slower pace than for most other reading material and with considerable personal involvement and activity. The methods that follow seem helpful to many students; they must, of course, be adapted to the learners with whom you are working.

1. Skim the material rapidly, or examine an outline, or the table of contents to see where the subject matter at hand fits into a larger picture.

2. Spend nearly all of your reading time going through the material in as slow and painstaking a way as necessary.

a) Have pencil and paper at hand. Work out examples. Fill in missing steps. Note questions, conjectures, and discoveries as they occur to you.

b) Reread as often as need be. Turn back to previous work and fit it in with the subject at hand. Look up definitions of any words not understood. Frequent regression is very much the rule in reading mathematics, even though frowned on in rapid reading.

c) Make sure you understand fully any symbols that are used.

3. Reread the material again rapidly to put it in context.

As you will readily perceive, the reading of mathematics cannot be passive. It involves both reading and doing in varying mixtures. Both learner and teacher should realize this and not be surprised if it takes longer to master four pages of mathematics material than forty pages of fiction. The teacher should read and master the material in just this way prior to setting an assignment for the student.

Merely outlining methods for reading mathematics will not develop competence. The teacher must devise good assignments and follow-up activities. The most effective of these involve listening in various ways to individuals explain what they got from the reading or how they worked out certain problems. Whether an explanation is objectively right or wrong, you will often be surprised by the shrewdness and understanding the student exhibits. A variety of approaches should be encouraged. Even completely wrong explanations give valuable insight into the learner's misconceptions and give clues to the help he needs in his reading of mathematics.

Most of us need to learn to listen. A neutral attitude and willingness to accept any contribution is very useful. One should avoid giving answers too soon, thus robbing the student of an independent discovery. It should be remembered that the ability of a student to grasp an idea often outstrips his ability to put it into words.[1] Hence, the teacher must develop an intuition about what the student intends to say but cannot say.

As with all reading, the teacher should provide experiences to give meaning to words and ideas that cannot be satisfactorily conveyed in books alone. This is true at all grade levels. The widespread feeling that it is not "respectable" for students beyond the third grade to experiment with concrete materials and models is a great handicap to their understanding. Often the best way, at any level, to help a student understand his reading, certainly in mathematics, is to direct him to suitably devised concrete models to work out his misunderstandings.

[1] Gertrude Hendrix, "Learning by Discovery," *Mathematics Teacher*, LIV (May, 1961), 290–99.

In following up and evaluating reading assignments in mathematics, the aim is to expand the repertoire of means by which the student can acquire understanding by his own efforts. The more such means he has at his disposal, the less he will be inclined to simply throw up his hands when he does not immediately see the meaning of a given problem or bit of exposition.

It will help a student in reading mathematics materials to be made aware of the various technical and contextual aids to his mathematical reading. Definitions, assumptions, and especially important ideas frequently receive special typographical treatment via italics, indentations, bold type, or underlining. Material thus emphasized should serve as a signal that a key point is at hand and as a warning to the reader to find out why it is regarded as important and how it fits in. Other aids include the table of contents, glossaries, lists of symbols, summaries, and the index. With some experience the student should become aware that mathematical exposition has its own characteristic style, and this in itself can be a very helpful guide.

Students should, however, be warned against relying on context in the conventional sense. In ordinary reading the student often learns that he need not worry too much about individual words, for the context will give the meaning. But one of the hallmarks of modern mathematics is careful definitions of words, so that in many cases it is not context but the words themselves that give meaning to the material.

LEARNING NOT TO READ

Having discussed ways of developing competence in reading mathematics, let us turn the tables and indicate how we can effectively teach a student *not* to read mathematics. One of the most effective ways in which this can be done is to perpetuate the widespread myth that mathematics is hard, mysterious, incomprehensible. This can be done in many subtle ways. How many times does a child hear an adult remark brightly (even with pride) , "Oh, I never could understand mathematics"? One shudders when one hears a teacher say, "If you will read your mathematics lesson, then you can read something you *like* from the story shelf." Or again, "We have to do our arithmetic now, but as soon as we finish you can work on your projects." Surely such implicit bribes suggest that mathematics cannot be enjoyed and, hence, teach our students not to become really involved in reading it.

A well-meaning but misguided practice that teaches students not to read is that of grouping examples by "type," with a method for obtaining answers to all problems of the type. At best, this makes a student careless in his reading. At worst, the student just memorizes responses to certain patterns of words and symbols, and this is *not* reading. Furthermore, such automatic responses will fail as often as they succeed, as soon as one leaves the world of carefully contrived textbook examples. A teacher can overcome materials that emphasize such categoriza-tion by making varied assignments and contriving frequent examples where the prescriptions do not work.

A sure way to teach students not to read is to place almost exclusive emphasis on operational skills. If in spite of reading assignments and pious talk about understanding, a learner perceives that what is really required is that he be able to provide numbers in response to various combinations of symbols, then he will almost certainly learn *not* to read the material between problem sets. While skill in computation is one objective of school mathematics instruction, it is ridiculous to see it as the primary goal of six to eight years of work. Genuine discovery on the part of the learner and a feeling for the logic, structure, and richness of arithmetic and mathematics are relatively much harder to achieve than memorization of a catechism of methods and results. Its achievement requires that a child be taught to read mathematics.

CONCLUDING STATEMENT

When all is said and done, the most important thing a teacher can do to develop competence in reading in mathematics is to build the confidence of the student in his ability to read, understand, and perform mathematics. Well-founded confidence, when the student is faced with material that takes slow and patient reading to master, wins half the battle. Every success builds the student's confidence in his ability to succeed, and the importance of this confidence cannot be overstated.

CHAPTER XIV

THE DEVELOPMENT OF EFFECTIVE, FLEXIBLE READERS

*

HELEN K. SMITH

*

WHEN WE consider the fact that only recently two men orbited the earth one hundred twenty times — or a distance of some three million miles — within a period of eight days, we realize that we live in an age of unbelievable speed. Although only a few people have the opportunity to pilot spacecraft around the globe, the remainder of us have a wide variety of means of transportation and speeds of traveling from which to choose. We can fly to London or Paris within a day's time, or we can take a leisurely trip by ship if our schedule permits. We can keep appointments in San Francisco or New York comfortably within a matter of several hours' flying time, or we can travel to these places at a slower pace in our own automobiles. We can sometimes obtain an over-all glimpse of the landscape when we fly, and we can observe many details as we drive. The mode of speed we choose depends upon our purpose in traveling, the difficulty of the way, and our familiarity with the highway and our destination.

A mature reader's approach to different kinds of reading can be compared with different means of transportation. Skimming is like traveling on a streamline train: a person sees only high spots or what he wants to see and does not heed the details. We skim when we wish to locate a name, date, word, or phrase; we may skim to gain a rapid impression, a hazy overview, or the location of the answer to a question.

Fast reading of easy and enjoyable material is similar to the fast driving of a car on the open highway. The way is easy, and the obstacles are few. The reader is not attempting to memorize details or organize ideas; instead, he is pleasantly trying to arrive at his destination of enjoyment in reading or of gaining the principal ideas of the selection.

We drive more slowly when the population is dense, when the traffic is heavy, or when the road requires caution. In reading, when the ideas are difficult or thought-provoking, when critical reaction is necessary, or when we do not have background knowledge for the subject matter, we need to read more slowly with more deliberation than we do at other times.

COMPONENTS OF READING FLEXIBILITY

Flexibility in reading is usually defined as the adjustment of rate and approach, or the ability to "shift gears," in harmony with one's purpose, the difficulty of the material, and one's background or knowledge of the subject matter. Purpose for reading may be defined in at least two ways: first, the broad general purposes, or life purposes and motives, for which a reader selects and reads particular selections or books; and second, the desired behaviors in the area of comprehension to be attained in the educational enterprise. Examples of the first kind are reading to meet the practical demands of daily living, to satisfy different moods through vicarious experiences, and to further or promote professional or avocational interests. Examples of the second kind of purpose include understanding the main idea, noting sequential order, making generalizations, and anticipating outcomes.

The difficulty of the content is determined by the vocabulary and concept load. Other factors, such as the writer's style or the literary type of the selection, may add to the difficulty.

One's previous knowledge of the content or of ideas related to the content can influence one's approach to reading. If a person is very familiar with the ideas being presented, he will naturally be able to read with more ease than if he is unfamiliar with the content.

Flexible reading, then, implies versatility of reading rates and differentiated approaches. Arthur I. Gates defined the best reader as "the one who comprehends the material with a rather high degree of accuracy for the purpose in mind." [1] Flexibility is a com-

ponent of effective reading and receives major emphasis in this chapter.

The idea of flexibility in reading is not new. One may recall that Francis Bacon wrote the following in his essay, "Of Studies": "Some books are to be tasted, others to be swallowed, and some few to be chewed and digested: that is, some books are to be read only in parts; others to be read, but not curiously; and some few to be read wholly, and with diligence and attention." Bacon, then, in the early 1600's was advocating different approaches to different books.

Through eye-movement photography Clarence T. Gray and Charles H. Judd and Guy T. Buswell studied the relationship of purpose to reading with a limited number of subjects. [2] Gray noted that his adult subjects read differently when they read prose and poetry to answer questions upon the content and when they read prose for the purpose of reproducing the content. Because these subjects made differentiations between the two purposes in reading, Gray concluded that they approached different reading purposes with different mental sets. Judd and Buswell also found that the change in purpose of reading resulted in different mental processes for some subjects; others, however, exhibited a lack of flexibility in adapting their method of reading to the end in view. These in-

---

[1] Gates, *The Improvement of Reading* (New York: Macmillan Co., 1950), p. 367.

[2] Gray, *Types of Reading Ability as Exhibited through Tests and Laboratory Experiments* ("Supplementary Educational Monographs," No. 5; Chicago: University of Chicago Press, 1917); Judd and Buswell, *Silent Reading: A Study of the Various Types* ("Supplementary Educational Monographs," No. 23; Chicago: University of Chicago Press, 1922).

vestigations were limited to the more mechanical aspects of the problem and did not yield details of reading processes except for the number and length of fixations, regressions, and time spent in reading. Although the foregoing studies by both Gray and Judd and Buswell were exploratory in nature and limited to a small number of subjects, they exerted a strong influence on expert opinion and the research which followed.

Experts have frequently stated that one's approach to different kinds of reading should vary but have given relatively few definite suggestions as to ways in which this should be done. William S. Gray early suggested that the different processes in reading were dependent upon one's purpose for reading. He ably explained how the processes might vary with different purposes:

The purpose of one's reading determines to some degree the processes involved in comprehension and interpretation. For example, analysis, selection, and judgment are very prominent when one is reading to discover important points and supporting details or to find passages related to a given problem; association and organization are essential when reading to grasp the author's organization or to supplement or validate previous experiences; critical evaluation is important when appraising the worth, relevancy, or consistency of statements, and when weighing the validity of the evidence presented; association, organization, and retention are prominent in reading to reproduce or to make specific use of the facts apprehended; and emotional responses to the events and situations presented are prominent when one is reading to develop appreciation or literary taste.[3]

Accuracy of interpretation and depth of comprehension are dependent, at least in part, upon one's purpose. For example, when reading for general impressions or the over-all idea, the reader need make little attempt to clinch or remember details. In such reading the general drift of the selection may be grasped without full analysis or recall of all the details. The reader is not required to weigh critically any of the elements, and he may skip brief parts of the material without causing harm to the realization of his purpose. This kind of reading should be fluent, yet accurate, rather than slow and laborious.

Reading for an implied main idea, on the other hand, is an exacting kind of reading requiring the person to note, weigh, and relate the details, to understand the literal meaning, and to determine by means of the author's implications the central thought of the selection. The reader is thus required to read slowly and intensively and perhaps to reread portions.

A versatile reader in the elementary or high school or college does not read all content-area subjects in the same manner. There is evidence in certain fields, such as science and mathematics, that students who have learned to read slowly and carefully are higher achievers than the ones who read fast-

3 Gray, "The Nature and Organization of Basic Instruction in Reading," *The Teaching of Reading: A Second Report*, Thirty-sixth Yearbook of the National Society for the Study of Education, Part I (Bloomington, Ill.: Public School Publishing Co., 1937), p. 69.

er.[4] On the other hand, some literary selections and social studies materials can be read rapidly for general ideas; others may require rereading, pondering over each sentence, and relating ideas to one's previous experiences.

Good readers do not necessarily read an entire selection for the same purpose and at the same rate. They should be able to set up initial optimum speeds for reading a selection for a specific purpose, but obviously, they may need to change their pace and approach during the reading of a selection. Just as the driver of the automobile may heed road signs warning him of danger, winding roads, or construction ahead, so may the reader find obstacles in his comprehension of materials. The good reader slows his speed within a selection when he encounters difficult phrasing, unknown concepts, references to previous reading, and ideas to be remembered. On the other hand, he may read faster or may skim materials when the content has little to do with his purpose or when he is familiar with the ideas from earlier experience. Even though there is a tendency for one to read poetry or scientific materials more slowly than short stories or social studies, much variation within each kind of reading is desirable and necessary.

THE ASSESSMENT OF FLEXIBILITY

One of the roadblocks in the development of flexibility has been the lack of assessment instruments. Without

adequate means of evaluating how students read materials for different purposes and for different levels of difficulty, teachers may be unable to see and correct weaknesses in their reading.

Standardized reading survey tests do not provide for the evaluation of flexibility. If rate of reading is included in a test, the score is usually based upon one kind of reading, and no purpose is suggested to the examinee. Sometimes teachers find it necessary to administer two reading rate tests, one on easy reading and another on study-type reading. If students read both kinds of materials at approximately the same rate, one can only conclude that they are inflexible readers.

Teacher observation and informal tests, especially in the content areas, may yield much information concerning how students read. Teachers can observe which students read everything slowly and which ones glide over the materials hastily; they can note their students' habits of surveying materials, taking notes, using reference materials voluntarily, or merely turning the pages.

A teacher can also check his students' flexibility informally by using appropriate selections from different levels of textbooks or basal readers. In this way the difficulty level, the ideas, and the questions can be geared to the experiences and the characteristics of the immediate group of students.

Experimenters who are especially interested in flexibility of rate have developed tests, but most of them, unfortunately, have not been published.

The Reading Clinic at the Univer-

4 Eva Bond, *Reading and Ninth Grade Achievement* ("Teachers College Contributions to Education," No. 756; New York: Bureau of Publications, Teachers College, Columbia University, 1938), p. 58.

sity of Chicago has for many years used a test developed by Buswell.[5] His adaptation of the Van Wagenen-Dvorak comprehension test is composed of twelve paragraphs taken from the intermediate, junior, and senior divisions of the test. The test provides some information concerning the student's flexibility of rate in reading selections at different levels of difficulty, with the purpose of answering questions remaining constant.

More recently, Charles T. Letson devised a test to determine which of two factors, the difficulty of the material or the purpose for reading, influenced the rate of reading to a greater degree.[6] In George Spache's reading flexibility test for college students and adults, the examinee is asked to read the same selection three times for three different purposes.[7] William D. Sheldon, assisted by Braam, developed a tool to assess the approaches students make when reading articles of four different types: general fiction, philosophy, familiar technical material, and unfamiliar technical material.[8]

The only published flexibility tests

are two by McDonald and others.[9] The *Inventory of Reading Versatility* (Educational Developmental Laboratories, 1962) is designed to measure the ability of high-school and college students and adults to adjust their rate to three different purposes; and *Reading Versatility Test* (Educational Developmental Laboratories, 1961) is designed to assess the same abilities of pupils in the fifth to ninth grades.

The results of the aforementioned tests are interpreted by the number of words the students read per minute and by the number of comprehension questions they answer correctly. All are concerned with flexibility of rate but not with the procedures one uses to vary one's rate. The differences in the construction of these tests probably reflect the different definitions of flexibility held by these experimenters.

J. Harlan Shores, Vernon E. Troxel, and Paul W. Koester developed purposeful reading tests in the content areas of mathematics and science.[10] Each investigator developed questions relevant to two of the following purposes: main idea, answering questions

---

[5] Leone M. Burfield, "Remedial Reading in the College," in *Clinical Studies in Reading I* ("Supplementary Educational Monographs," No. 68; Chicago: University of Chicago Press, 1949), pp. 41–59.

[6] Letson, "The Relative Influence of Material and Purpose on Reading Rates," *Journal of Educational Research*, LII (February, 1959), 238–40.

[7] Spache, "Diagnostic Tools," *Exploring the Goals of College Reading Programs*, Fifth Yearbook of the Southwest Reading Conference for Colleges and Universities (Fort Worth: Texas Christian University, 1955), pp. 121–22.

[8] Sheldon, "Diagnostic Techniques and Tools," *Exploring the Goals of College Reading Programs*, Fifth Yearbook of the South-

west Reading Conference for Colleges and Universities (Fort Worth: Texas Christian University, 1955), pp. 116–17.

[9] McDonald, "Flexibility in Reading," in *Reading as an Intellectual Activity*, International Reading Association Conference Proceedings, ed. J. Allen Figurel (New York: Scholastic Magazines, 1963), VIII, 84.

[10] Shores, "Reading Science Materials for Two Distinct Purposes," *Elementary English*, XXXVII (December, 1960), 546–53; Troxel, "Reading Eighth Grade Mathematical Materials for Selected Purposes" (Ph.D. dissertation, University of Illinois, 1959); Koester, "Reading Science Materials for Two Specific Purposes at the Sixth Grade Level" (Ph.D. dissertation, University of Illinois, 1960).

on the selection, ideas in sequence, understanding directions, and finding best explanations for events.

The "Test of Purpose," still in experimental form, attempts to investigate the procedures high-school students use when they read for different purposes. In addition to answering questions on the selections, the examinees have the opportunity to indicate on a check list the procedures they used, such as comparing ideas in the test with others they had acquired or experienced before; rereading words, sentences, and/or paragraphs; skipping parts; forming sensory images; and the like. A reading inventory has been devised as an additional check upon procedures of ninth-grade students and has been used in conjunction with the "Test of Purpose." [11]

INSTRUCTION IN FLEXIBILITY

There is a dearth of research concerned with methods and instructional materials that can be used to teach flexible reading at every educational level. The reported research has dealt with the development of rate or rates of reading of older students who have been identified as inflexible readers.

In the absence of research, expert opinion and observation of practice have provided suggestions for systematic instruction at all grade levels. It is generally agreed that adjustment of reading techniques to different reading situations should ideally begin in the lower elementary grades and be extended through high school and college in the developmental programs. Students should be taught early how to read selections in the different curricular fields in harmony with their own experiences and purposes.

The following generalizations concerning instruction can be made from the literature and can be applied at any grade level:

First, students should be taught how to read for many purposes. As examples of such purposes, the primary pupil and the high-school student should have many opportunities to read to distinguish important from unimportant details; to identify stated and implied main ideas; to gain sensory impressions; to anticipate outcomes or ideas; and to make generalizations and draw conclusions.

Instruction should allow opportunity for thinking about purposes that are to be followed during and after the reading process in accordance with the maturity of the reader. No one purpose should be overemphasized to the exclusion of other purposes. Guy L. and Eva Bond have written that it is "unfortunate that many teachers stress a type of reading which is among the most infrequently used by adults. . . . The practice of asking questions demanding memory of details encourages students to use this reading technique at the expense of others." [12]

Until students can set their own purposes, teachers should help them establish and clarify the purposes most appropriate to each assignment. If the teacher has no particular purpose in

[11] Helen K. Smith, "The Development of Evaluation Instruments for Purposeful Reading," *Journal of Reading*, VIII (October, 1964), 17–23.

[12] Bond, *Developmental Reading in High School* (New York: Macmillan Co., 1941), pp. 83–84.

mind, George Spache doubts that the assignment is justifiable.[13] A student cannot be expected to show any degree of comprehension or interpretation if the assignment is purposeless.

Second, students should be taught early how to set their own purposes for reading. This instruction should continue in high school and college. Beyond the middle grades, students should also be aware of appropriate rates of reading for different purposes. After a preview of the materials, they should ask themselves such questions as "What is my purpose?" "What do I expect to get from it?" "How can I best arrive at my goal?" "Do I need all the information given for my purpose?" Such questions as these help the reader form appropriate mental sets for reading.

Third, teachers should ask a wide variety of questions requiring different kinds of responses. These questions should be in harmony with the purpose of a reading assignment. There should be questions both before and after reading. The foregoing questions must be appropriate to the prestated purpose, so that the student may exhibit his understanding of the types of ideas for which he has been instructed to read. If questions asked by the teachers are not in harmony with the stated purposes, students lose faith in the instructions given to them and become confused about the demands made of them.

Questions should be asked to help students understand situations, clarify details, and sort out ideas, not to par-

rot the words of the book. At all levels *why* questions should not be neglected for the *who* and the *what* questions. Open-ended ones will help students formulate answers based upon their own thinking. A teacher can get the kind of comprehension he wants by the kinds of questions he asks.

Fourth, materials and activities should be abundant and diversified, so that the students can have many opportunities to develop flexibility. Obviously one textbook is not sufficient. Students need to recognize that some materials are more difficult and penetrating than others; and they need to know how to cope with them.

Fifth, the ultimate aim of flexible reading instruction is the self-direction and independence of the reader. Increasingly, students should learn to adapt their approach to the selection, to test themselves on whether their rate is appropriate for their goals, and to note that their reading techniques for assignments are different than those for leisure reading.

In spite of the frequent suggestions for developing flexible reading in developmental programs, there is evidence that many students and adults do not adjust their techniques to their purpose. J. Harlan Shores concluded that his sixth-grade subjects had not yet achieved the flexibility of rate and comprehension that characterize the able adult reader when he reads for different purposes.[14] They reported using the same techniques for each of two purposes: main ideas and ideas in

13 Spache, *Toward Better Reading* (Champaign: Garrard Publishing Co., 1963), p. 77.

14 Shores, "Are Fast Readers the Best Readers? — A Second Report," *Elementary English*, XXXVIII (April, 1961), 236–45.

sequence. Sister M. Herculane found that eighth-grade students varied insignificantly in speed and techniques according to purpose.[15] No student could define or explain accurately the concept of flexibility of reading rate. Approximately 90 per cent of the students were aware of the need to determine the purpose and speed; they did not, however, use this knowledge in actual performance. The writer found that, in a twelfth-grade population, good readers used a greater variety of approaches than did poor readers when reading for two different purposes: details and general impressions.[16] It appears, however, that the good readers in this study had learned on their own to make adjustments in their reading, as they were not able to remember any instruction they had received in flexible, purposeful reading.

A successful technique used to develop flexibility of rate has been used in the University of Chicago Reading Clinic for many years with high-school and college students and adults.[17] A diagnostic examination is first given to determine the nature of the person's reading problem. Then rate instruction is offered to students who have mastered the mechanics of reading but are not reading as fast as they could

be. It should be remembered that if handicapped readers are pressured into reading faster only frustration can result. Therefore, at the clinic, if the diagnosis points to only a rate problem with no deficiencies in word recognition, vocabulary, or comprehension, the goal of instruction is flexibility of rate, not merely increased speed. For more mature readers who read at a habitually slow rate, a pacer provides extrinsic motivation and helps them push themselves to read easy materials more rapidly. Because students may tend to read study-type materials at a rapid pace when they are receiving rate training, it is considered important to provide opportunities each day for them to read somewhat more difficult selections which are similar to textbook materials. They frequently need to be taught to hold their speed down for this kind of reading. This is the beginning of flexibility of rate. The more efficient readers are generally able to read easy materials twice as fast as study-type materials after they have received instruction.

The foregoing procedure was used by Addie Stabler Mitchell in her study of rate training of college sophomores.[18] She found that her experimental group made significant gains over the control group in rate of reading. She also found that the experimental group made significant gains in flexibility of rate but that the control groups did not. One of her eleven con-

[15] Sister M. Herculane, O.S.F., "A Survey of the Flexibility of Reading Rates and Techniques According to Purpose," *Journal of Developmental Reading*, IV (Spring, 1961), 209.

[16] Helen K. Smith, "The Responses of Good and Poor Readers When Asked to Read for Different Purposes" (Ph.D. dissertation, University of Chicago, 1965).

[17] Helen M. Robinson and Helen K. Smith, "Rate Problems in the Reading Clinic," *Reading Teacher*, XV (May, 1962), 421–26.

[18] Mitchell, "The Effects of Rate Training on the Academic Performance of Good Readers at the College Level" (Ph.D. dissertation, University of Chicago, 1965).

clusions was that the ability to shift gears in accordance with the demands of the material can be substantially enhanced through formal rate instruction which emphasizes the development of different rates of reading rather than a single rapid rate. Informal experimentation in the Reading Clinic recently indicated that able sixth-grade pupils could also profit by such training.

As has been stated before, there is little reported research concerned with the development of flexibility of approach. The purpose of a study which is being completed at the present time at the University of Chicago is to determine the effectiveness of direct, planned instruction in reading for high-school students who did not reveal on tests any adjustment of their reading to different purposes. For this study, purposes for reading embrace the following comprehension skills: details, main ideas, sequence (including time, place, and logical order), comparisons and contrasts, cause and effect relationships, generalizations, mood, sensory imagery, characterization, persuasion, fact and opinion, and anticipation of events or ideas.

The study was conducted for one year among ninth graders in a suburban high school; fourteen classes were experimental, and fifteen, control. In the experimental classes each purpose was introduced by means of especially prepared instructional materials which included an explanation of the purpose of each selection, detailed suggestions and examples of ways to read for specific purposes, and practice ma-terials in which the students were told specifically what they were expected to gain from their reading. The questions which followed the reading of the selections were in harmony with the directions and the purpose for reading. Guides were also prepared for the teachers.

The results of the foregoing study show that purposeful reading can be taught to ninth-grade students. Experimental students were able to identify the most appropriate purposes for which selections should be read and to read for each purpose significantly better than control students. They also learned to adjust techniques to purposes.

CONCLUDING STATEMENT

The need for the development of effective, flexible readers is great today. We are surrounded by a vast quantity of books, magazines, and newspapers. Students and professional people as well are required to select and to read a variety of materials. The person who can adjust his reading to his purpose, to the difficulty of the material, and to his background knowledge of the subject should be able to select the most appropriate materials, to read them with ease, to read more of the things he wishes to read, and to broaden his perspective.

As Edgar Dale has stated. "The person educated for flexibility will see the world in a fresh inventive way. He will not be chained to the immediate, the customary, the habitual. He will not be dependent on someone else to plan his route and show him how to get

there. He will chart his own course." [19]
The reader educated for flexibility

19 Dale, "Educating for Flexibility," *News Letter*, (Ohio State University, Bureau of Educational Research and Service), XXVIII (January, 1963), 1.

will also be able to travel into time and space, to realize when he has arrived at his destination, and to know that there are then new roads to travel and new goals to achieve.

CHAPTER XV

DEVELOPING PURPOSEFUL AND FLEXIBLE READING

*

IN KINDERGARTEN THROUGH GRADE THREE

SISTER MARIE COLETTE, O.S.F.

*

IN KINDERGARTEN and the primary grades, purposeful and flexible reading builds upon a foundation of listening and picture interpretation. Exercises in listening for different purposes lead logically to, and provide readiness for, reading for different purposes.

Several types of listening exercises suitable for first grade were described by Sister Ethel Cole in her master's thesis.[1] One of her suggestions relates to getting the main idea by listening to context clues. The teacher reads a short paragraph and asks "What was it all about?" or any similar question to elicit the main idea or topic. Listening to follow directions is another suggestion. Children enjoy this exercise because it can involve large-muscle activity. For example, "Take a piece of chalk, draw a circle on the board, divide it in half, and put a capital A in each half." Another exercise is listening to recall specific details. This can be varied by setting up listening purposes beforehand, for example,

"When you hear the name of a wild animal, make the sound you think he would make." Listening can also be done in order to classify objects. The teacher may direct the children, "If I say *jacks*, you might say *jacks and ball*, because jacks and ball go together. Try to think of the closest thing that will go with the word I shall say."

Following a series of clues to emerge with a central thought can be accomplished through listening to riddles. Another skill may be practiced by reconstructing story events after listening. Still another facet of listening is listening to draw conclusions. An interesting method of presenting this skill is for the teacher to stimulate one side of a telephone conversation, structured to give clues to an event. The children respond by guessing what happened prior to the telephone call.

PICTURE INTERPRETATION

Teacher guidance in picture interpretation provides children with background for interpreting the printed page. One aspect of picture interpretation is learning to identify the mood, for example, "loneliness" or "curiosity." Pictures used for interpretation of

---

[1] Sister Ethel Cole, "The Effect of Intensive Instruction in Listening Comprehension with Different Intelligence Groups in Grade One" (M.A. thesis, Cardinal Stritch College, 1961).

mood should be uncluttered by distracting details, but they do not have to be selected from children's books. "Christina's World," by Andrew Wyeth, for example, readily elicits appropriate responses such as "wanting" and "reaching."

In creating titles for pictures, children practice judgment and reasoning, which they will need later to identify the main idea of a paragraph or a longer selection. Other activities involving picture interpretation were suggested by Sister Marie Joan in a master's thesis.[2] One of these, making booklets of animals, toys, and furniture and labeling the objects, increases sight vocabulary without word drill. Another worthwhile practice involves pasting an interesting picture on tagboard. A sheet of primary writing paper is placed below it with a title and a list of words that may be used by the children to compose a short story about the picture. As another activity involving interpretation, charts may be made by the children of things that are thought of in pairs. The pictures may be drawn by the children or collected from discarded magazines.

Recently, three books designed to develop receptive and expressive language have been published, using delightful cartoon pictures. One of these books consists of ninety pages of 8½ x 11 pictures for storytelling. The other two books contain a variety of language activities related to cartoon strips, including story sequence practice.[3]

[2] Sister Marie Joan O'Keefe, "An Evaluation of an Enrichment Program in Reading for the Superior Group in First Grade" (M.A. thesis, Cardinal Stritch College, 1961).

FLEXIBILITY

The concept of flexibility in reading at primary-grade levels has several facets. One of these is the difference between silent and oral reading. In order that the children develop true silent reading, as free as possible from vocalization, the teacher needs to remind them in various ways, such as, "Read it with your eyes and your mind" and "See if I say anything when I read silently." Another important aspect of flexibility is difference in approach, stories versus other materials such as science and health books. The latter should not be read in the same way that narratives are read. When reading factual material, children can be asked to convert headings into questions, for example, "What do we want to learn about birds' nests?" and "Where do puffins live?"

Reading to summarize information is another common purpose for reading. This may be practiced on a chart or a simple time line. The headings of the chart can be guides to reading selectively to find specific information. For instance, "What happened in the morning?" "Where did they go after lunch?" and "What did they do just before going home?" are questions which may be developed from the headings, "Morning," "Noon," and "Night" on a simple time line. Another aspect of flexibility is the ability to skim for specific words or phrases in answer to questions. This can be

[3] The text of the *Julie and Jack Series* is by Sister Mary Walter, O.S.F., and the cartoons are by Marvin Townsend; the series is available from St. John School for the Deaf, 3680 S. Kinnickinnic Avenue, Milwaukee, Wisconsin, 53207.

taught at first with questions using the same words or phrases that the children find on a page of their books; after they grow adept at this, the questions may employ words other than those on the page.

Weekly classroom newspapers can be used for a variety of reading purposes. In nearly every issue there are word recognition aids in the form of attractive pictures with labels. These are valuable for making topical dictionaries, for example, "Words That Tell about Space," "Words about Animals," and others. Devices useful for word synthesis, sometimes found in classroom newspapers, are "scrambled letters" and "jumbled syllables." In the former, children may rearrange letters into familiar words, and in the latter, they may reconstruct three or four two-syllable words from a random sequence of syllables. Crossword puzzles are another aid in developing orientation to letter sequence within words. Of course, these puzzles promote meaning vocabulary, too, as do pictures accompanying stories. For example, is the milkmaid's dress striped, dotted, or checked? Stories and short plays in the weekly newspapers lend themselves to another purpose — dramatization or oral reading for enjoyment.

Of primary importance to primary-grade children is the encouragement of efficient use of reading and study time, for small children are frequently dawdlers. The teacher can lead a group toward the idea of budgeting time by planning to accomplish a certain reading task before recess time or before the end of the afternoon. Although direct emphasis on rate of reading would

be unwise, occasional use of short, timed exercises remind children of the desirability of reading as rapidly as necessary to accomplish their purposes.

CRITICAL READING

Critical reading involves different purposes than those underlying the reading tasks mentioned above. In reading critically, the young child will be asked to judge: "Could this be true?" "Did they do what was right?" "Is the ending what you thought would happen?" Critical and creative reading can be developed in young children chiefly through the skilfulness of the teacher's questions. If the teacher can elicit thinking about the over-all organization of a story, or plot, in addition to responses about specific facts, and if she can interest pupils in following a character throughout the story, she is laying the groundwork for mature, creative, interpretive readers.

Primary-grade children can also learn to collate material from two or more sources, under the teacher's direction. They can compare two accounts of the same event; for example, descriptions of the life cycle of the turtle as presented in their science book and as given in a trade book.

REFERENCE SKILLS

To use basic reference books, children need to learn about the library, about the parts of a book, and about the alphabet. It has been wisely stated that the first thing to do when teaching children to use the library is to give them a task requiring the use of the library. William D. Sheldon has identified certain learnings as appropriate to various grade levels. He suggests that kindergarten children can learn to handle books correctly, learn to note book titles and authors, and become aware of code markings on books. He identifies the following learnings as desirable in the primary grades: experience in using tables of contents to ascertain whether a book contains needed information, and knowledge that books are placed in certain order on the shelves, that the card catalog is used by older children and adults to locate books, and that the library has newspapers, magazines, and other materials in addition to books.

Kindergarten children may learn the titles and authors of favorite books and that their parts are called chapters. Primary-grade children should acquire additional learnings about the parts of a book: how to use tables of contents to find stories in school books and to find the parts of a book that will answer a specific question or questions; how to classify books according to their topics; and how to use a simple glossary.

In learning to use the alphabet for reference work, children progress from knowledge of letter names through complete knowledge of alphabetical order, ability to alphabetize by the first and then the second letters of words, and ability to divide a simple dictionary into three parts.[4]

In addition to the reading-study skills described above, primary children should also acquire some "non-book" reference skills. George D. Spache lists map and globe skills contained in a bulletin issued by the Board of Education of Prince George's County, Maryland, which is most useful in presenting a sequence of skills from grades one to six.[5]

CONCLUDING STATEMENT

In reviewing the variety of reading purposes which primary-grade children can and should be taught, it is obvious that each day in kindergarten through grade three offers multiple opportunities both for reading to learn and for learning to read.

[4] Sheldon, "How To Develop Study Skills from Kindergarten through Grade Six," Curriculum Letter No. 62, Wesleyan University, Middletown, Connecticut, 1965.

[5] Spache, *Reading in the Elementary School* (Boston: Allyn & Bacon, Inc., 1964), pp. 207–11.

* * *

IN GRADES FOUR THROUGH EIGHT

J. HARLAN SHORES

*

TO ASK how rapidly a person should read or what he should comprehend is useless. These questions would never be asked by anyone with even an elementary understanding of the nature of the reading process. Neither speed nor comprehension goals are meaningful apart from specific materials or apart from the purposes for which they are read. People read some materials rapidly for some purposes. The same people read other materials, or the same materials, slowly for different purposes. People comprehend some materials easily for some purposes and other materials, or even the same materials, poorly for other purposes.

Where, then, does the concept of flexibility enter this picture? Flexibility as defined here, and as usually defined in the literature concerned with the reading process, is the ability to adjust reading skills to varied materials and purposes for reading. It may be important to note at this point that the flexible reader is not necessarily the good reader any more than the rapid reader is necessarily the good reader. One cannot be a good reader without being a flexible reader, but one can be a flexible reader without being a good reader. If a reader had all the reading and thinking skills at his command, if he knew how and when to use each singly and in combination, he would be both a flexible reader and a good reader. Lacking as we all are in both thinking and reading skills, we attack the problem on three fronts. We learn to think more adequately. We develop our reading skills, and especially those necessary for different materials and different purposes. And we become more flexible in choosing the best skills and abilities for the reading job at hand.

CURRENT PRACTICE

Before we can turn to suggestions of specific methods and techniques for developing purposeful, flexible reading, it is important to see how these aspects of reading are treated in current programs of measurement and instruction.

Looking first at general achievement tests in reading, we find that the reader is usually asked questions requiring understanding of the main ideas, the "significant" details, and of the inferences that may be made. It would seem then that these are his purposes for reading. As far as purpose is concerned, however, these measures are practically meaningless for three reasons. First, the reader does not discover these purposes until after he has completed the reading since the questions are at the end. To read purposefully, he would need to be extremely "testwise" and read the questions first or to reread the selection once he knows what he is being asked. Most test directions discourage these two practices. Secondly, the test scores do not indicate how well or how poorly the reader has read for any one purpose. He may have read well for main ideas and poorly for details. He may get both main ideas and details but be unable to make inferences from his reading. All this is wrapped up in a single score. A third difficulty with the general reading test as far as purpose is concerned is that ability to read for many significant purposes is not measured. How well can he read to follow directions? To understand a bar graph or a timetable? To determine whether the material is pertinent to his question? Can he keep a series of ideas in mind in proper sequence? Is he able to read critically? These are obviously only a few of the unmeasured purposes for reading.

Before we leave measurement, the relationship between reading rate and comprehension must be considered as these relate to both purpose and flexibility. Some reading tests measure only comprehension with liberal time allotment. Thus, there is no possibility of discovering whether the reader's rate is in keeping with the task. Other tests impose rather rigid time limits. With these tests we don't know whether we have a measure of rate or comprehension or both, and again, we do not know whether the rate is flexible with the purpose. Still other tests measure rate and comprehension separately. With these, the comprehension measure is often a power test, with the questions getting more difficult, while the rate portion asks questions so simple that the answers are nearly apparent without reading the selection. These provide no indication of rate for relatively difficult materials for relatively challenging purposes but only for simple materials for a minimal and ill-defined purpose.

It should be understood that these rather sweeping criticisms of general reading tests apply to their usefulness in measuring either ability to read for varied purposes or flexibility in fitting the skills to the purpose. What we want to know is how rapidly a person can do a particular job and with what comprehension. Over a series of jobs, we also want to know whether he varies his rate and techniques to the requirements of the task. General reading tests do not provide answers to these questions. Perhaps one reason for lack of adequate attention to purposeful reading is the confusion beyond the primary grades between the teaching of reading and the teaching of literature. As a content field, literature is neither more dependent upon reading skills nor more useful in developing reading skills than are science or the social studies. In fact, one probably needs to read for more varied purposes in the latter fields. To teach reading skills largely in connection with literature both restricts the range and narrows the perspective of purposeful reading.

When one asks what a reader does when he reads, there is little point in trying to differentiate between reading skills and study skills. Such arbitrary distinctions lead to the neglect of many skills involving reading that are important to the content fields. One way of shirking the job of teaching purposeful, flexible reading is to say, "Those are not reading skills; they are study skills." If they involve reading and are subject to improvement, they are reading skills and should be taught as a part of the reading program. That some of these skills may best be taught in connection with the program of science, social studies, or language arts does not deny their importance to the total reading program. The great advantage of assigning reading skills to subjects other than reading on the grounds that they may be more efficiently taught there is lost completely if the reading skills get low priority and consequent neglect among the objectives of the subject.

METHODS AND TECHNIQUES

The first and most important curriculum decisions regarding the skills of purposeful and flexible reading are to decide which skills to teach and to give these the priority they deserve among objectives. A checklist of purposeful reading skills is not difficult to make. Some of these are listed as parts of the developmental reading program in the intermediate and junior-high school grades. Others are listed as basic study skills in the language arts curriculum, and still others are found in the literature on reading in the content fields. To bring these lists together and have them at hand would be useful. Chapter ix, "The Combined Program for Intermediate Grades," of George D. Spache's *Reading in the Elementary School* will provide an excellent starting place.[1]

Regardless of how complete such a checklist might be, it cannot provide priorities for the development of skills in any one school. Perhaps a good way to start determining priorities is to ask what skills students need in this school. What are they required to do with reading? Must they locate information? Must they organize information? Must they think critically about what they read? Must they memorize detail? If we are asking them to do these things, these particular skills should have high priority for instruction.

Materials and tests for use in teaching purposeful reading skills are scattered and fragmentary. The labora-

tory-type boxes of Science Research Associates and Educational Developmental Laboratories may be useful practice materials for some of the skills.[2] There are also a few tests published in these areas.[3] However, for many of the purposes for which one must read, there are neither published tests nor materials. Although it would be helpful to have commercial materials packaged and ready for use, those developed in a workshop situation by teachers may be more useful. Both tests and teaching materials can then be directly related to learnings in the content fields.

The weaknesses noted in general reading tests for measuring purposeful, flexible reading need not appear in teacher-made tests. Since the tests are also practice exercises, testing time is not a major problem. The expense, of course, need be no more than for other hectographed or mimeographed materials. In these tests the student should know in advance his purpose for reading, the comprehension demands should be in keeping with the purpose, and the elapsed time should be measured for both an original read-

[1] Published in Boston by Allyn and Bacon, Inc., 1964.

[2] *Basic Skills Kit* (Organizing and Reporting Skills Kit, 1962; Graph and Picture Study Skills Kit, 1961; Map and Globe Skills Kit, 1964), prepared by Science Research Associates, Inc., Chicago, Illinois; *EDL Study Skills Library* (Science, Social Studies, Reference Skills), prepared by Educational Developmental Laboratories, Huntington, New York.

[3] *Gates Basic Reading Tests* (Teachers College, Columbia University; rev., 1961); *Iowa Tests of Basic Skills* (Houghton Mifflin Co., 1964); *SRA Achievement Series* (Science Research Associates, Inc., 1961); *Stanford Achievement Test* (World Book Co., 1953); *A Test of Study Skills for Grades 4–9* (Steck Co., 1940).

ing and for rereading and question-answering. To do this is not difficult. First we decide what skill is to be developed — what the student is to do. We then tell him this and develop one or more appropriate questions to measure his ability to do this specific job. For example, if the skill to be developed is that of getting the main idea from a passage, we tell the student in advance that he is reading to get the main idea. The comprehension task is met when he can recall or recognize the main idea. Since this demand is probably met with one question, the reliability of such a measure is undoubtedly low; but if he does this kind of job twenty or more times during a period of instruction, the teacher will be able to judge whether this is a job he can do.

It is also important to know how long it takes to do a job. If the teacher has a stack of 8 x 10 inch numbered cards and exposes one of these each five or ten seconds in order, beginning at a specified time perhaps a minute before the most rapid reader might finish, it is a simple matter to have each student record the number that is showing when he finishes a first reading. His instructions would then be to answer the question, rereading if necessary, and again to record the number showing. Even before this test is given, the teacher could count the number of words in the passage and make a chart indicating words per minute for the exposed numbers. If this technique is used frequently, the school may wish to buy an Automatic Elapsed Time Indicator for more accurate measurement and to free the teacher from constant attention to the cards.[4]

A rough indication of flexibility comes from a comparison of reading rates over different materials and different purposes. Although this evidence is quite objective in demonstrating the over-all effect of adjusting rate to purpose and material, is does not indicate the type of adjustment that the student is making. Questionnaires, interviews, or just "talking it over" provide less objective data but may give a better picture of flexibility.[5]

CONCLUDING STATEMENT

Probably the best starting place for actual instruction in purposeful and flexible reading is an analysis of reading tasks by teachers and students. How would a good reader do this job? This approach suggests, of course, that we would do well to teach elementary school children much more than we do about the nature of the reading process so that they would know when they are reading well for a given purpose.

After a person can read something for some purpose, we should begin to extend and make the skills more useful. While still in the primary grades, the child can learn to read for a particular fact and to read some material more rapidly for a less demanding purpose. As he gets into the content fields more deeply, teachers should ask themselves, "What reading skills does a

[4] Manufactured by Franklin Research, 1922 Bonita Ave., Berkeley, Calif.

[5] J. Harlan Shores, "Reading of Science for Two Separate Purposes as Perceived by Sixth Grade Students and Able Adult Readers," *Elementary English*, XXXVII (November, 1960), 461–68.

student have to be able to do the kind of work expected in this field? Does he need to locate information, determine its pertinence, outline, and read outlines? Does he need to know how to read a map or a bar graph? Are we expecting him to recognize differences in values or points of view or to find errors in reasoning?" Such purposes come from the objectives, from the lessons in the content fields, from textbooks, and from teaching units.

We should then plan to teach individuals and groups to do these reading jobs. They are most easily done in connection with assignments. They may be practiced in real jobs and drilled when the need for further practice is apparent. Instead of the frighteningly complex problem it once seemed, the development of purposeful reading with flexibility is simply learning to use the right tools for the right job and to do so efficiently.

✳ ✳ ✳

IN GRADES NINE THROUGH FOURTEEN

OLIVER ANDRESEN

✳

OF ALL the areas of research in the field of reading, that of reading comprehension has been subjected to the least amount of investigation, especially at the high-school and college levels. For the last three years the Reading Research Center at the University of Chicago has been conducting a study in the area of reading comprehension at the high-school level under the direction of Helen K. Smith. This study is supported by a government grant from the U. S. Department of Health, Education, and Welfare. Basically, it is an investigation of an experimental teaching process in which a group of ninth-grade students have been taught to read for different purposes. The experimental group was matched and compared on scores derived from pre- and post-instruction tests with the scores of a control group that did not receive special instruction. Although the data have not been fully analyzed, indications are that teaching students to read for different purposes enhances their reading comprehension significantly.

Prior to this experiment, other reading authorities have also published ideas for teaching in this area. James M. McCallister has identified and advocated the teaching of paragraph types according to their purpose and location within a selection.[1] Joseph Gainsburg advocates the outlining by reading students of certain paragraph

[1] McCallister, "Using Paragraph Clues as Aids to Understanding," *Journal of Reading*, VIII (October, 1964), 11–16.

types.[2] H. Alan Robinson, Leitha Paulson, and Oliver Andresen have written on the value of analyzing paragraphs according to type when in search of the author's meaning.[3] In general, these writers contend that in order to comprehend a selection at the receptive level the reader must give himself intelligent self-direction while searching out the author's meaning.

This writer was the research associate for the government study at the University of Chicago that has been described above. This past year he also taught a developmental reading class for college students at the University of Chicago. Drawing on the thinking of the Chicago study along with that of the reading authorities just mentioned, he has designed a method of teaching reading comprehension at the senior high-school and college level. The purpose of this paper is to present this teaching method.

TEACHING READING COMPREHENSION
AT THE UPPER LEVEL

This writer contends that in order for a student to give himself intelligent self-direction in reading for understanding he must perform two tasks. First, he must look for the struc-

[2] Gainsburg and Samuel I. Spector, *Better Reading* (New York: Globe Book Co., 1962).

[3] Robinson, "A Plan for Helping Teachers Relate Reading and Writing Instruction," in *Reading and the Language Arts*, ed. H. Alan Robinson ("Supplementary Educational Monographs," No. 93; Chicago: University of Chicago Press, 1963), pp. 224–27; Paulsen, "Developing Reading and the Language Arts Efficiencies in the Content Areas: In Corrective and Remedial Classes," in *ibid.*, pp. 92–97; Andresen, "Interrelating Reading and Writing: In Grades Nine through Fourteen," in *ibid.*, pp. 131–37.

ture with which the author has organized his ideas. Then, he must look for the relationship among those ideas and determine its nature. With the performance of these tasks, the reader should have a grasp of the author's ideas.

The basic structure for presenting ideas is that of a main idea and details. In other words, in any type of selection, an author's organization will consist of a main idea substantiated by details. The effective reader looks for the details and the main idea supported by them; but he must do more for a complete understanding of the author's thinking. The reader must look for two basic relationships. First, he must look for the relationship between the main idea and the details. For example, he should ask himself whether the main idea or the details should demand more of his attention. He should also look for the relationship among the details. He should determine which are the primary details, commanding the greater part of his attention, and which are the secondary details, requiring only cursory notice. When he has attended to the details, the main idea, and the relationships involved, he should have unraveled the meaning in the selection.

OTHER TYPES OF
ORGANIZATIONAL STRUCTURES

The basic pattern of a main idea and details can be varied by more complex organizational patterns. This writer suggests that there are four of these and that they ought to be taught in the order in which they are described below. This order has already been established through the thinking and research of Helen K. Smith.[4]

Sequence. The first of these complex organizational structures is sequence. In a sequence, a relationship of one detail to the next is of primary importance; and therefore, the details in a sequence demand particular attention by the reader. Most authorities state that sequence can be subdivided into three types. The type that most readily comes to mind is that of time. An example of this type is the customary chronological sequence of historical events. The second type is that of space. An example of this type is a description of the relative position of objects in a room. The third type is that of logic. An example of this type is a presentation of steps in a mathematical problem.

Certain signal words can serve as clues to the reader that one of these types of sequence is present. Examples of signal words for a time sequence are dates or such words as "first," "second," and "finally." Examples of signal words for a space sequence are "in front," "in the middle," and "at the end." Examples of signal words for a logical sequence are "best," "second best," and "least."

In reading for the purpose of determining sequence, the reader should be taught to note such signal words and to follow the author's thinking through the steps of the sequence. Only then should he focus his attention on

4 Smith, "Sequence in Comprehension," in *Sequential Development of Reading Abilities,* ed. Helen M. Robinson ("Supplementary Educational Monographs," No. 90; Chicago: University of Chicago Press, 1960), pp. 51–56.

the main idea which is being presented by the sequential structure.

Comparisons. The next kind of organizational structure is comparison. The term comparison connotes the relating of both similarities and differences between two or more items or ideas. A comparison, therefore, usually has not only a main idea but two or more subordinate ideas which are being compared.

Signal words and phrases that often serve as clues to the reader that a selection contains a comparison are "but," "on the other hand," "similar to," and "in contrast to."

In order to read for a comparison effectively, a student should note such signal words and phrases. As soon as he realizes that the author is employing comparison, he should look for the two or more subtopics being compared and note the relationship among these topics. Finally, he should attend to the main idea which the author is developing through the comparison.

Cause and effect. The third kind of organizational structure is that of cause and effect. Similar to a comparison, the cause and effect structure contains a main idea based on two subtopics — one the cause, the other the effect of the cause. Some signal words indicating that cause and effect are present in a selection are "because," "therefore," and "consequently."

To read for cause and effect effectively, a student should be taught to note these signal words. When he realizes that his mind is entering a cause and effect situation, he should look for the subtopic which is the cause and the subtopic which is the effect and for the relationship between the two. Then he should place intellectual emphasis on the main idea which is derived from the cause and effect.

Generalization, summary, or conclusion. The last kind of organizational structure is generalization, summary, or conclusion. Because these three types of presentation are so similar in their structure, they can be studied as one organizational pattern. In this kind of structure, the flow of the author's thinking leads from the main idea rather than to it. The climax of the selection is the concluding or generalizing statement. Occasionally, this statement may also serve as the main idea of the selection. A generalization or conclusion, however, usually can be distinguished from a typical main idea in that the generalization contains a presentation of the author's opinion.

Some signal words indicating a generalization are "hence," "thus," and "in conclusion." A student should be taught to note these words and then to follow the author's thinking from the main idea through the details to the final statement.

OTHER CLUES INDICATING TYPES OF ORGANIZATIONAL STRUCTURE

There are other types of clues indicating organizational structures besides signal words. Titles and first sentences can inform a perceptive reader of the organizational pattern serving as the structure of the selection. For example, the title *Why Napoleon Was Defeated at Waterloo* indicates to the reader that the discussion following will be primarily organized by a cause and effect pattern. An opening sentence such as "The earth is surrounded by four strata of atmosphere" indicates that the discussion will be organized primarily as a space sequence. By the use of such clues, the reader can direct his attention more efficiently to the author's ideas.

Under most circumstances the reader will seldom find only one structure in a selection. Usually, a combination will be present. For example, a sequence may lead to a generalization, or a comparison may be the cause of an effect. Further, abbreviated structures may be found in larger ones — somewhat like the small wooden Chinese dolls that contain ever smaller replicas within each part. In other words, an entire chapter of a textbook may be organized primarily as a cause and effect. Yet, within this chapter there may be a section organized as a comparison, which in turn may contain paragraphs organized in a sequence, or as main idea and details, or some other pattern.

CONCLUDING STATEMENT

Finally, the student should understand that in any one of these structures the main idea can be either stated or implied. Consequently, during instruction he will need experience in identifying a main idea by inference when the author has chosen not to state it directly.

With awareness of these structures and with knowledge of the reading processes that should be applied for an effective understanding of the ideas presented in them, the student should soon develop the ability to grasp the author's meaning successfully.

IN CORRECTIVE AND REMEDIAL CLASSES

HAZEL HORN CARROLL

*

To meet the needs of retarded readers, a remedial class should be flexible; that is, it should be adjustable, and it should be versatile. Any reading class should have as its goal the development of efficient readers. Efficient readers should have versatility, and they should have the skills to attain and maintain this quality.

A purposeful remedial class is one in which the teacher has worthwhile goals and plans systematically to achieve them. Perhaps the most important of these goals is the assessment of the strengths and weaknesses of the individual students. This assessment should be followed with specific assignments in line with the findings. The students, as well as the teacher, should have worthwhile purposes. This "purposing" of the students is sometimes called motivation. It has been the experience of this writer that a student can be motivated to try almost any assignment, if he knows he needs it and if he feels he can succeed in it.

LEARNING NEEDS AND LEVELS

An effective way for the teacher and the student to learn the student's needs is by oral reading of graded paragraphs. This type of reading can also give knowledge of reading levels. It is essential for the student's assignments to be planned at the right levels if he is to meet the success that will be his motivation for continued learning.

The selections may be chosen from basal readers by the teacher or they may be taken from an inventory such as the one contained in the appendix of *Reading Evaluation*.[1] The information gained from such reading can be tabulated in an easy-to-use form. The checking of specific errors during the oral reading analysis will help the student understand his needs, since this checking is his record of errors.

Oral reading instruction also affords an opportunity for the teacher to adjust his teaching to the levels and needs of the students. A tabulation sheet can be kept by the instructor to alert him to teach particular skills when the need arises. Guidance in the application of word attack skills is frequently needed by many remedial students, and it can be given most effectively in the oral reading experience.

DEVELOPING VERSATILITY

In *Making Better Readers*, by Ruth Strang and Dorothy K. Bracken, a chart of reading speeds and approaches is given.[2] The authors list four rates: skimming (the fastest), speeded reading, study reading, and careful and reflective reading (the slowest). They indicate that skimming is used to locate

[1] Mary C. Austin, Clifford L. Bush, and Mildred H. Huebner, *Reading Evaluation* (New York: Ronald Press Co., 1961).

[2] Strang and Bracken, *Making Better Readers* (Boston: D.C. Heath & Co., 1957), p. 120.

information, to find main ideas or to find out "what happened next," and to survey. Speeded reading is reading rapidly for certain details or main ideas. Study reading is reading for maximum understanding by putting a study plan such as Survey Q3R to work. Careful and reflective reading is used to follow directions or perform an experiment, reflect on content, evaluate, enjoy, or read aloud to share an aesthetic experience. Each rate and purpose are used with different kinds of materials. Consult the chart in *Making Better Readers* for an easy-to-use guide.

The chart can be used as a basis for selection of materials and assignments to help pupils become flexible readers. Attention should be given to planning of instruction and to practice in all four of the reading rates. Provision can be made within the corrective or remedial class for each student by spending more time on the type of reading in which his needs are greatest. Multilevel materials are available to help in improvement of each rate and purpose. A careful selection of material will assist the student in attaining success.

A list of materials for junior and senior high-school students follows. It includes some of the multilevel materials that are available in addition to some materials for teaching special skills. It should be considered only an example of how materials may be organized for a particular reading level.

WORD SKILLS

Word Clues, G-7, H-8, I-9, J-10, K-11, L-12, EDL (Educational Developmental Laboratories), Huntington, N.Y.

Flash-X, EDL

Spelling Magic, Webster Division, Mc-Graw-Hill Book Co., Inc., 1154 Reco Ave., St. Louis, Mo.

New Webster Word Wheels, Webster Division, McGraw-Hill Book Co., Inc.

Improve Your Own Spelling, McGraw-Hill Co., Inc., 330 W. 42d St., New York

SRA Spelling Word Power Laboratory, IIa–IIb–IIc, 6–7, Science Research Associates, 259 E. Erie St., Chicago, Ill.

Words Are Important, 7th grade up, C. S. Hammond Co., Maplewood, N.J.

Vocabulary Growth: Divide and Conquer Words, Coronet Learning Program, Coronet Films, Coronet Bldg., Chicago, Ill.

Syllable Game, Gelles-Widmer Co., 7530 Forsyth, St. Louis, Mo.

Tachist-O-Filmstrips, *Learning through Seeing*, Sunland, California

English Vocabulary Cards, Visual Education Assoc., Inc., 207 S. Perry, Dayton, Ohio

Basic Reading Skills workbooks, junior & senior high school, Scott-Foresman & Co., 433 E. Erie St., Chicago, Ill.

Stereo-Reader Service, Keystone View, Meadville, Pa.

Basic Reading Skills, Scott-Foresman & Co.

Tactics in Reading, Scott-Foresman & Co.

COMPREHENSION

Reading for Meaning, 7–12, J. B. Lippincott Co., Philadelphia, Pa.

EDL Study Skills Library, Science Laboratory, G-7, H-8, I-9, EDL

EDL Study Skills Library, Social Studies Laboratory, G-7, H-8, I-9, EDL

Reading for Understanding, junior-senior high school, college-adult, SRA

Using the Context, E. F. Barnell Loft, Ltd., Rockville Centre, N.Y.

Cyclo-Teacher, Field Enterprises Educational Corp., Chicago, Ill.

SRA Reading Laboratory (graph and picture study skills), IIIa–7, 8, & 9, IVa–college preparatory, SRA

Controlled Reading Filmstrips, GH—7 and 8, IJ—9 and 10, KL—11 and 12, MN—college, EDL

Skimming and Scanning, EDL

How To Become a Better Reader, by Paul Witty, SRA

How To Study, junior and senior high school, SRA

How To Study in College, Houghton-Mifflin Co., 53 W. 43d St., New York

Listen and Read Program, GL—junior and senior high school, MP—college, EDL

Basic Reading Skills, Scott-Foresman & Co.

Tactics in Reading, I and II, Scott-Foresman & Co.

English 2600—high school, *English 3200*—advanced, Harcourt, Brace & World, Inc., 757 Third Ave., New York

RATE

SRA Reading Accelerator, SRA

SRA Better Reading Books, 1, 2, 3, SRA

SRA Reading Laboratory (timed) SRA

Controlled Reading Filmstrips, EDL

Skimming and Scanning, EDL

BOOKS

Teen-Age Tales, D. C. Heath & Co., 285 Columbus Ave., Boston, Mass.

Real Books, Doubleday & Co., Garden City, N.Y.

SRA Pilot Library

Reader's Digest (soft cover)

Reader's Digest (condensed)

Literature Sampler, Learning Materials, Inc., 100 E. Ohio St., Chicago, Ill.

CONCLUDING STATEMENT

Corrective and remedial classes need to be flexible and purposeful. To make them so, instruction must be adjusted to fit levels and needs. It must include assignments on reading at different speeds for different purposes.

Specific attention must be given to developing confident attitudes in students. Confidence is a foundation stone for purposefulness. A gain in confidence will be the by-product of success in learning, which, as has been suggested in this article, is made possible by an adjustment of instruction to specific needs. But there is a greater gain to be won when the teacher gives short lectures aimed at releasing energies and unblocking abilities. Such a subject as "I Can" may sound trite, but a good talk based on it can achieve wonders.

All activities should be based on the theory that "nothing succeeds like success." If this is done, all remedial students will feel like the one who said at the close of a semester. "Do you want to hear a 'brain' read? I hardly ever miss a word now. And when I finish something I know what the score is."

CHAPTER XVI

ADMINISTRATIVE RESPONSIBILITIES FOR VIEWING
AND EVALUATING RECENT DEVELOPMENTS IN READING

*

THE ROLE OF THE READING CONSULTANT
IN BUILDING A FUNCTIONAL READING PROGRAM

SIDNEY J. RAUCH

*

THE SPECIFIC roles of the reading consultant have been listed by H. Alan Robinson and Sydney J. Rauch as (1) a resource person, (2) an adviser, (3) an in-service leader, (4) an investigator, (5) a diagnostician, (6) an instructor, and finally (7) an evaluator.[1] Although all seven of these jobs have their special values in building a functional reading program in a school system, we will concentrate on two of them.

THE READING CONSULTANT AS AN
IN-SERVICE LEADER

How is a good reading program built in a school system? From the administrator's and supervisor's point of view, the answer seems obvious: Give me a good teaching staff. However, there is another possible answer: Assign a well-trained reading consultant who has the ability to impart his knowledge and dedication to other

[1] Robinson and Rauch, *Guiding the Reading Program: A Reading Consultant's Handbook* (Chicago: Science Research Associates, Inc., 1965), pp. 1–3.

teachers, supply him with the necessary time and materials, and give him whole-hearted co-operation and respect. Then chances for success are excellent. Omit any one of the three factors — the well-trained consultant, the necessary time and materials for the job, or the co-operation and respect — and the chances for success are seriously diminished.

Implicit in this design is the clarification of the consultant's responsibilities in a school system. No lasting results can be expected if the majority of the consultant's time is devoted to remedial teaching, thus depriving scores of teachers responsible for hundreds of pupils of his services. The extent of reading retardation in a school system will therefore be a primary factor in determining the consultant's responsibilities. The greater the extent of retardation, the more imperative the need for in-service training.

The more one reads about various types of reading programs and the more one observes and evaluates programs in action, the more one becomes convinced that the ultimate success of any program is dominated by two factors. These are (1) the amount of time specifically devoted to the teaching of reading, with special emphasis upon the teaching of skills; and (2) the moral and material support given to reading instruction by the administrators and supervisors responsible for the program. Again, the need for in-service training, seems to be underscored.

In her description of the elementary-grades reading program in the New York City school system, Helene M. Lloyd indicates the immensity of the task in terms of pupils (600,000) and staff members (20,000). To achieve a successful reading program in such an environment, there was only one possible answer: in-service training. More specifically, Mrs. Lloyd tells of a six-pronged "Action Program," of which Action One was as follows:

Reading improvement has been given top priority at the supervisory level. For each of the past four years, the principals of each of our 580 elementary schools has had reading improvement as his major objective for the year. He has iterated the supervisory procedures by which he has planned to move ahead the school's program of reading instruction. These procedures are, of course, in-service training at the functional grass roots level. Our supervisors have themselves participated in special courses, workshops, and conferences to enable them to increase the effectiveness of their in-service effort in behalf of better reading.[2]

2 Lloyd, "Meeting the In-Service Needs of Elementary Teachers in Reading Instruction," in *Improvement of Reading through Classroom Practice*, International Reading Associ-

Since an effective in-service training program must be given top priority, the selection of a reading consultant by a school system must be decided primarily upon ability to conduct such a program. No matter how impressive a record a candidate has as a remedial or classroom teacher, he should not qualify automatically as an in-service leader. For this, we have to look for qualities of leadership, professional background, teacher-training skills, and effective personal relationships.

In organizing an effective in-service program, the following guidelines by Robinson and Rauch are recommended:

1. The program must reflect the realistic needs of the pupils, the staff, and the community. This involves careful observation, consultations, and analysis on the part of the consultant before he begins his program. The consultant should capitalize on the interests and efforts of such groups as grade-level chairman, subject-area specialists, and other resource personnel.

2. An in-service program that threatens the security of staff members cannot succeed. The consultant must be sensitive and realistic in his demands upon the teaching staff. Programs that require too much of the teacher's "free" time are likely to breed resentment and failure. At the same time, participants in the in-service program should have the opportunity to share in both the planning and the evaluating of the program.

3. Programs that try to accomplish

ation Conference Proceedings, ed. J. Allen Figurel (Newark, Del.: International Reading Association, 1964), IX, 208.

too much in too short a time will not have lasting results. It is better to concentrate on one grade level or one subject area at a time rather than attempt to reorganize the entire system-wide program in one year. A successful program in a limited area will mean much more in the long run than questionable progress on a broad scale.

4. The active support of teachers who are reputed to be extremely capable instructors and who are respected by other teachers greatly helps the reading consultant in organizing and conducting the in-service program.

5. In-service reading programs that involve persons who teach in a subject area must reflect the goals and objectives of that area. To help ensure fuller co-operation from content-area teachers, the consultant should use the materials of their subject to demonstrate the application of specific reading skills.[3]

THE READING CONSULTANT AS AN ADVISER

A primary responsibility of the reading consultant is to be aware of recent developments in the field of reading, and to relate this information to his particular school system. Since these are times of ferment and experimentation in the reading field, most teachers want to know whether any of the newer methods or approaches can be beneficial in their immediate teaching situations. Within recent years, such developments as programed instruction, the Initial Teaching Alphabet, the linguistics approach, the resurgence of the Montessori schools, and the demand for formal, systematic

reading programs in kindergarten (and even for the prekindergarten child) have created a certain amount of uproar in our press. Unfortunately, the sensational has often been highlighted, and the results of limited and informal experimentation have been reported as the "answers" to all our problems. The situation has been exaggerated by the existence of enthusiastic, fervent, and vocal supporters of each new method or development. As Walter Barbe has so aptly put it,

It is a strange but very real fact that all new programs in reading seem to be successful. Started with careful planning and based upon an understanding of the goals to be accomplished, every report in the literature of different methods reports more success with the new procedure than with the old. Almost amusing is the fact that those trying one method report better success, while others, rejecting that method but trying the different method, report better success. Is this not perhaps the best indication that like everything else, too much doing of the same thing makes it become routine and often sterile. And when teaching becomes routine, it is both more difficult for the teacher and less effective for the children. In discussing one particular program, Willard C. Olson observed that "change in itself appears to be beneficial." And so, perhaps a plea for flexibility, if not for change itself, is in order.[4]

Thus, it is up to the educator — and the reading consultant, in particular — to analyze and carefully evaluate the reports of new developments so as to protect our schools and children from

---

[3] Robinson and Rauch, *op. cit.*, pp. 47–48.

[4] Barbe, *Educator's Guide to Personalized Reading Instruction* (Englewood Cliffs, N. J.: Prentice-Hall, Inc., 1961), p. 6.

the vagaries and pressures of public opinion.

For too many years, unfortunately, it has been common school policy to treat the teaching of reading as some esoteric practice that is beyond the ken of the average parents. This "hands-off" policy has been responsible for a good deal of the suspicion and unrest on the part of parents when invited to discuss their children's reading. This lack of information about methods and the use of accompanying materials has also made many parents more susceptible to inflammatory press reports criticizing the teaching of reading. It is not only the consultant's responsibility to inform parents of the school's philosophy and methods of teaching reading but also to prepare teachers for parent conferences. One of the most frequent complaints aired by parents is that they were informed *at the end of the school year* — usually by a mimeographed form — that their child was to be retained in his present class because of poor reading. "Why wasn't I told about this sooner?" or "Why wasn't he given special help?" are the justifiable complaints.

To avoid such breakdowns in public relations, the consultant can help the teacher to communicate more effectively if the following practices are followed: (1) Prepare carefully for the conference: (2) be a good listener; (3) answer questions completely; (4) be tactful but realistic; (5) ask the parent for help; (6) be positive; (7) keep the vocabulary simple; and (8) invite parents to observe reading lessons.[5]

CONCLUDING STATEMENT

Our students have to be *taught* to read. The major responsibility of the reading consultant is to give the average classroom teacher all possible practical preparation — by way of theory, methods, and materials — for the teaching of reading.

[5] Robinson and Rauch, *op. cit.*, pp. 7–8.

* * *

THE SELECTION AND EVALUATION OF MATERIALS FOR A COMPREHENSIVE READING PROGRAM

GRACE BOYD

*

WHEN selecting materials for any phase of a reading program in a particular school system, the following factors need to be considered:

First, the people of the community, — their level of learning, their expec-tations for their children, their stability or mobility in the community, and the strength and sincerity of their interest in the educational program of the schools.

Second, the children — their achievement capacity, their environmental backgrounds, and their readiness for developing learning skills.

Third, the school administrative and supervisory staff — the professional goals of members of this group, their willingness to work together toward a common philosophy of education, their interpersonal relationships, and the role they play in the selection and evaluation of teaching materials.

Fourth, the members of the teaching staff — their professional competence, experience in teaching, length of service in the system, and their willingness to devote time to professional tasks beyond the hours children are in school.

Fifth, the organization of the schools — the number of children housed in one building, the age and grade levels represented, the sizes of class groups, and the physical facilities of the classrooms and of the school buildings.

Sixth, the amount of money available in the school budget to be spent for books and materials of instruction.

EXPERIMENTATION WITH MATERIALS

In the schools of Cicero, Illinois, the reading program is closely interrelated with all areas of the curriculum. Administrators provide teachers with many opportunities for professional growth. Representatives of the faculty are granted the privilege of attending and participating in conferences, from which they report back on their experiences. A curriculum library is well supplied with professional books and current periodicals which may be used in the library or borrowed for study and for use in classrooms. Publishers have supplied sample copies of whole series of textbooks that teachers may examine. From time to time committees are organized to study a particular phase of the curriculum and the materials used in that curriculum.

There has been an active reading committee for a period of several years. The members of this committee represent all grades in each of the ten schools in the system. In addition, two principals are active, contributing members. A teacher of first-grade children and a reading consultant have served as co-chairmen. A recorder has helped to prepare a summary of each meeting, which is sent to all committee members and principals. The purposes served by this committee are (1) to become familiar with recent professional literature and to encourage reading by teachers, (2) to gather and disseminate information about the reading program in all schools, (3) to inspire interest and enthusiasm for improving practices and to celebrate successes that are reported, (4) to encourage experimentation with materials and procedures by those who have worked out a well-organized plan, (5) to share in the evaluation of materials for teaching reading, and (6) to assist in planning for changes in the reading program and for purchase of new materials.

The first activity of the reading committee was to survey recently published professional materials. An annotated bibliography was made available to all those interested, not only to the members of the committee. The committee learned of a number of experimental activities that were being carried on by teachers in the schools. Some of these teachers were invited to attend a committee meeting and tell of their work. Summaries of some of these reports follow.

1. After thorough study, and after discussion with the principal and reading consultant, an experienced teacher of fourth-grade children tried an individualized program for teaching reading. Children with special needs were brought together in small, flexible groups for intensive teaching of skills. Work-type materials were assigned to those who needed them. A group intelligence test and a standardized battery of achievement tests were administered in September before individualization was started. Scores made on achievement tests given the following September, as the children entered fifth grade, ranged from 3.9 to 9.5 and gave evidence of excellent individual improvement. This report gave impetus to many teachers to use a variety of reading materials and to individualize their teaching within the framework of the basal program of the district.

2. A teacher of third-grade children carried on a study over a period of two years in which she compared the amounts of measureable improvement made by two comparable groups of children. For one group, the books provided for independent reading were almost all of the supplementary textbook type. For the other group, the books provided for independent reading were almost all attractive trade books drawn from the building library. Both groups were given the bas-

al instructional program. The scores on standardized tests, given at the beginning and end of this experiment each year, gave evidence of a greater gain on the part of those children who had read library books.

3. A teacher of seventh and eighth grades conducted a vocabulary study with her students. Members of her classes prepared a variety of interesting and beautifully illustrated booklets which gave evidence of rich vocabulary development. Among these were menu folders listing unusual items. Some of the creative writing took the form of Japanese haiku poetry.

As the reading committee members brought information from such reports to the attention of others in their schools, many teachers were stimulated to think critically of their use of materials. There was interest in greater flexibility of effort to meet individual needs. Impetus was given to the evaluation and selection of materials.

SELECTION OF MATERIALS

The reading-instruction program in all grades in the Cicero schools is built around the use of a basal series of readers, supplemented by materials suited to individual needs. In the selection of a basal series of readers, there is much to consider. Slow learners need reading materials that they can use successfully, whereas bright achievers need challenges.

Recently published materials for teaching children to read are certainly taking on a "new look," so that it is necessary for choices to be made very carefully. It has become customary for new materials to be put to the test of classroom use before being bought for all schools in the system. This past spring it became necessary for a choice to be made between two basal series that have been used experimentally from kindergarten through grade two in two of the Cicero schools. Three devices for evaluation were used: (1) discussion sessions; (2) evaluation forms or check lists with space provided for comments; (3) study of standardized test scores that compared achievement with capacity.

Responses on the evaluation forms prepared by the reading consultant were particularly valuable. Teachers' responses revealed keen insights into the needs of children and ways of teaching to meet these needs. They expressed clear thinking and critical judgment accompanied by specific, thoughtful suggestions for improvement. Although the positive comments outweighed the negative, the specific suggestions certainly merited attention, and teachers were assured that their evaluations and suggestions, both in their discussions and as reflected on the checklists, would be discussed with the authors of the series and with the representatives of the publishers.

In analyzing the reading scores in relation to the mental capacity of each child, measurable differences in the adequacy of the two basal programs were not revealed. At the end of first grade, the reading achievement scores on the standardized tests were somewhat disappointing. They ranged from 1.3 to 2.4. However, these same children progressed in grade two so that scores at the end of the year ranged

from 2.7 to 4.2, with the bulk of the scores ranging from 3.1 to 3.8. In comparing the successes attained by each series of basal readers, all evidence indicated that both presented excellent programs, thoroughly planned and adequately supplying the help needed by teachers. Each of the two series also had strengths and weaknesses. In the final analysis, it seemed clear that the progress made by children reflected the earnest, energetic work of teachers using good tools for teaching.

Although a single basal series of readers has been selected by the administration, on the basis of the evaluation and recommendation of the teachers and supervisory staff, it is understood that the classroom teacher is the key figure in the use of materials and in the guidance of the learning experiences of the children. There must be such flexibility within the general framework of the program of instruction. Participation by teachers in the study of pupil achievement, potential, and interests results in careful selection and purposeful, enthusiastic use of materials by both teachers and pupils. Materials are sometimes selected in place of the accepted basal readers and sometimes in addition to the usual program, depending upon the variety of materials and time available in the total program for the teaching of reading.

Many publishing companies are responding to the need for easy-to-read books of high interest and low vocabulary for those students who read below level for their age and grade expectancy. Aids in the selection of such books are to be found in many professional publications, such as *A Teacher's Guide to Children's Books* (Charles E. Merrill, 1960), by Nancy Larrick; *Good Reading for Poor Readers* (Garrard Publishing Co., 1964), by George Spache; and *Toward Better Reading* (Garrard Publishing Co., 1962), by Spache. Many recent studies of children's reading needs are reviewed regularly in such magazines as the *Reading Teacher* (International Reading Association), *Elementary English* (National Council of Teachers of English), *Educational Leadership* (Association for Supervision and Curriculum Development), and *Childhood Education* (Association for Childhood Education International).

THE SCHOOL LIBRARY AS A RESOURCE CENTER

Flexibility in the use of materials demands a much greater variety than can be made available in one classroom. Books and materials for daily use need to be changed often as children achieve more ability to use them, as interests emerge, and as there is need for enrichment of experience through reading. Educational television and radio programs, field trips, interschool activities, and discussions of current events extend children's interests and stimulate their efforts to seek more information from books and printed materials. This need can be supplied best through a school library which is a well-stocked center of instructional materials, housing a great number of books, periodicals, and audiovisual aids.

Selections of materials for the library should be made by the librarians with the help of the teachers and the students. Choice should be based upon (1) the librarian's knowledge of books and understanding of children, (2) requests and suggestions from those concerned with all areas of the curriculum, and (3) lists of recommendations from many reliable sources, including the American Library Association, the National Council of Teachers of English, the International Reading Association, the Association for Childhood Education International, the Child Study Association of America, the Illinois Reading Service, and the Bulletin of the Center for Children's Books (University of Chicago).

Well-chosen books entice the student to want to read and enrich his speaking vocabulary. They also encourage parents to read to their children. Parents who wish guidance in the purchase of books to enjoy with children are directed to the recently revised edition of *A Parent's Guide to Children's Reading* (Doubleday, 1964), edited by Nancy Larrick. The local public library and bookmobile also provide rich resources in books and movies.

Responses made by students can help librarians evaluate the materials on hand and indicate needed additions. Responses may take on many forms such as brief reports including evaluative statements, recommendations of readings for others to enjoy, lists of favorite authors, and individual reading record charts. One glance over these records permits one to see where interests are strong and where there has been little exploration.

For the evaluation of audiovisual

materials to be purchased, Cicero teachers and their classes attend previews and prepare evaluation forms, provided by the district library counselor. If they think that a particular piece of equipment will provide needed assistance, the purchase is made for their particular school. Re-evaluation by the teachers, after using the equipment, determines whether this material should be purchased for other schools in the system.

CONCLUDING STATEMENT

In our local situation we believe that selections of materials have been sound because of the evidence that they are being used effectively. In a recent exhibit of science projects, one was impressed with the amount of research that had been necessary to acquire the information that was presented. The explanations accompanying the exhibits were concise and well organized.

Children and young people are enjoying reading for many purposes in Cicero. The circulation of books for reading outside of school indicates a ready desire to turn to books. Parents report that children are choosing to read and to be read to. There are delightful examples of creative expression in many forms that have resulted from wide reading.

It is impossible to try out every series of books in classrooms in order to make selections. We can, however, turn to much recently published information that is based on research and sound evaluation procedures. Two sources of inestimable value in judging materials merit attention. The Sixtieth Yearbook of the National Society for the Study of Education presents help from many authors. Particular information concerning materials for instruction is given by Helen M. Robinson.[1] A very recent publication by H. Alan Robinson and Sydney J. Rauch, *Guiding the Reading Program: A Reading Consultant's Handbook*, contains briefly stated criteria for selecting and evaluating reading materials.[2] All who supervise and assist teachers will find in these two sources much practical help.

[1] Robinson, "Corrective and Remedial Instruction" in *Development in and through Reading*, National Society for the Study of Education Yearbook, Part I (Chicago; National Society for the Study of Education, 1961), pp. 368–69.

[2] Published by Science Research Associates, Inc., Chicago, Ill., in 1965.

INITIATING, STIMULATING, AND EVALUATING RESEARCH IN READING WITHIN A SCHOOL SYSTEM

JOSEPH E. BRZEINSKI

*

PROGRESS in reading instruction can be fostered by creative innovation and careful evaluation. The importance of sound educational research properly conducted within a school system is now recognized by administrators, teachers, and the general public. This is a relatively recent development. Traditionally, school systems were viewed as consumers of research rather than as producers.

Such a conception influenced research practices. In the past, most sophisticated educational investigations were directed by research specialists associated with colleges or universities. Often, this research dealt with limited numbers of subjects in laboratory settings under optimum conditions. Research conducted in near ideal circumstances frequently was judged to have little value for actual classroom practice. Even when its worth was recognized, its diffusion into American schools proceeded at a rather slow pace. The innovation had to be explained and preparations made for its initiation into the schools.

Research at the public school level consisted almost entirely of informal trials or the collection of descriptive statistics. In the former case, most classroom research suffered from weaknesses caused by lack of planning, insufficient control of important vari-

ables, and inadequate evaluation often colored by the subjective judgment of the experimenter. Mere collection of statistical data, although helpful, did not provide answers to really important educational questions.

When educational innovations were few and change proceeded in a leisurely fashion, former research approaches were adequate. Currently, however, there is relatively little time to evaluate the myriad suggestions for educational progress in general and for the improvements of reading in particular.

Administrators, supervisors, and teachers faced with the problem of quickly determining which of the many new reading approaches are best suited for their schools need valid evidence in a comparatively short time. To secure this information, a new kind of research approach is emerging. Public school systems are beginning to initiate, stimulate, and evaluate reading research in co-operation with curriculum specialists and research advisors from outstanding universities. Because public school classrooms represent a realistic setting, sophisticated research conducted at this level holds much promise. As an example of this type of research, steps taken in the Denver, Colorado, Public Schools during a reading research project may be of general interest to administrators, consult-ants, and supervisors.

Recognizing the importance of a sound foundation for reading and faced with many proposals for change, the Denver Public Schools gave con-sideration to improvements which might be made in the teaching of be-ginning reading. Two possibilities emerged: strengthening the methods used to teach beginning reading, and introducing reading at earlier ages than was usual.

Contemplation of these possible courses of action raised many ques-tions and led to a review of related re-search. The time spent examining pre-viously completed research was ex-tremely worthwhile. It revealed those areas where substantial research evi-dence has resulted in general agree-ment and other areas where research has been incomplete or incomprehen-sive. Armed with such information, the school system (1) had an over-all view of the state of knowledge, (2) was able to avoid duplicating previous efforts, and (3) could determine the direction of additional research.

Review of the previous literature suggested the conclusion that many generally accepted beliefs concerning early reading instruction rested upon rather tenuous evidence. Additional research seemed warranted. Prelimi-nary planning was started. Initial steps were taken to insure the adequacy of the proposed research in terms of two sets of criteria: (1) the soundness of ed-ucational methodology, and (2) the va-lidity of the research design.

Basic to sound educational method-ology are carefully planned materials appropriate for a particular age group. Because of the importance of experi-ence in this regard, two well-known reading authorities were requested to construct the necessary beginning reading materials. Paul McKee and M. Lucile Harrison agreed to become as-sociated with the project. They brought competency gained from widespread authorship of children's reading materials as well as knowledge of reading readiness, as reflected by a number of publications in this field.

In keeping with the policy of the Denver Public Schools that curriculum change must be based on sound trial, prefatory use was given these newly de-veloped methods and materials. Expe-rience showed that they could be used with kindergarten children. The test-ing period also provided a basis for modifications and improvements. The new procedures were evaluated in terms of such factors as their differ-ences from established procedures, the cost of the instructional materials, the amount of school time required, and the likelihood that pupils would profit educationally from them.

While the soundness of the educa-tional innovations was being tested, the adequacy of the research meth-odology was also being weighed. Taken into consideration in this proc-ess were such factors as the numbers of pupils and teachers that would be involved, the likelihood that the pro-posed research could be carried out and that valid answers to questions would be obtained, and the potential value of the results to teachers and pupils.

For further assurance of the adequacy of the design, experienced research advisers were consulted. Wilbur Schramm, of the Stanford Institute for Advanced Communication Research, constructed the paradigm of the research design. Other competent research specialists were consulted as required.

Once the preliminary evaluation indicated that the proposal met the standards that had been established and stood a reasonable chance of effecting educational improvements, a research proposal was drawn up. The organization of the proposal will be apparent in the following review of its elements.

The problem was briefly stated in terms of its general significance to education. This step was of vital importance, for it was the primary justification for carrying on the proposed research. The rationale also included reference to potential local benefits.

Six major hypotheses and several subsidiary questions were formulated. A brief statement was made concerning their relationship to the problem. The Denver study was primarily concerned with the effect of teaching beginning reading at earlier ages than normal in the school system.

A summary of pertinent research was prepared. The purpose was to establish the importance of prior research and to show in what ways the proposed study would extend present knowledge. This summary also helped to guide the current investigation.

The actual procedures to be followed were detailed in such a way that the experimental design, its antecedent and criterion variables and its methodology became clear. The selection of the population sample and its composition was decided upon. Plans were laid concerning the types of data, the methodology, and the evaluative instruments. The methods of analysis for the final evaluation were also determined. A time schedule was prepared incorporating approximate target dates for the completion of various tasks or phases of the study. A project budget for materials, facilities, personnel, and other research costs was drawn up.

The completed project application was approved by the school board and submitted to the Cooperative Research Branch of the U. S. Office of Education for consideration. Following a determination by the U. S. Office of Education that the project met their standards and that partial financial support would be forthcoming, the research was placed into operation.

STIMULATING RESEARCH

Whenever research is undertaken in schools, it is essential that the community be informed of its nature. In the initial stages of the Denver project, the support of the school board, key P.T.A. personnel, and the participating teachers was sought. As the research was placed into operation, the newspapers, the remaining parents, teachers, pupils, and the general public were provided with details of the project. These efforts to inform were extremely well received and provided the necessary factual basis upon which opinions could be formed.

Parents, for the most part, wanted reasonable assurance that their children would benefit regardless of the research roles assigned to them. The general public was concerned with financial costs. Upon learning of the matching funds that were available to enable the district to develop needed curriculum materials economically, they appeared to be reassured and generally reflected pride in the project.

Teachers were quite interested in the research project. Although most recognized that participation in the study provided opportunities for personal growth and professional improvement, their enthusiasm was tempered by several considerations. Most important, the early introduction to reading ran counter to the beliefs of many kindergarten teachers. Others were concerned about their ability to use the trial methods and materials. Teachers at later grade levels, who would become participants in the study as it progressed, were worried that materials they had developed and become accustomed to might not be usable in the future. All were, of course, concerned with the welfare of the pupils participating in the study.

Awareness of these doubts led to plans for the involvement of the instructional staff in the project. Consultants were provided to help teachers become proficient in the use of the new methodology. Instructional materials were developed with staff assistance to supplant those previously used. In-service meetings provided an opportunity for discussion of the project and for familiarization with the trial materials. Teachers were reassured that comparisons between schools or staff members would not be made — that the sole purpose of the testing and evaluation was to gather facts on which to base a subsequent decision. As a result of these efforts, teachers were motivated to participate. Their co-operation and wholehearted participation strengthened and improved the research materials and methodology.

EVALUATING THE RESEARCH

Data were gathered by several means. Well-known standardized tests were used extensively to collect information on reading progress and academic achievement. Awareness of the limitations of standardized tests led to the construction of experimental or specially prepared tests and evaluative techniques, which required a certain degree of creativity. As with most nonstandardized evaluative techniques, their value depended on establishing their reliability and validity.

The data were subjected to an analysis of variance. Because of the large numbers of subjects and the many variables, the statistical analysis was programed for a computer.

Interim results have been quite favorable to teaching reading at early ages. Communication of this information to interested persons resulted in the consideration of tangential projects. In co-operation with the Carnegie Corporation, research was undertaken to investigate whether parents could help prepare their young children for reading.

It can be seen that initiation, stimulation, and evaluation of research tend to generate interest in additional research. Through this process, new instructional materials are produced, and evidence is gathered upon which intelligent administrative decisions may be made regarding the worth of reading innovations.

* * *

STIMULATING EFFECTIVE READING INSTRUCTION IN THE TOTAL CURRICULUM

EARLE W. WILTSE

*

TWO PROBLEMS require the attention of the administrator who is organizing a school-wide approach to reading improvement. The first is related to the need for involving the entire teaching staff in reading improvement, and the second is related to the techniques which all teachers must use in order to help students become better readers.

Here and there over the country there is evidence that individual teachers and, in some cases, entire departments, are making excellent progress in developing and improving the reading ability of high-school students. An English department, for example, may be helping students improve their ability to read critically. Isolated science teachers may be using techniques to develop vocabulary. In still other schools librarians may be making available comprehensive lists of reference materials for children of varying abilities. One teacher may stress speed; another, comprehension. Several schools may specialize in the remedial phase of reading improvement. Many reading laboratories are equipped with all of the latest gadgets to improve speed and comprehension. But the number of schools in the United States having comprehensive programs of reading improvement at all levels, in all classes, in all departments of a school, are indeed few and far between.

The total teaching staff can be involved in reading improvement by the following actions:

1. *Appoint a reading co-ordinator with time to plan and organize.* Although it is important that the superintendent and the principal recognize the importance of reading improvement and give it leadership and encouragement, these people are expendable. Many of the innovations an administrator takes into a school disappear with his departure, and new innovations are introduced by his succes-

sor. Thus, since reading improvement is so fundamentally a part of a well-organized modern high school, its implementation should not be left to the administrator alone. It requires the guidance and direction of a knowledgeable person who can give full time to reading improvement on a permanent basis, at least in our larger high schools. The importance of such a person is not reduced in the smaller high schools even though he may also be required to do some teaching.

2. *Provide a budget for promotion of reading.* The size of the budget will depend upon financial resources and the extent of the program. Funds are required for such things as the purchase and scoring of tests, reading materials, teaching machines, slides, projectors, film strips, clerical assistance, and so on. It is possible to secure federal and state funds through the National Defense Education Act, the Economic Opportunity Act of 1964 and the 1965 Elementary and Secondary Education Act. The budget should include funds for professional materials, travel, workshops, and institutes.

3. *Maintain a program of in-service training for all teachers.* The role of the secondary-school teacher is rapidly changing. Whereas he once taught subject matter, he now teaches students how to read subject matter. Teachers recognize that the abilities necessary to read science are not the same as those needed to read social science or mathematics. They are aware of these differences, but they are often at a loss to know what to do about it.

A carefully planned in-service program of meetings and workshops prior to the opening of school to explain the reading program will assist in orienting new teachers. Reading improvement is not accomplished in one or two years. It is a long-term process, and a sensitized teaching staff is its *sine qua non*. Every high-school teacher needs a course in reading instruction as part of his training and refresher courses as part of local, in-service orientation programs.

4. *Organize reading strategy committees.* In districts with more than one school an over-all strategy committee may plan and promote such school-wide activities as (*a*) preparing, pooling, and sharing bulletins; (*b*) appraising the several elements in the reading program; (*c*) planning film strips for class use; (*d*) writing a study-habits manual; (*e*) attending monthly meetings; and (*f*) setting the goals for each year. This last gives the program a new look each year. (Our school system has set such annual goals as establishing effective habits of study, developing critical reading, and building vocabulary for each subject.)

The reading committees in each building have the responsibility of carrying out the plans of the strategy, evaluating progress, and suggesting improvements. They should also promote reading improvement at departmental and general staff meetings.

5. *Expand library facilities.* Most library budgets are not adequate. Budgets have not kept pace either with the growth in knowledge or with the increasing cost of library materials. If the library is to be the center of learning in a school, careful attention must be given to its plan of organization, ac-

cessibility of materials, adequacy of facilities, and ways of stimulating their
use.

HELPING ADOLESCENTS TO
BECOME BETTER READERS

There is no royal road to learning.
Reading improvement is hard work.
The following elements should exist
in all well-organized, ongoing high-
school reading programs.

1. *The reading center.* There should
be a well-equipped attractive area in
every school to which students may go
for help in becoming better readers. It
should contain the latest equipment as
well as a wide variety of reading materials. The teacher or teachers should
have special training in reading instruction. This center should attract
college-bound students as well as those
who need remedial instruction. Remedial instruction loses its stigma when
the slow readers find that the centers
are also used by the best readers to
improve their reading ability.

2. *Vocabulary development.* Every
teacher is responsible for developing
the vocabulary that is needed in his
own discipline. This is not difficult to
do. It does not require any complicated knowledge of reading. Reading
speed and comprehension will improve
as students learn the meaning of the
unusual vocabulary that appears in the
daily lessons.

3. *Reading in the subject-matter
fields.* Certain reading skills (for example, following directions) can be
taught better in one discipline (science) than another. Subject matter
teachers should be able to isolate them
and to work on their separate development. For help in examining these

skills, teachers may turn to chapter ii
in Shelley Uman's *New Trends in
Reading Instruction.*[1] There are general reading abilities that are common
to all types of reading, and these can
be used as the basis for discussing and
establishing local lists to be implemented by the teaching staff. Much
growth can result from the exchange
of ideas and sharing of experiences in
staff meetings.

Here are three examples of experiences that could be shared, selected
from a list of fifteen summarized by
English teachers in our school system.

a) Ruth Nickelson approaches vocabulary with an intent to discriminate the meanings of words that appear synonymous. For example, "aversion" and "repugnance." "Ver" means
to turn; an aversion is therefore a turning away. "Repugnance" is the stronger word because it comes from the Latin *pugnare,* "to fight." This approach
repeated many times throughout the
year leads to better readers and to more
appreciative readers.

b) In the December, 1960, issue of
the *English Journal* there was a list of
twenty-five recommended novels for
teen-agers. Twenty-four of these twenty-five are currently in our high-school
libraries. Mrs. Muckle has read each of
them and has kept a notebook on each
one as well as a card file. Since the interest and ability range of the novels
is extensive, she has found some suitable for slow readers and some better
suited to able readers. She has taken
class time to comment on these books.
Reading interest has increased.

[1] Published by Bureau of Publications,
Teachers College, Columbia University, in
1963.

c) Another teacher distributed the following mimeographed guide sheet for use in an English class:

Reading Improvement

Do you read in the same way when you study science, social studies, mathematics, and literature? You shouldn't. You read different types of material in each subject for different purposes. You need to learn the reading skills that each subject demands.

A. In your science book, you find chapters that tell how living things are *classified* or grouped. You must be able to compare and contrast as you read. For example, you must remember what simple-bodied plants — such as algae — are like so that you can understand how seed plants — such as flowers — are more complex. Other chapters *explain* processes, such as cell division. Others, found in experiments, have you follow directions and reach a conclusion.

B. In social studies, you need to know how to connect dates and events and remember them in order, how to look for the *cause* of an event — such as the American Revolution — and its *effects*.

C. Mathematics should be read differently from the above two subjects. You must be able to form a mental picture of the problem as a whole. Then you must analyze each separate part of the problem: Which details are important? How are they related? What facts can you use in the process of solving the problem?

D. Literature is different from these three subjects, and so it demands new skills. Your *purposes* in reading literature should be for enjoyment, understanding, and appreciation. You need to develop three skills:

1. *Literal comprehension.* — We get only the direct message as it is stated in so many words in the text.
2. *Interpretation.* — We sense meanings that are less obvious, reach conclusions on our own, conclusions which are only *suggested, not stated* in the printed lines.
3. *Critical reading.* — We use the above two but go further and *evaluate* or pass judgment on the writer's skill.

Much can be done to develop a favorable climate for reading improvement. The art department can develop attractive posters for use on bulletin boards and in classrooms. The reading center can stress the need for setting reading speeds on the basis of the nature and purpose of a selection by means of reading clubs. Members may be awarded silver and gold medals indicating their reading rate and comprehension ability. Paperback bookstores stimulate the reading of supplementary materials in subject-matter fields.

CONCLUDING STATEMENT

There should be a comprehensive program of reading improvement in every school that involves all teachers at all levels and in all areas of the curriculum. This comprehensive approach to reading improvement requires leadership, motivation, co-operation, and planning. Nothing less than an all-out attack will be sufficient.

METHODS OF HELPING TEACHERS PREPARE EFFECTIVE READERS

MARGARETHE F. LIVESAY

*

ALTHOUGH primary teachers are per-haps better trained for their re-sponsibilities in the teaching of read-ing than teachers at other levels, they also need help in recognizing pupil needs and in applying those methods that will prevent reading disabilities. The ability to recognize degrees of readiness and to give the kind of in-struction needed at the time must be developed. Classroom teachers need an opportunity to observe many more children in many more situations than is possible in their own classrooms. They need assurance that giving a child time to learn well each task in the developmental process is more im-portant than "finishing" a text or a prescribed curriculum.

Grouping to meet individual needs is effective only if the groups are flex-ible, not only within the classroom but also across grade lines. This requires teacher communication and affords an opportunity to keep the consultant in the classroom. While the consultant as-sists in one classroom, the teacher is freed to be an observer in others. As well as time for planning, teachers need time to share ideas and interpre-tations of pupils' needs. If Johnny is ready for a certain skill which Teacher C is planning to develop with Group 3 next week, Johnny should be with that group. In order for this to be ar-ranged, however, his teacher must be aware of Teacher C's plans. The con-sultant should assume the role of grouping co-ordinator until such time as teachers can work independently.

The effectiveness of grouping at any level depends in part on the skill of the teacher in helping students achieve independence in the use of *meaningful* practice materials. This is also the key to the use of programed materials. To develop this independence takes time, time in which it may seem that no teaching is taking place. Actually each student will be learning to take some of the responsibility for his own learn-ing, and the dividend for the teacher is time gained to work more closely with individuals and smaller groups. Faster learning groups should be started first so that the teacher can spend more time with those groups re-quiring her closer attention.

STUDY SKILLS IN THE CONTENT AREAS

Intermediate teachers are faced with curriculums overflowing with content. At the same time their training has given less attention to their roles as teachers of reading skills. Often they look upon the teaching of reading as the time spent on the basal reader, which has become increasingly devoted to the skills necessary for independent reading for pleasure. Students enter-ing junior high school who are con-sidered good readers are often found weak in textbook reading skills. High-school teachers are frequently heard to complain that their students cannot read their texts. College freshmen fail because of their inability to cope with the demands made upon them by textbook reading.

The time to begin the teaching of textbook reading skills is when pupils are first introduced to textbook materials in the intermediate grades. At this level, the teaching of reading can and should be a continuous, all-day affair. Well-structured practice materials will be needed, but the basic aim is the effective reading of the textbook itself. Reading skills can be taught and practiced while subject matter concepts are being learned.

Since many teachers are not aware of the technique of Survey Q3R,[1] its introduction provides an excellent opportunity for the use of the demonstration lesson. The demonstration lesson is most effective when it is given in the teacher's classroom with his own group of pupils. Not only does the observing teacher see technique in practice, but he has an opportunity to observe his own students in an environment different from, yet oriented to, his own classroom. The lesson should of course be in the context of the unit being studied.

There are a variety of ways to present vocabulary study. A selection of

difficult or new words, in the context of actual sentences from the textbook, can be a part of the readiness step of the lesson.[2] These words can be given to the class on a study sheet or separately to individuals who are then responsible for presenting the word to the class. The primary aim is to develop the habit of looking over any textbook assignment for difficult words *before* reading.

Unfortunately, those qualifications that make good secondary teachers of content-area subjects do not necessarily make good teachers of reading skills. Generally competent readers themselves, they find the phenomenon of a high-school student who cannot read the textbook difficult to understand and even more difficult to cope with. They must be helped to see that their most successful teaching of subject matter comes when they help students to read independently in a subject. Rather than insist that these teachers teach reading, however, the consultant should attempt to improve methodology in science, social studies, or whatever the subject area. If the teacher builds background, establishes meaningful concepts, gives purposeful assignments, directs reading to relate details to main ideas, asks for rereading to establish proof of facts, and demands discussion and evaluation of what is read, he will be teaching his subject well. He will also be providing for the development of reading skills.

The reading consultant can work with subject-area teachers through department meetings. As these teachers

[1] Francis P. Robinson, *Effective Study* (rev. ed.; New York: Harper & Bros., 1961), chapter ii.

[2] *Five Steps to Reading Success in Science, Social Studies, and Mathematics* (New York: Metropolitan School Study Council, Teachers College, Columbia University, 1960).

plan, the consultant can help them see how such skills as outlining, analyzing paragraphs for key and related ideas, and summarizing can vitalize textbook material. Where the textbook is weak, the use of reference materials should be suggested. Teachers may need assistance in recognizing those portions of the text which can be adapted to skill practice. When the consultant visits the classroom, it should be for the purpose of becoming acquainted with specific needs of the learners, with the subject matter, and with the teacher's approach to his subject. This knowledge will be invaluable in helping the teachers of a department plan actual lessons which are subject-centered but which also provide for reading skill development.

One social studies department, working through the ninth-grade teachers — since all students were enrolled in ninth-grade world geography — made a concerted effort to improve social studies reading skills. It was hoped that habits would be established that would function in later, more advanced courses in social studies. Meeting monthly with the consultant, the ninth-grade teachers planned lessons designed to teach needed skills — use of Survey Q3R, outlining, skimming for fact, discriminating between fact and opinion, and interpreting illustrative materials. Working in a similar manner, a science department stressed the recognition of patterns of writing in science, reading directions for experiments, noting details, and making inferences. In both cases, a supplementary reading list of both fic-

tion and non-fiction books was developed to help the reluctant textbook reader learn important concepts through independent reading. It was thought that perhaps in this way the student would also come to recognize that the content was a part of real life and not just the next day's assignment.

In a school organized for team teaching, there is an excellent opportunity to work for reading skill improvement, as suggested by Carlin in chapter vi. If the school is using large group–small group instruction, the possibilities are increased. Observing a large-group session, the consultant selects the reading skills needed for effective small-group follow-up and independent study. Since the small groups are formed as homogeneously as possible, the skill needs will vary from group to group. The consultant then joins the team in planning sessions, suggesting where opportunities for skill development are inherent in the lessons and where individuals might be given additional practice materials.

Secondary teachers can make much more use of the individualized assignment than they do at present. This device utilizes the skills of each student, allowing each to contribute something to the learning of all. While the more skilful search out information beyond the textbook, even the weakest reader can be helped to find specific facts, locate a place on a map, interpret an illustration, or obtain a book from the librarian for class use. To make this device work, the teacher must be helped to know both materials and the students as readers. Each assignment must include, as its very core, the purpose for reading. At first, the teacher will need to state this purpose repeatedly, but as students become more mature readers, they will develop the habit of recognizing their own purposes. And along with establishing the *why*, there should be a recognition of the corresponding *how*.

WORKSHOPS MUST BE MEANINGFUL

Workshops can be a most effective way of providing in-service training. To be meaningful, they must be planned to integrate theory with practice. They must meet both needs and interests. Summer school programs for students needing additional help or time to develop reading skills can provide a practical opportunity for teachers to learn. With the consultant as director, students may be grouped according to reading needs, with consideration given, if possible, to chronological age, physical size, and interest levels. Concurrently for a three-week period, a teacher workshop may be held under the direction of the same consultant. The afternoons may be spent in seminar sessions devoted to discussion of the theory of reading instruction, interpretations and implications of recent research, methods, materials, and evaluation. Each teacher participant may be assigned four or five students to work with during the morning class hour and should have the balance of the morning for independent reading, examination of materials, and

planning. Participants should also have the opportunity to observe demonstrations of both method and materials and to share with one another their experiences.

Working with small groups, these "student" teachers will have an opportunity to do individual testing, to follow through with an item analysis of the tests, to try out new materials and methods, and to study student reaction to them. These are things they do not have an opportunity to do in the regular classroom, often overcrowded, during the school year. The students in such a program benefit from the small-group experience, too. If there is a college or university nearby, arrangements might be made for college credit for the participating teachers. At any rate, professional credit should be granted. Building principals and administrators should be encouraged to participate along with the teachers. Their own preparation in the field of teaching reading may be weak; and they can profit from the opportunity to gain a teacher-student point of view.

In addition to knowing techniques and materials, teachers need to know the learners and the backgrounds from which they come. They need to know the reasons for their skill strengths and weaknesses as well as the fact that they exist. Since a complete case study of every student is not practical, each teacher should be helped to do at least one thorough study a year. The very process will make him a more conscious observer of the other members of the class. Such information can be cumulative, and the consultant can assist in the interpretation and sharing of the information. Albert J. Harris presents a good outline for a case study.[3] From the case study, the teacher can be helped to deal with special reading problems in his own classroom. He can learn how to make use of the special services personnel available in the school system — the nurse, the speech specialist, the school social worker, psychologist, and psychiatrist — and simi-

lar service personnel and situations in the community.

CONCLUDING STATEMENT

Effective readers? Not without the help of effective teachers. And to help teachers become more effective is the responsibility of effective educational leadership. Whenever possible, this should come from an active, creative consultant who is specially trained and has been given the time to work with teachers, to examine and try materials, to develop methodology, and to interpret research.

[3] Harris, *How To Increase Reading Ability* (4th ed.; New York: Longmans, Green & Co., 1961), pp. 311–14.

CHAPTER XVII

PRESENT STATUS OF READING INSTRUCTION

*

RUTH STRANG

*

WHO KNOWS what goes on behind the closed doors of classrooms all over the country? Many sound proçe-dures were first advocated decades ago, but just how prevalent they are we do not know.

Nation-wide surveys give glimpses of present practice. *The Harvard Report on Reading in Elementary Schools* comes nearest to giving us an adequate picture.[1] Based on questionnaires and observations and covering more than a thousand elementary schools, this report shows present practice as teachers and administrators described it to the investigators. For example, we learn that about 95 per cent of the primary teachers surveyed and 88 per cent of those in the middle grades are using basal readers. Almost as great a proportion supplement the basal readers with a variety of children's books. Many facts of this kind can be learned from surveys. However, we must remember that the most common practice is not necessarily ideal.

We are more interested in learning about successful procedures than about common practice. We are looking for descriptions of programs and procedures that have been put into practice with certain groups of students and have been considered successful by the persons who initiated and developed them.

In our search for successful reading programs, procedures, and materials, we turn to reports and reviews of research such as Helen M. Robinson's exceptionally helpful annual summaries of the broad field of reading,[2] and H. Alan Robinson's reviews of reading research in high school and college.[3]

We must admit, though, as George D. Spache and Arthur S. McDonald have pointed out in this proceedings, that the results of much research are inconclusive. "No significant difference" is a familiar refrain. Since it is impossible to control all the variables that affect learning in the language arts, any comparison-group type of research is bound to be inconclusive, no matter what statistical principles are

[1] Mary C. Austin *et al., The First R: The Harvard Report on Reading in Elementary Schools* (New York: Macmillan Co., 1963).

[2] For example, Helen M. Robinson, Samuel Weintraub, and Carol A. Hostetter, "Summary of Investigations Relating to Reading, July 1, 1963 to June 30, 1964," *Reading Teacher,* XVIII (February, 1965), 331–428.

[3] For example, H. Alan Robinson and Allan F. Muskopf, "High School Reading — 1963," *Journal of Reading,* VIII (November, 1964), 85–96.

used in handling the data. Moreover, group comparisons may conceal or neutralize individual differences. Would it not, then, be more helpful to know how effective a given procedure is with a given group of students in a given situation than to be told whether it is, in general, better than another method? We could gain such insight from a "simple research design" that involves (1) an initial comprehensive study of the students, (2) a detailed, accurate account of the methods and materials used, and (3) an appraisal of the students' progress in reading. This kind of investigation bridges the gap between unevaluated description and experimental research.

From these three sources — surveys, descriptions, and reports of research — we may obtain some knowledge of the present status of reading instruction.

CURRENT EMPHASES

Four emphases are currently in evidence: the emphasis on research, the emphasis on the importance of reading, the emphasis on children from educationally and culturally disadvantaged homes, and the emphasis on the preschool years. Large sums of money are now available for research. Though this aid will facilitate more extensive, more intensive, and more thoroughly controlled studies, it will not ensure their significance to education. At present everyone in our higher institutions of learning, and even in our public schools, may be under too much pressure to conduct studies, regardless of the state of his theoretical knowledge or of his familiarity with the pitfalls involved in applying the

scientific method to educational problems. We hope that research in the future will have a more beneficial impact on reading practice than it has had in the past.

A broadening of research design is evident from studies recently reported by classroom teachers. Some use the case study method; others describe ways in which practical problems were solved; still others evaluate reading materials on the basis of pupils' responses to them in the classroom. Instead of trying to isolate the effect of a single procedure, some of these studies report the complex outcome of a total teaching situation, which is objectively and accurately described.

The second emphasis, on the importance of reading, is presented in chapter i of this proceedings. McSwain's ideas are given support by Francis Keppel, who has written: "Every examination of the problems of our schools of poverty, every question raised by troubled parents about our schools, every learning disorder seems to show some association with reading difficulty."[4] The relation between reading disability and leaving school prematurely was clearly shown by Ruth C. Penty.[5] The preponderance of those leaving school early (49.97 per cent) were in the lowest quarter on the basis of reading ability; only 14.5 per cent in the highest quarter left before completing the senior year. When interviewed sev-

[4] Keppel, "Research: Education's Neglected Hope," *Journal of Reading*, VIII (October, 1964), 8.

[5] Penty, *Reading Ability and High School Drop-outs* (New York: Bureau of Publications, Teachers College, Columbia University, 1956), p. 20.

eral years after they had dropped out of school, students of average intelligence gave reasons such as the following:

I didn't think that I was getting any place in school. I was working part time . . . and I wanted to work full time. . . . I had trouble reading and understanding assignments. I couldn't remember what I read and didn't like to recite as I wasn't sure of myself.[6]

More recently, Daniel Schreiber, director of the NEA School Drop-out Project, declared that the greatest factor in school drop-outs is reading retardation. Many studies have shown that the average drop-out is two or more years retarded in reading.

Similar evidence is available on the relation between reading retardation and discipline problems, juvenile delinquency, emotional disturbance, and unemployment. There is a reciprocal relation between reading and personal values. Reading develops values; and conversely, the reader's value system determines to some extent what he reads and the way he reads.

The third emphasis is on concern for the educationally and culturally disadvantaged. The educational retardation that is associated with cultural deprivation has received increased attention during the past few years, as in this analysis:

The root of the problem is the slum pupil's failure to learn reading skills in the primary grades. Poor reading, in turn, becomes the major cause of school dropouts and subsequent unemployment. Inability to read adequately corrodes the child's self-concept and can cause a drop in intelligence test scores.[7]

The earlier the retarded reader is recognized, and the earlier his difficulties are corrected, the better. Major government programs to reduce poverty and unemployment recognize that "reading is the key."

The March, 1965, issue of the *Reading Teacher* and the April, 1965, issue of *Education* were devoted primarily to articles on the educationally and culturally disadvantaged. An understanding of the characteristics of these children and of the conditions under which they have grown up is necessary if we are to provide the experiences they need to improve their reading.

The fourth current emphasis is on the early years — on the importance of developing visual and auditory perception and of providing experiences that will contribute to growth in meaningful vocabulary and in spoken language.

There is growing evidence of the importance of the preschool years for reading development. Samuel Kirk has found a relationship between lack of early intellectual stimulation and later mental deficiency. M. D. Vernon, Helen M. Robinson, Marianne Frostig, and others have shown the relation of proficiency in visual and auditory perception and discrimination to success in beginning reading and to school adjustment. Studies of disadvantaged and bilingual children have shown the need for verbal stimulation during

6 *Ibid.*, p. 43.

7 Stanley Krippner, "Materials and Methods in Reading," *Education*, LXXXV (April, 1965), 467.

the preschool years and of the possibility of satisfying this need with summer kindergartens in which the child can learn to listen, to speak English, and to become amenable to school routine. "Project Headstart" has given a dramatic and widespread impetus to the development of readiness for school during the preschool years.

The effectiveness of an experiment in the Denver Public Schools in which five-year-old kindergarten children were taught to read is discussed by Joseph E. Brzeinski in chapter xvi. Boys and girls who started learning to read in kindergarten and then moved into an appropriately adjusted program in the primary grades have shown some evidence that reading instruction is of value at this age. No evidence has been obtained that it damaged eyesight or interfered with social and academic adjustment. There is some question, however, whether the "adjusted program" alone might not have been equally effective. The experiment is continuing through the fourth grade.

A program to teach reading to still younger children was also initiated by the Denver Public Schools, assisted by leadership groups of parents. Television programs were the means of instruction, supplemented by a guidebook for parents. This program, too, showed some evidence of effectiveness. Evaluation of this kind of program is made almost impossible by inability to control the many variables: parent-child relationships, parental interest and teaching skill, the children's individual capacities to learn, their previous experiences, and many other factors. In both Denver projects, too little attention seems to have been given thus far to individual cases in which reading disabilities have developed.

The majority of schools give readiness tests in the first grade. We do not know how many schools use the results of these tests to differentiate prereading experiences for individual children, but we suspect that the majority of first-grade teachers still go through a routine readiness program with all their pupils. It is as unwise to subject some children to needless prolongation of the readiness stage as it is to neglect readiness altogether. Every child should have the opportunity to progress in reading at a pace commensurate with his ability.

The best use of the preschool and kindergarten years is to develop all the prerequisites for success in reading and, if the children are socially, physically, and mentally ready to read, to begin reading instruction regardless of their chronological ages. There is need for more experimentation with formal instruction in the early years and for follow-up studies of the results.

PRESENT STATUS OF READING PROGRAMS

In the elementary school, the regular classroom teacher is the teacher of reading. Recognizing the importance of getting children off to a good start in reading, administrators are making the greatest efforts to improve reading instruction in the primary grades. They are recommending that every prospective elementary teacher have at least one course in reading and that every teacher in the primary grades have two courses. School principals are selecting first-grade teachers with greater care than previously providing orientation for new teachers, and furnishing continuing in-service education for all teachers. Innovations such as the ungraded primary unit, individualized reading, and team teaching are being introduced in some schools. To assist all teachers and to meet the needs of severely retarded readers, some administrators are employing a combination reading teacher and consultant in their elementary schools.

Surveys in different parts of the country have reported that various kinds of reading programs have been introduced in from one-third to two-thirds of the secondary schools. In the past, these programs have emphasized the remedial aspects of reading. There is now a discernible trend away from programs that are primarily remedial. Throughout the state of Pennsylvania, a developmental reading course is required for all students in the seventh and eighth grades.[8] We also appear to be moving toward more effective teaching of reading in the subject areas. At the present time many schools present a comprehensive program of reading instruction in every subject, a developmental reading course, special reading groups or a reading center, and individualized instruction.

Parallel with this broadening concept of the reading program is the changing role of the reading specialist. The reading teacher who works exclusively with a limited number of retarded readers is gradually changing into a reading consultant who spends most of his time in assisting — and learning from — subject teachers as they attempt to improve their methods and materials for teaching the reading of their subjects. This alliance between the reading specialist and the subject teacher serves to combine the abilities and knowledge of both in the service of better reading.

Although administrators say, "Let there be reading programs" — and reading programs are created — the persons assigned to carry them out are, for the most part, unprepared for this responsibility. The large majority of high-school English teachers feel poorly prepared to teach reading. There is serious lack of specialized training in reading, even among those responsible for supervising, directing, and teaching reading programs. Mary C. Austin, in the first Harvard reading survey, recommended "that a course in basic reading instruction be required of *all* prospective secondary school teachers."[9]

In the professional literature at least, reading is being considered as a part of the total curriculum rather than as an isolated segment of the school program. H. Alan Robinson and Allan Muskopf noted that less than one-fifth of the articles on high-school reading in 1963 were descriptions of separate programs; almost two-fifths were concerned with reading

[8] Sheldon Madeira, "Pennsylvania's Mandated Reading Program," *Journal of Developmental Reading*, V (Summer, 1962), 221–26.

[9] Austin *et al.*, *The Torch Lighters: Tomorrow's Teachers of Reading* (Cambridge, Mass.: Graduate School of Education, Harvard University, 1961), p. 147.

instruction as part of the ongoing school curriculum.[10]

PRESENT STATUS OF
MATERIALS OF INSTRUCTION

A revolution in beginning reading materials has been set in motion by criticism of the prevalence of (1) uninteresting stories, (2) overcontrolled vocabulary, (3) neglect of instruction in phonics, and (4) content foreign to the lives of non-suburban children.

To meet these criticisms and thus make beginning reading more attractive and more rewarding, existing basal reader series have been revised and new series have been put on the market. Every effort has been made to incorporate humor, adventure, suspense, and modern non-fiction material into the new basal readers.

As children's speaking vocabularies increase with their television viewing, we find that they actually know quite a few more words than are included in the basal readers. The increased availability of supplementary reading also extends their vocabulary. The new linguistic readers control sound-letter (phoneme-grapheme) associations rather than number of words. Thus their vocabulary load tends to be larger than that of the other basal readers.

Neglect of phonics has been the most popular complaint of parents. At present phonics is in a state of flux. Two emphases, however, seem evident: (1) sound-letter associations are being introduced earlier and more directly, and (2) more time and attention are being given to the teaching of phon-

10 Robinson and Muskopf, op. cit., p. 86.

ics. Instead of teaching fifty or one hundred fifty sight words to begin with, teachers are calling attention immediately to words that begin with the same consonant sounds. This practice helps children to learn sight words more quickly and also introduces them to the linguistic principle of translating letter forms first into sounds and then into meanings.

Evidence of the increased attention to phonics is found in the teachers' guides and supplementary materials of recently revised basal series and in the apparent popularity of separate phonic systems such as the *Phono-visual* (Phono-visual Products, 1961), the *Phonetic Keys to Reading* (Economy, 1964), and Sister Carolyn's *Breaking the Sound Barrier* (Macmillan, 1960). The phono-visual method is based on an analysis of speech sound; the *Phonetic Keys to Reading* features phonic rules — a method of which linguists disapprove. *Breaking the Sound Barrier* presents phonics as a thinking process.

Some teachers are putting word recognition skills on a thinking level; that is, they encourage children to discover for themselves the relationship between sounds and symbols and to think actively about the meaning of the words they are reading. For example, the teacher may show the words (1) *scare*, (2) *score*, and (3) *scar* on a chart and ask:

Which are meant to frighten?
Which is something left after a cut is healed?
Which tells the number of points won in a game?

Or the teacher may present the sentences, "Before I could have breakfast this morning, I had to go to the store. I bought a quart of milk and a dozen rolls." The unfamiliar words *milk* and *rolls* are inferred from the context after a discussion of other possibilities.

To meet the criticism that beginning reading material has been too remote from the life experiences of many children, Detroit's Great Cities Improvement Studies developed a series of readers featuring Negro children and Negro homes. By showing somewhat better conditions than underprivileged children are accustomed to, the books may raise the readers' sights and help them identify with improved conditions. The success of this series, published by Follett Company, may be due to the interest and humor of the stories rather than to the color of the characters. The *Bank Street Readers*, published by the Macmillan Company, aim to reflect life typical of various environments, economic situations, occupations, and family settings. The content of these books is psychologically meaningful to the child. It does not make the disadvantaged child feel rejected or alienated.[11]

An even greater revolution is taking place with respect to other materials of instruction. This development has been accelerated by government appropriations for equipment and materials other than textbooks. Included are mechanical aids such as special films, film strips, slides, overhead pro-

11 John H. Niemeyer, "The Bank Street Readers: Support for Movement toward an Integrated Society," *Reading Teacher*, XVIII (April, 1965), 542–45.

jectors, tape recorders, and a variety of pacing devices. The audiovisual aids are being used to supply needed background experience for reading, to show students how to acquire certain skills, to capture their attention and interest, to help them analyze their own performance, and to give them other kinds of assistance. The pacing devices for students who have acquired basic vocabulary and comprehension skills are often motivating — they help the student develop the ability to react faster rather than increase his recognition span.

Kits and collections of materials are being published in increasing quantities. Some of these, like the *Little Owl*, the *Young Owl*, and the *Wise Owl* series (Holt, Rinehart and Winston) and the *Scholastic Literature Units* (Scholastic Magazines), have a recreational emphasis. Other kits such as the *SRA Reading Laboratories*, the *EDL Study Skills Libraries* in science, social studies, and library skills for grades three to nine, the Scott, Foresman *Tactics in Reading* for corrective training, and many others are intended for instructional purposes. There are also collections of excerpts from books and selected small libraries that have considerable appeal and value. Many teachers have long been using the Dolch games (Garrard Press) and more recently the EDL Flash-X and the Linguistic Blocks (Scott, Foresman), which give fascinating scientific practice in sentence building.

In addition to ready-made collections of books and excerpts, we have thousands of trade books on all levels

of difficulty and in all fields of interest. Despite this wealth of appropriate
supplementary reading material, however, the basal reader is still the only
book used in many classrooms. Government spending may be changing
this as well as other aspects of instructional practice.

Paperbacks are being widely used.
Witness the large number and variety
of books being published by the Scholastic Book Service of Scholastic Magazines and other book clubs, the Doubleday Signal books, the Dell editions
of classics, and many others. Some
teachers are beginning to substitute paperbacks for bound anthologies, as
suggested by David Sohn in chapter vii.

Workbooks do not seem to be following this upward swing in variety
and interest. Although they are useful
for giving additional practice to students who need it, students are being
encouraged to read more and more
books on their own, and it is becoming less common to use workbooks
with an entire class.

Although at first glance the newer
programed materials seem to resemble
workbooks, they are actually quite different. Each program is theoretically
based on expert initial analysis of the
content and the skills involved in
learning. These materials vary in quality, however; and research has shown
that results are affected by the type of
programing, the type of students involved, and the classroom conditions.[12]
It should also be noted that there is
little evidence that students learn

12 Lee J. Cronbach, "What Research Says
about Programed Instruction," NEA Journal,
LI (December, 1962), 45–47.

more by making programed responses
than they do from reading silently a
well-organized selection or listening to
a straightforward lecture. The rationale for this type of instruction seems to
be the direct opposite of the philosophy of learning as discovery and inquiry. Critical reading is discouraged
by programs that reward the student
for agreeing completely with the pro-
gram-makers. However, by teaching
the tools of thought, it may be that
programed materials free the teacher
to spend more time on adventurous
problem-solving.

The Initial Teaching Alphabet
(ITA) is intended for use in the initial
stage of reading instruction. Experiments in England and in this country
have shown that children can make
the transition to traditional orthography quite easily. We should ask, however, whether other methods might
not establish as much self-confidence
on the part of beginning readers —
which is the strong claim of ITA.
Some linguists achieve the same thing
by introducing only consistent sound-
letter associations at first and ensuring
mastery of each one by sufficient practice on it in words, sentences, and stories.

The idea of associating each of the
forty-four sounds of English with a different color and responding to the col-
or rather than to the form of the letters
seems fantastic at first glance. It also
seems contrary to a fundamental law
of learning — that we should not teach
associations that will have to be discarded later. The underlying principle, however, is similar to that of ITA

— initial success in pronouncing words builds self-confidence, which, in turn, evokes greater effort and motivates achievement.

The advantage of language-experience charts is that they are dictated or written by the children themselves. Thus they constitute reading material that is personally significant to the children and relatively easy for them to decode since it employs their own vocabulary and sentence structure. As the teacher edits and corrects misspellings, the child learns the connections between sounds and letters. The language-experience approach is especially useful in teaching children from non-English-speaking homes. A modification of this approach has been used successfully with older retarded readers in science, social studies, English, and shop classes, when they have found the textbooks provided for them are far too difficult. The teacher first explains and discusses the content of a small section of the book. Then the pupils give their account of it, organize the ideas suggested, and write it in their notebooks. Thus each student has his own special edition of the text.

Reading for personal and social development, though recognized as one of the most important aspects of reading, is left largely to incidental discussions of the motives and actions of characters in literature. The superficial response of one class to the question, "Why do you think the author wrote this story (a simple adventure story)?" is probably not typical: "To teach us a lesson." Perhaps this situation will change, with the quantity of material now available for the study of human relations, including relations that prevail among peoples of other races, countries, and creeds.

OTHER ASPECTS OF READING INSTRUCTION

We might venture the statement that the outstanding characteristic of the teaching of reading today is *lack* of instruction. Practice and testing crowd out specific instruction. Pupils are told to get the main ideas and to remember important details, but they are not shown how to do this. They are expected to locate and interpret context clues without being given specific instruction in how to locate various kinds of context clues and how to use them in interpreting character and plot.

In fact, the amount of reading instruction usually begins to decline in the intermediate grades. When asked about reading instruction, Danny, a fourth-grade boy, replied, "The teacher just tells us to read. And if you can't understand it, you're in trouble." How much instruction and practice in reading are actually given in the intermediate grades? We do not know. We suspect that Danny's answer would apply in many classrooms. An evaluation of the contents of the *Reading Teacher* for 1964 showed that only 1.1 per cent of the space had been given to the intermediate grades, as compared with 19.1 per cent to the elementary grades as a whole, 15.3 per cent to junior high school, 12 per cent to senior high school, and 17.5 percent to college.

To be sure, there have always been teachers who skilfully and intuitively guided students' learning. If all teachers did what the best teachers now do, the teaching of reading would be vastly improved.

It is difficult for many teachers to bridge the gap between theory and practice. How many times do teachers use a given method or technique without being aware of the purpose for which they are using it or the kind of learning that is supposed to result from it? The large majority of subject teachers for example, tend to emphasize the acquisition of facts to the exclusion or neglect of instruction in how to learn.

The independent study approach and the individual contract plan put more responsibility on the pupil. Young adolescents want to be independent. They want to see results, to have objective evidence of progress. They prefer to compete with themselves rather than with their classmates. These are some of the factors that contribute to the success of independent study plans. One plan, described by Marjorie Royer in chapter vi, stresses the principle of teaching, reinforcing, and applying the reading skills that the student needs in order to understand a given selection.

The use of psychologically planned preliminary verbal instruction is just beginning to be explored. This approach should include (1) directing the student's attention to the learning that is expected, (2) recalling previous knowledge or skills that will be useful to him in this situation, and (3) guiding him in the specific learning process.

Individualized reading is here to stay as part of the total reading program. Although research has not shown that individualized reading causes differences in achievement, the students who participate in these programs do read more books. Both teachers and students express satisfaction with the programs. The students are responsible for setting specific reading goals and keeping a record of their progress toward them. The best features of the individualized program — the quantity of self-selected reading and the frequent teacher-pupil conferences — can be combined in various ways with basic reading instruction.

Linguists have been critical of teachers' instruction in reading. Three of their criticisms are (1) the discrepancy between phonics and scientific phonetic analysis, (2) the lack of attention to the primacy of the spoken word and the many meanings conveyed by intonation, stress, and rhythm, and (3) the failure to recognize the importance of sentence structure in conveying meaning. The impact of linguistics on the teaching of reading is evident in (1) the incorporation of linguistic ideas into widely used revisions of basal readers — for example, the Scott, Foresman series; (2) the new linguistic readers; (3) the use of Paul Roberts' two high-school textbooks by English teachers; and (4) increased publication of books and articles that deal specifically with the relation of linguistics to the teaching of reading. The impact is weakened, however, by the constantly changing theories of the linguists themselves. The logic of Aristotle and

Plato may soon supplant the linguistic emphasis of Bloomfield and Fries.

CONCLUDING STATEMENT

At present reading instruction offers many objectives, many theories, many procedures, many kinds of instructional material. Teachers are often bewildered by so many conflicting choices. The organizing principle is still the child, however — his physical and mental capacities, his linguistic abilities, his listening comprehension, his self-concept, his values and goals.

There are as many different reading programs as there are teacher personalities. We may broadly characterize these personalities as follows:

The set-in-his-ways teacher — the old time basal reader is good enough for him.

The insecure, perhaps inexperienced teacher — the teachers' guide is his Bible, and he follows all its precepts and suggestions to the last detail. This book of the law never departs from his desk, and he meditates on it day and night.

The diagnostically oriented teacher — completely converted to the principle of individual differences, he may spend more time understanding his students than he does in using the understanding to help them.

The pioneer teacher — any new device or method appeals to him; he will try anything once.

The creative teacher — he dislikes to follow beaten paths. Divergent thinking is the most satisfying to him; it is his cognitive style.

The scientific, problem-solving teacher — he analyzes the teaching situation, obtains an initial understanding of his students' reading, appraises the available materials and methods in relation to his students' needs and individual stages of development, and constantly evaluates the procedures he uses.

An overview of reading instruction as it is practiced today [13] may encourage teachers to keep using the methods and materials that have facilitated their students' over-all reading accomplishment. It should also suggest ways in which they can incorporate new ideas into a still more effective program.

[13] Helen M. Robinson (guest editor of the reading supplement), "Reading '65: An Overview of Current Practices," *Instructor Magazine*, LXXIV (March, 1965), 56–110.

CHAPTER XVIII

LOOKING AHEAD IN READING

*

HELEN M. ROBINSON

*

TODAY IT is most hazardous to attempt to predict future developments in reading. In the past, such predictions could be made with some degree of confidence because changes
came about gradually and trends were
more likely to continue. Now we are
in the midst of a period of phenomenal discovery of the nature of the
world about us and of the role and
place of man in this world. What we
consider truth today becomes out-
moded tomorrow. Since reading is a
function of, and a tool for change, in
the social order,[1] the extremely rapid
changes we are witnessing and anticipating add to predictive errors.

While preparing this paper, I have
frequently wished for a crystal ball so
that I might foresee even a few of the
more significant problems and issues
for reading instruction, and the use of
reading, in the next decade. Unfortunately, the crystal ball has eluded me.
This paper, therefore, is subject to all
of the limitations of the scope of one
human mind.

READING FOR WHAT?

The most obvious reason for learning to read is to secure an education.

Formal schooling is increasingly prized
today by the general public. In addition, our political leaders are looking
to education as a means of increasing
employment, strengthening the economy, and helping to maintain our nation's leadership. Whether education
is capable of accomplishing all of these
tasks can be questioned, but we do not
question the basic role of reading in
acquiring school learning. Beyond
school years, reading will surely be one
of the most powerful means of continued learning. Thus, for the future,
as in the past, reading will be basic to
formal education and to further education throughout life.

We are in the midst of a technological revolution in which I see no end
to the possibilities of mechanization.
Powerful and complicated machines
run other machines, which in turn do
the work formerly done by many men
and women. Thus, "brawn power" is
rapidly disappearing from the labor
market and "brain power" is in increasing demand. A high percentage of
unemployable adults are unable to
read well enough to be retrained for
available jobs. The manpower short-
age is of highly skilled men to operate
the machines, to repair and service
them, and to design others which will
be even more complicated. In the fu-

<hr>

[1] See Nila Banton Smith, *American Reading Instruction* (Newark, Del.: International
Reading Association, 1965), for comprehensive
treatment of this topic.

ture, therefore, an obvious need is for higher levels of reading competence on the part of all children and youth, so that they may meet the demands of the technological age ahead and be sufficiently versatile to adjust to change as it comes.

At the same time, we are living in the nuclear age. The political problems facing the world demand a citizenry which is better informed, more understanding and tolerant of those unlike us, and better prepared to help solve social problems. Our pressing problems must be solved amicably or we may never have a second chance. Reading is one of the several means of developing the understanding and strategy to survive the nuclear age.

Our tremendously complicated society, largely collected in crowded urban centers, will continue to make great demands on personal and social adjustment. We can anticipate that reading will be an increasingly important aid in the solution of personal and social problems.

An examination of current union demands portends a reduced work week with an accompanying increase of leisure time. But according to Sebastian de Grazia, there is a marked difference between time free from employment and leisure time. He points out that "the benefits of leisure are the benefits of cultivating the free mind."[2] Instead of cultivating the mind, De Grazia produces evidence to show that American adults use their free time largely in the acquisition of consum-

[2] De Grazia, *Of Time, Work and Leisure* (New York: Twentieth Century Fund, 1962), p. 413.

er goods. In fact, he concludes that leisure is a *useless hope*. Perhaps as teachers we might ponder this conclusion and re-examine our reading instruction to determine whether reading in the future could not be made a means of cultivating the free mind.

The mass media are competing for the free time now available to children and adults. According to most surveys, television occupies a large portion of the time of those who have little education and shares the time formerly devoted to reading among college graduates. Obviously, television and radio bring the latest news of the world, almost as it is made. Newspapers and magazines can no longer compete for this role. Whatever functions they eventually adopt, teachers must continue to project the unique role of reading in the age of varied means of mass communication.

Other examples of the future demands that may be made of reading could be given. However, the foregoing comments, coupled with all that has been said in the other chapters of this proceedings, illustrate the problems and uncertainties which complicate easy predictions and disrupt trends. It seems clear that in a future of rapid change the role of reading, and consequently, the goals of reading instruction, will have to be constantly re-examined. Accompanying the new goals will be changes in what, when, and how we teach reading to reach these goals.

WHAT WILL COMPRISE READING?

In looking ahead to the many possible roles of reading in a changing world structure, it is apparent that reading will have to be broadly conceived and defined if it is to serve as a means of learning and of cultivating leisure time. In chapter ix Malmquist has described reading broadly and in detail. He cites William S. Gray in identifying the four major aspects of reading: (1) effectively perceiving words, (2) obtaining the stated and implied meanings, (3) reacting critically to the content, and (4) assimilating ideas acquired with previous experience.[3] In describing the four strands, Gray emphasized the importance of an attitude of inquiry and the use of inductive and deductive thinking to gain new insights, discover new principles, correct false impressions, and discover fresh patterns of organization. The act of discovery on the part of the reader may very well be basic to high motivation for continued reading. The four major strands, with the many subskills that have been identified, are not steps or levels since all may occur almost simultaneously, each reinforcing and motivating higher levels of competence in the others.

Today some writers and speakers argue that reading is simply learning to decode by understanding the phoneme-grapheme correspondences. Their concept of reading embraces only word perception. Beyond this level, they argue, the process of construing meaning and reacting to it is essentially the same for what is read,

[3] Gray, "The Major Aspects of Reading," in *Sequential Development of Reading Abilities,* ed. Helen M. Robinson ("Supplementary Educational Monographs," No. 90; Chicago: University of Chicago Press, 1960), pp. 8–24.

heard, or seen. However, even though the processes appear to be quite similar for the different modalities of perception, the higher level aspects of reading are essential to achieving the objectives of reading and their development can therefore not be left to chance.

In chapter xiv Smith identifies some of the aspects of reading required to develop flexibility. And there are also specialized skills and abilities required for reading in the different content areas, as Brother Leonard points out in chapter xii. In order to meet the future demands on reading, all of these abilities will surely have to be included in our conception of reading.

WHOM SHALL WE TEACH?

As we look ahead it seems likely that we shall teach all children, youth, and adults to read at their own highest levels of competence. We shall not be satisfied to develop only minimal competence on the part of any person. We *dare* not be complacent.

Obviously, much remains to be learned about some segments of our school population if we are to develop universal competence. Today we read and hear a great deal about the limitations imposed by perceptual disorders and minimal brain damage. Often students are given these labels without adequate study or conclusive evidence. Some of the most challenging students are the perceptually handicapped and the culturally disadvantaged. Progress in understanding their problems appears likely to be rapid in the next few years.

"Perceptual handicap" is a term applied loosely to children with many characteristics. In some instances, it appears to be a label such as word-blindness, strephosymbolia, and alexia were in the past. Such labels have often excused teachers from further responsibility for teaching reading rather than motivated them to greater efforts. Adequate procedures for identifying the type and extent of perceptual disorders and the most suitable instructional techniques to overcome them are essential if we are to help these children and reassure parents who have been alarmed by a vague diagnosis.

The culturally disadvantaged form a substantial proportion of the poor readers of our school populations. Research and experimentation will soon begin to offer promising leads which will have to be developed, evaluated, readapted, and applied.

A new look at reading potential is in order if we are to increase efficiency in reading on the part of all, especially the able readers. They, too, need to be taught to read with a breadth and depth of understanding harmonious with their level of intellectual maturity. If we just applied all that we know today about reading, the results would probably be astonishing.

At present we often only give lip service to teaching reading beyond the first six grades. In many instances, only remedial reading is offered for those who read below grade level. And yet, evidence is already available to show that even the best students can improve their reading if they are given appropriate instruction. Only a few high schools, and fewer colleges, offer a broad developmental program. In

the future, therefore, I predict that a sequential and developmental reading program will be extended from the elementary grades through the early years of college for all students.

Meanwhile, adults who are dissatisfied with their reading accomplishments will continue to seek instruction. It seems likely, therefore, that children who are younger than our present school-entrance ages, all those of school age, and many adults will be taught to read in the immediate years ahead.

WHAT MATERIALS SHALL WE USE?

When reading materials are mentioned, most teachers think of basal readers and workbooks. In the future we shall correctly consider all printed and written materials as potentially useful for reading instruction.

As Edgar Dale has said,

Textbooks are highly important teaching tools, but in the rush of present-day experimentation on television, they seem to have been forgotten. As far as I know, no major foundation has made an important grant to improve textbooks. Certainly the ease of using a textbook and the permanently available material which it contains make it extremely valuable.[4]

In all probability, therefore, basal readers will continue to be among materials in use. There are likely to be changes in content and in the accompanying guides, however, as we acquire greater insight into the process of learning and teaching. The use of a

[4] Dale, "Teaching with New Media," *News Letter* (Ohio State University, Bureau of Educational Research and Service), XXIV (March, 1959), 3.

single basal reader for all pupils in a particular grade is rapidly disappearing because it is based on the now discredited assumption that all pupils must progress through the same stages, with the same materials, although perhaps at differing paces. The able reader finishes first and is often rewarded by being given another basal reader at the same level so that he can learn the same skills and abilities again. Most basal readers are geared to the learning pace of the average pupil. The slow learner and the retarded reader may arrive at a certain level one or more years later than the average student only to find that their years and interests have outgrown the selections.

Already on the horizon, and portending future developments, are basal readers with editions both for able and for less competent learners. This modest beginning may foreshadow a variety of other parallel programs. For example, when we know more about students whose parents speak another language and students whose experiences and language have been sharply curtailed, we may be able to provide special materials adapted to their unique needs.

The traditional workbook, which is often used for busywork, will become increasingly important — so much so that teachers will allow time to correct them and to study students' answers as well as discuss with each his particular errors. They may even be self-correcting, but in all probability they will fail to be self-teaching. The workbooks will provide practice in applying skills and abilities that have been introduced in class. They may supply dif-ferent types of materials to permit students to compare and contrast styles of writing — for example, factual versus fictional reports — and they may even provide the opportunity for critical reading. They will have periodic reviews and informal tests which will permit conscientious teachers to diagnose each student's independent efforts.

These traditional materials will be supplemented by a generous supply of trade books, magazines, and pamphlets. The classroom collection will vary in difficulty and cover a wide range of interests. Each student will be able to find materials that contain just the information he seeks, to live vicariously through real or fictional characters, or to note how others solve personal problems similar to his own. Personal reading which is satisfying not only provides much-needed practice in a variety of materials but strengthens interest in reading as an independent activity. Only as students read widely will they be prepared to exercise judgment and refine their taste for good literature.

The textbook in science, social studies, home economics, or other subject area is also material for reading at elementary, secondary, and college levels. Although the primary purpose of such textbooks is to gain information or to learn how to solve problems, each depends heavily upon reading. Content-area teachers have obviously mastered the specific reading skills and abilities used in their fields but are often unaware of them and feel unprepared to teach them to their students. Yet students must learn how to do thoughtful reading of different types or they will fail to acquire the knowledge and attitudes essential to continued growth in specific areas. Single textbooks seldom satisfy the curiosity engendered by a competent teacher; so they will be supplemented by a large variety of reference materials and a whole school library of related materials.

It also appears that careful examination of the content in various subject-matter areas may permit the separate introduction of specific skills, followed by their integration into the preparation of various lessons. Some of the earliest attempts to prepare such materials for high-school English teachers look very promising indeed. Perhaps they can be extended to other areas, too.

Undoubtedly some of the skills to be learned will be programed. Students who are absent from school for several days can be directed to a machine with the appropriate program of the steps or skills they missed. Others who need to develop particular competencies in order to forge ahead may be directed to other programs. In view of the tremendous strides we have made in recent years, one might be tempted to predict that we will learn how to program all instructional materials for reading. From where I stand, I cannot see that far into the future.

Related audiovisual aids will surely be standard equipment in tomorrow's classroom. The tape recorder set up in a small adjacent workroom will permit individuals, or even small groups, to read orally and monitor their own expressions. Special plans may be prepared by the teacher for other groups.

With an opaque projector students without adequate experiential backgrounds will be able to use our wealth of pictures and illustrations to gain experience vicariously. Electronic devices yet undiscovered may become significant aids to the future teacher, who will undoubtedly be an electronic technician.

To sum up, the classroom of the future will contain myriad materials to tempt the reluctant reader and to spur the able reader to breadths and depths of understanding and pleasure. Materials for *all* learners, adapted to their unique interests and abilities will be a necessity, not a luxury.

WHICH METHODS SHALL WE USE?

Before addressing myself to this question, it is essential to point out that the choice of method is determined by the particular aspect of reading. Clearly, the methods used to introduce a child to reading differ markedly from those used by the high-school teacher to help students read mathematics or those used by the English teacher to enhance appreciation of literature. Therefore, to discuss specific methods of the future requires specification of goals. Within the limited space available, therefore, it will be necessary to confine my comments to methods in general, with a few exceptions.

Undoubtedly, many of the methods we use today will continue to be effective with a large majority of children and youth. Some methods now employed, however, will gradually be replaced by ones that help children learn more quickly. As more is learned about the fundamental processes of learning and teaching, radical changes in parts of our reading programs may be anticipated.

Today's bitter arguments about methods for beginning reading instruction are likely to continue, largely because we see strong personal commitments to one or another of the methods. Indeed, research may reveal that the teacher's confidence in a given method is basic to success in using it. If so, then perhaps we will be sufficiently flexible to permit teachers to use those procedures with which they are most successful.

Likewise, research dealing with the basic aptitudes of young children appears to be pointing to different constellations of abilities. It is possible, therefore, that in the school of the future, pupils who are likely to profit most from a visual, phonic, linguistic, or kinesthetic approach will be assigned to the teacher who is most competent and comfortable in that approach. When both professional educators and laymen really understand individual differences, individuals may be free to learn by the methods best suited to them without being considered peculiar or incapacitated in some other way. Application of what is already known should break that lock step of expecting all students of a given age to profit from identical types of instruction.

As we increase the competence of younger pupils, we shall be faced by the necessity of providing effective methods for teaching the higher level reading skills, which are almost totally ignored in today's heated arguments.

Nevertheless, isolated researchers are probing these areas and beginning what will undoubtedly be the new horizons of the future. We are beginning to acquire information on creativity, for example. We are beginning to study critical reading, including the nature of the process itself, so that in the future methods for teaching it may be devised. We are giving more than lip service to the development of flexible readers who can adapt their procedures to the purposes for which they are reading and to the difficulty of the materials. We are seeking ways to develop reading skills and abilities without destroying the learner's ultimate desire to read. In the immediate future, teachers will be experimenting with different methods for reaching all of these goals.

But the new information coming from such embryonic studies will be insufficient. Furthermore, unanticipated ideas will emerge from such research and experimentation. Therefore, it seems clear to me that change in methods and instructional procedures will become the rule rather than the exception. Although we see radical changes occuring today, the reasons for future change will be different. Today some school systems change methods of teaching because of parental pressure or because another school has made a change. In contrast, future change will result from research. School people will spark the changes, and they will also educate the public concerning the values of appropriate innovations.

Furthermore, ways will be found to combine methods for teaching so as to take full advantage of the values and diminish the deficits of any one method. Of course, the methodological ingredients will vary with the level of accomplishment of the learners.

The methods used at any given level will be a function of the instructional sequence in use. Very little research has been done to determine the most appropriate sequence for developing the different aspects of reading. Most teachers now begin with the simplest levels of each of the major aspects, which are taught concurrently. Recently, Eleanor J. Gibson has suggested a sequence requiring emphasis upon single skills: "Learning to differentiate graphic symbols; learning to decode letters to sounds; and using progressively higher-order units of structure." [5] Obviously, the methods used to teach this sequence would be quite unlike that of the traditional classroom.

In describing a linguistic approach in chapter xi, yet another sequence was proposed. Which is the best? How do we know? Very soon, research should compare the ultimate success of contrasting sequences to determine any differences. Sequences other than those now in use will reorder instructional methods at the very least and may perhaps alter major approaches.

HOW WILL READING BE APPRAISED?

In all probability, reading competence will be assessed by school personnel, by parents, by the lay public, and as today, by the press. To be sure, each will use different standards and tech-

[5] Gibson, "Learning to Read," *Science*, CXLVIII (May 21, 1965), 1067.

niques. Nevertheless, better co-operation and increased mutual understanding could relieve many current tensions.

In light of the new curriculum which will inevitably evolve, many new techniques will be needed to determine reading competence. I foresee the use of new standardized tests, informal tests, rating scales, interviews, interest inventories, records of books read, and self-evaluation procedures.

Standardized tests of the future will be different in form and scope from those of today. They will surely abandon the narrow range of skills and abilities presently included. An informal analysis of several current standardized reading tests reveals almost exclusive emphasis, at the elementary level, on literal meaning. Furthermore, the secondary- and college-level tests show minimal departure from this narrow objective. New tests will assess reading readiness, word perception, power of interpretation, ability to react critically and emotionally to selections, ability to select the appropriate purpose and the most effective way to read a particular selection, rates of reading different types of materials, oral reading, and many other abilities. Reading skills and abilities in the various content areas will also be tested, either as a part of general reading tests or in the respective areas. Without doubt, means will be found to assess understanding of credibility of sources, appreciation of language and literature, and other of the new elusive reading abilities.

The format of reading tests may change from the usual multiple choice to that requiring original thinking. This change may be made possible by the use of the complex new electronic devices capable of scanning written materials and noting correct responses. Ambiguous responses will still require human judgment.

Informal tests may continue to be an effective means for making quick assessments in order to place pupils in proper classes, for determining specific strengths and weaknesses in reading, and for fitting materials of varying levels of difficulty to learners of varying abilities. Rating scales and interviews will be used more extensively as we come to recognize fully the contribution of interests, attitude, self-concept, and experience background to the ability to read.

Records of personal reading of books, magazines, and other materials have often been cumbersome and faulty. Ingenuity will bring more dependable and pleasant means for determining both the extent and the quality of reading. This aspect is exceedingly important because, after the school years, reading competence is of little value if it is not used. Habits of usage should be developed, maintained, and extended throughout the school years.

Self-evaluation is now practiced in programed instruction. It is equally feasible to have self-evaluation procedures available to learners in forms other than programed books. Imagine the school of tomorrow with a battery of evaluative devices to which students may turn whenever they feel that they are ready. Because they appreciate the information they can attain, they will

follow directions, score their tests, and punch the information into a computer. In a few seconds, the student may receive a profile suggesting that he pay greater attention to some specific areas and praising him for progress in others. Such a system would provide for true independence and self-guidance in learning to read.

WHO WILL TEACH READING?

Those gifted men and women who believe that reading is an essential part of living and who can inspire all pupils by example will be our future reading teachers. To achieve this goal, it is necessary that we begin now to attract the most able young people to the teaching profession. Furthermore, the prospective teachers who enjoy reading and appreciate literature will have these two related abilities broadened and enriched in their college programs. They will become familiar with children's literature and literature for adolescents as well as for adults.

In addition to knowledge about and appreciation of literature, prospective teachers will learn the psychology of reading and become familiar with the methods and materials for teaching reading effectively. Instead of learning cookbook recipes as many do today, prospective teachers will learn the values and limitations of methods and materials. Imbued with the spirit of inquiry and the need for experimentation, our new teachers will enter schools as interns, where they will be further inspired while they acquire the details of teaching under the guidance of master teachers. Given such excellent prospects, administrators will find ways to stimulate and reward growth in teaching competence.

These teachers will be truly professional teachers who know *why* they carry on given activities as well as *how* to do them. They will be free to experiment with less effective parts of the instructional program and to adapt their materials and methods of teaching to the needs of their particular pupils. They will inspire confidence in parents and suggest ideas to them rather than change their direction because of parental pressure. Teachers with such training may be a part of a team in which their competency with reading will be utilized to the full.

SHALL WE PROVIDE SPECIAL HELP FOR TEACHERS?

In the foreseeable future, few teachers will approach the ideal just described. Even those few must have the help and support of flexible administrators and competent, imaginative supervisors.

A new specialist called the reading consultant is emerging on the educational scene. In co-operation with the general supervisor, the principal, and the superintendent, the reading consultant will be a key person in improving the total reading program and interpreting it to the public. Because the training of the reading consultant emphasizes inquiry and the solution of practical problems through interpretation of the most recent research, these specialists will reduce the lag between new knowledge and practice.

The reading consultant will keep abreast of new developments in organization of classes, in effective methods for teaching reading, and in materials for the use of teachers. Promising ideas may be tried and evaluated without fanfare or commitment to maintain or defend them. Thus some materials and procedures will constantly be discarded in favor of others.

Continuous in-service training for experienced teachers will, therefore, be supplemented by intensive orientation of new teachers. Results of broad appraisals of the reading progress of all learners will be conveyed to teachers so that practices may be altered to meet individual needs. In this way, reading retardation can be significantly reduced. Only a small percentage of students with serious difficulties will need the help of trained remedial teachers.

At the same time able students will be stimulated and given the techniques essential to forge ahead. The reading consultant will strive constantly to help teachers develop maximal reading competence on the part of each student. Since reading is closely related to the other language arts and is the foundation for acquiring information in the content areas, the consultant will study these areas, too, and be ready to assist teachers who need help.

As school systems have become larger and more complex and as knowledge has increased, the generalist finds it increasingly difficult to keep abreast of new developments in all areas. The reading consultant's job will therefore be to keep the administrative staff sufficiently informed so that its members can make wise decisions about curriculum, instruction, and other aspects of the school program where reading is fundamental.

CONCLUDING STATEMENT

Much of what has been said is utopian. I submit that we must hitch our wagons to a star and begin to climb toward it. In the opening chapter, McSwain reports that only man can dream or imagine tomorrow. Let us exercise man's unique function. Come dream with me!

Let us create the best materials and procedures and promote the highest levels of reading that we can imagine. To do this, we must temper imagination with realism — submit ideas to scrutiny based on what we know and can learn about children and youth and about the reading process.

In the spirit of inquiry, let us try innovations; at the same time, let us give them a *fair* trial as McDonald suggests. in chapter viii. We must make sure that change brings permanent improvement in the overall reading growth of children and youth. Clearly, then, our goals must be set, and continuous appraisal of how near our young people are to these goals shall be the rule.

In the future, as in the past, reading will make a significant contribution to the self-fulfilment of the individual and to the good society. I cannot predict the precise role of reading in a society changing as rapidly as ours. Hence, many questions are posed but remain unanswered. However, it seems safe to predict that reading will be defined broadly as an intellectual activity. Our larger goal will be maximal reading competence, accompanied by permanent interest and deep appreciation of literature, on the part of all children, youth, and adults. Every effective means that we can imagine will be adopted to achieve this goal. In the hands of our future citizens lies the destiny of mankind. To prepare these future citizens to meet such a challenge is the educator's privilege and responsibility.

CHAPTER XIX

NOTEWORTHY BOOKS PUBLISHED SINCE THE 1964 READING CONFERENCE

*

FOR ELEMENTARY-SCHOOL PUPILS

SARA INNIS FENWICK

*

RECENT developments in reading, as well as in other areas of the curriculum, have as one common characteristic the identification of a broad range of reading goals and the need for a variety of materials for reading — variety in subject content, appeal, form of writing, format, and level of difficulty. It is an interesting fact of publishing history that the writing and production of trade books for children has always closely paralleled the evolution of new trends in education. There is an indication of such influence in the list of noteworthy books that follows.

The concern of educators to find reading materials that will appeal to children whose academic interests and motivations have been impaired by a culturally disadvantaged environment is strongly reflected in this year's list. For the younger children, there are books with the appeals of recognition and minority group identification. Two books by Ezra J. Keats have these qualities. *Whistle for Willie* is a picture book, similar in its bold bright colors and striking design to this art-

ist's earlier book, *A Snowy Day*; Willie has brown skin; but no reference to race for any of the characters is made. Keats's most recent book this year is a simple retelling of the American tall-tale legend of John Henry, the greatest railroad builder in history, with the same bright colors and humor in text and picture. Similar appeals of minority group identification are made for the middle-grade children by Mina Lewiton's *That Bad Carlos*, a story of a family that moves from Puerto Rico to New York, and by a very readable biography of Martin Luther King, subtitled *The Peaceful Warrior* by Ed Clayton. The same needs must have been in the minds of the authors and publishers of *Berries Goodman*, by Emily C. Neville, a story of suburban segregation as seen through the eyes of a Gentile boy and his Jewish friend, and two biographical works, *Breakthrough to the Big League*, by Jackie Robinson, and *They Showed the Way: Forty American Negro Leaders*, by Charlemae Rollins.

Books that are useful because of well-handled urban settings include,

228

for younger children, June Behrens' *Soo Ling Finds a Way*, which tells in picture-book format of the impact of modern technology in the form of a laundromat, and for older readers, *The Green Laurel*, by Eleanor Spence, which although set in Australia tells realistically of problems of moving into a temporary housing community that would be the same for a pre-adolescent girl in any country.

Two stories of courage that should speak eloquently to pre-adolescent readers are *The Shadow of the Bull*, by Maia Wojciechowska, winner of the Newbery Medal for the most distinguished contribution to literature for children, and *Far Out on the Long Canal*, by Meindert De Jong.

A most illuminating study of a pre-adolescent girl is *Harriet the Spy*, by Louise Fitzhugh. Adult reviewers have been divided in their opinions whether this book will speak to young readers with as honest a voice as it speaks to adults — however, it is a very penetrating, sensitive story of a girl whose recorded observations of her classmates and neighbors precipitate a considerable avalanche of trouble and unhappiness.

As in other years, this annual list does not include all of the most outstanding books of the year since the 1964 Reading Conference, but it does represent a selection of worthwhile books that should provide for a variety of needs and interests.

FOR KINDERGARTEN THROUGH PRIMARY GRADES

BEHRENS, JUNE. *Soo Ling Finds a Way*. Golden Gate, 1965 (the problem created for Soo Ling's grandfather's laundry by the competition from a laundromat; a read-aloud book).

BENCHLEY, NATHANIEL. *Red Fox and His Canoe*. Harper, 1964 ("I Can Read Books").

BERENSTEIN, STANLEY. *The Bike Lesson*. Random, 1965 ("Beginner Books").

BRIGGS, RAYMOND. *Fee Fi Fo Fum: A Picture Book of Nursery Rhymes*. Coward, 1964.

CAUDILL, REBECCA. *A Pocketful of Cricket*. Holt, 1964 (picture-book story of a boy and a pet cricket).

CRAIG, M. JEAN. *Spring Is like the Morning*. Putnam, 1965 (description of the coming of spring).

DE REGNIERS, BEATRICE S. *May I Bring a Friend?* Illustrated by BENI MONTRESOT. Atheneum, 1964 (read-aloud verses, with illustrations that won the Caldecott medal for 1965).

FATIO, LOUISE. *The Happy Lion and the Bear*. Whittlesay, 1964 (more fun in a picture book about the always charming Happy Lion).

FISHER, AILEEN L. *In the Middle of the Night*. Crowell, 1965 (what it is like for a small girl to be outdoors at night).

———. *Listen, Rabbit*. Crowell, 1964 (the joy of a small boy in watching a wild rabbit and finding its nest, in a picture book).

GANS, ROMA. *It's Nesting Time*. Crowell, 1964 ("Let's Read-and-Find-Out Books").

HOBAN, RUSSELL C. *A Baby Sister for Frances*. Harper, 1964 (a read-aloud picture book of gentle family humor).

———. *Bread and Jam for Frances*.

Harper, 1964 (another picture story about Frances, who has problems with her new baby sister) .

——. *Tom and the Two Handles.* Harper, 1965 ("I Can Read Books").

HOLMAN, FELICE. *Elisabeth, the Treasure Hunter.* Macmillan, 1964 (a simple introduction to seashore life in a story of treasure-hunting) .

JACOBS, JOSEPH. *Tom Tit Tot: An Old English Folk Tale.* Illustrated by EVALINE NESS .Scribner's, 1965.

KEATS, EZRA J. *John Henry, an American Legend.* Pantheon, 1965 (simple retelling of legend, with wonderfully colorful illustrations) .

——. *Whistle for Willie.* Viking, 1964 (picture book of a small boy learning to whistle) .

KUMIN, MASINE W. *More Eggs of Things.* Putnam, 1964 ("See and Read Story Books") .

LARUE, M. G. *Tiny's Big Umbrella.* Houghton, 1964 (for beginning independent readers) .

LEXAU, J. M. *I Should Have Stayed in Bed.* Harper, 1965 (for beginning independent readers) .

LIONNI, LEO. *Tico and the Golden Wings.* Pantheon, 1964 (a picture-book story of a bird who gave away his golden feathers) .

MATSUNO, MASAKE. *Chie and the Sports Day World,* 1965 (a read-aloud family story of modern Japan) .

SELSAM, MILLICENT E. *Let's Get Turtles.* Harper, 1965 ("I Can Read Books"; science for beginning readers) .

SEUSS, DR. *Fox in Socks.* Random, 1965 ("Beginner Books") .

SILVERSTEIN, SHEL. *A Giraffe and a Half.*

Harper, 1964 (nonsense in a cumulative text) .

UCHIDA, YOSHIKO. *Sumi's Prize.* Scribner, 1964 (a read-aloud story of a little Japanese girl's wish to win a prize) .

FOR MIDDLE ELEMENTARY GRADES

ANDERSEN, HANS. *The Nightingale.* Translated by EVE LE GALLIENNE. Illustrated by N. C. BURKERT. Harper, 1965 (handsomely illustrated edition of an old favorite) .

BAKER, BETTY. *The Treasure of the Padres.* Harper, 1964 (a contemporary setting of the treasure-hunting adventures in the Arizona desert of an Indian boy) .

BELPRE, PURA. *The Tiger and the Rabbit and Other Tales.* Lippincott, 1965 (new edition of a collection of Puerto Rican tales) .

CHRISTOPHER, M. F. *Catcher with a Glass Arm.* Little, 1964 (baseball) .

CLAYTON, ED. *Martin Luther King: The Peaceful Warrior.* Prentice, 1964.

CLEARY, BEVERLY. *Ribsy.* Morrow, 1964 (adventures of Henry Huggins' dog) .

CLEWES, DOROTHY. *The Holiday.* Coward, 1964 (English Penny visits France briefly as a stowaway) .

CONE, MOLLY. *A Promise Is a Promise.* Houghton, 1964 (story of an eleven-year-old-girl, with good presentation of Jewish family life) .

DE JONG, MEINDERT. *Far Out on the Long Canal.* Harper, 1964 (a nine-year-old boy, in a town of skaters and a family of champions, struggles to learn to skate) .

DUMCOMBE, FRANCES R. *Cassie's Vil-*

lage. Lothrop, 1965 (Cassie's home in a New York State village is about to be destroyed by a new dam) .

ENRIGHT, ELIZ. *Zeee*. Harcourt, 1965 (a lightly told fairy tale) .

EPSTEIN, SAMUEL and BERUL. *Hurricane Guest*. Random, 1964 ("Easy to Read Books"; story of a visiting English pen-pal in the excitement of a hurricane) .

ESTES, ELEANOR. *The Alley*. Harcourt, 1964 (mystery and detection set in a small faculty community, with good character portrayal) .

FADIMAN, CLIFTON. *Wally the Wordworm*. Macmillan, 1964 (a romp with a wordworm who eats through a dictionary) .

FITZHUGH, LOUISE. *Harriet the Spy*. Harper, 1964 (a study of an unhappy sixth-grade girl who practices spying by keeping a notebook of candid observations of her classmates and neighbors) .

FLOETHE, L. L. *The Islands of Hawaii*. Scribner, 1964 (simple introduction to the fiftieth state) .

FLORY, JANE. *Clancy's Glorious Fourth*. Houghton, 1964 (summer vacation fun for a trio of fifth-grade boys) .

FRASCONI, A. *See Again, Say Again: A Picture Book in Four Languages*. Harcourt, 1964.

GIDAL, SONIA. *My Village in Germany*. Pantheon, 1964.

———. *My Village in Morocco*. Pantheon, 1964.

GLUBOK, SHIRLEY. *The Art of the Eskimo*. Harper, 1964.

GOUDEY, ALICE. *Graywing*. Scribner, 1964 (the life of the herring gull, in slightly fictionalized form) .

HARNDEN, RUTH P. *The High Pasture*. Houghton, 1964 (in the Colorado mountains, a boy learns strength for hard tasks and hard truths) .

HOFSINDE, ROBERT. *Indians at Home*. Morrow, 1964.

JUDSON, CLARA I. *Andrew Carnegie*. Follett, 1964.

LEODHAS, SARCHE N. *Gaelic Ghosts*. Holt, 1964 (a collection of stories) .

LEWITON, MINA. *That Bad Carlos*. Harper, 1964 (a ten-year-old boy comes to New York with his family from Puerto Rico) .

LORD, BEMAN. *Mystery Guest*. Walck, 1964 (the new girl next door turns out to be a good football player) .

ROUNDS, GLEN. *Rain in the Woods, and Other Small Matters*. World, 1964.

RUSSELL, S. P. *Lines and Shapes: A First Look at Geometry*. Walch, 1965.

STEELE, WM. O. *The No-Name Man of the Mountain*. Harcourt, 1964 (a tall tale, fun to read aloud) .

SYME, RONALD. *Alexander Mackenzie: Canadian Explorer*. Morrow, 1964.

TREASE, GEOFFREY. *No Boats on Bannermere*. Norton, 1965 (good mystery with an English setting) .

WOOLLEY, CATHERINE. *Cathy's Little Sister*. Morrow, 1964 (warm and realistic family life; a sequel to other stories about Cathy Leonard) .

YATES, ELIZABETH. *Carolina's Courage*. Dutton, 1964 (a pioneer story of the adventures of a small girl, her doll, and the Pawnee Indians) .

FOR UPPER ELEMENTARY AND
JUNIOR-HIGH GRADES

ALEXANDER, LLOYD. *Book of Three*. Holt, 1964 (fantasy of a mythical kingdom and a struggle between good and evil) .

ALLEN, ELIZABETH. *The Loser.* Dutton, 1965 (a high-school girl's story of a boy friend who is a non-conformist) .

AYER, MARGARET. *Made in Thailand.* Knopf, 1964 (arts and crafts, plus information about cultural and economic life) .

BRAGDON, L. J. *Meet the Remarkable Adams Family.* Atheneum, 1964.

BURLINGAME, ROGER. *Out of Silence into Sound: The Life of Alexander Graham Bell.*

CAUDILL, REBECCA. *The Far-Off Land.* Viking, 1964 (pioneer story of girl on a flatboat expedition to French Lick) .

CAVANAH, FRANCES. *Triumphant Adventure: The Story of Franklin Delano Roosevelt.* Rand, 1964.

CHAUCER, GEOFFREY. *A Taste of Chaucer; Selections from the Canterbury Tales.* Chosen and edited by ANNE MALCOLMSEN. Harcourt, 1964.

COTTRELL, LEONARD. *The Secrets of Tutankhamen's Tomb.* New York Graphic Society, 1964.

DARLING, LOUIS. *The Gull's Way.* Morrow, 1965 (photographs and text tell the life of the herring gull) .

DUGGAN, ALFRED. *The Romans.* World, 1964.

EMERY, ANNE. *The Losing Game.* Westminster, 1965 (teen-age story handles the problem of cheating) .

FOOTMAN, DAVID. *The Russian Revolution.* Putnam, 1964.

FOSTER, GENEVIEVE. *The World of Columbus and Sons.* Scribner's, 1965.

GRAHAM, LORENZ. *North Town.* Crowell, 1965 (a Negro family moves north, and the sixteen-year-old son enters an integrated school) .

HODGES, CYRIL WALTER. *Shakespeare's Theatre.* Coward, 1964.

HUNT, IRENE. *Across Five Aprils.* Follett, 1964 (story of a family of divided loyalties during the Civil War) .

JOHNSON, ANNABEL. *The Grizzly.* Harper, 1964 (an eleven-year-old boy goes hunting with his father) .

JOHNSTON, JOHANNA. *Together in America: The Story of Two Races and One Nation.* Dodd, 1965.

KENT, LOUISE A. *He Went with Hannibal.* Houghton, 1964.

KYLE, ELISABETH. *Girl with a Pen: Charlotte Bronte.* Holt, 1964 (biography of Charlotte Bronte between the years of seventeen and thirty-one) .

LAFFIN, J. *Codes and Ciphers: Secret Writing through the Ages.* Abelard, 1964.

LEWIS, RICHARD. *The Moment of Wonder.* Dial, 1964 (selections from Japanese and Chinese poetry, with exquisite illustrations and book design) .

LIFE MAGAZINE. *Australia and New Zealand.* Time, 1964.

MEADER, STEPHEN W. *Stranger on Big Hickory.* Harcourt, 1964 (story of a boy's photography project for 4-H club) .

MEANS, F. C. *It Takes All Kinds.* Houghton, 1964 (two teen-age sisters find difficulty in accepting their own and their family's limitations) .

MELTZER, MILTON (ed.). *In Their Own Words: A History of the American Negro.* Crowell, 1964.

NEVILLE, E. C. *Berries Goodman.*

Harper, 1965 (a good story of an eleven-year-old boy and his friends against the background of suburban segregation and anti-Semitism) .

PETRY, ANN. *Tituba of Salem Village.* Crowell, 1964 (Tituba, a slave, was one of three women convicted of witchcraft in 1692) .

ROBINSON, JACKIE, and DUCKETT, A. *Breakthrough to the Big League.* Harper, 1965.

ROLLINS, CHARLEMAE H. *They Showed the Way: Forty American Negro Leaders.* Crowell, 1964.

SPELLMAN, JOHN A. *Printing Works like This.* Roy, 1964.

SPENCE, ELEANOR. *The Green Laurel.* Roy, 1965. (story of a pre-adolescent girl who is unhappy in a temporary housing community; winner of 1964 Australian Children's Book Prize) .

TREECE, HENRY. *The Burning of Njal.* Criterion, 1964 (retelling of an Icelandic saga of the eleventh century) .

TUNIS, EDWIN. *Colonial Craftsmen and the Beginnings of American Industry.* World, 1965 (comprehensive, authoritative, and very well illustrated).

WEBER, L. M. *Don't Call Me Katie Rose.* Crowell, 1964 (high-school sophomore is ashamed of her name and her family) .

WOJCIECHOWSKA, MAIA. *Shadow of the Bull.* Atheneum, 1964 (story of the courage of a young boy whose family expects him to be a great bull fighter; Newberry Award for 1964) .

* * *

FOR HIGH-SCHOOL AND JUNIOR-COLLEGE STUDENTS

SUSAN SAX

*

AN EARLY children's encyclopedia has an amusing diagram illustrating anatomy which shows a transparent man filled with little elves and brownies all of whom are sawing, hammering, and running about on purposeful errands. This was the period when legs were limbs, feet were extremities, and truth and reality were ugly and frightening. People passed away instead of dying, and little strangers (babies) arrived on the scene instead of being born. Babies were kept in swaddling clothes, and young adults were wrapped about in curtains of ignorance, deceit, and romanticized euphemism.

At that time it was felt that reading matter for young adults should be inspirational, always wholesome, and free from controversy or involvement in any sort of critical issue. Biographies, like funeral orations, contained mention only of the subject's good qualities. America was always right, the bad always repented, and the good were always rewarded.

Today, high-school and junior-college students demand more substantial fare. They want to explore current issues from every perspective and they will not permit condescension or dishonesty. They want to read the same books that adults read, not diluted and edited versions.

The titles on this list reflect issues of current concern on an adult level. If the list were placed in a time capsule, a future historian could deduce much about the political, social, and cultural climate of the world in 1965. He would know that the civil rights issue is being discussed in America; that East-West world relations are tense; that Africa is undergoing change and arousing interest; that divorce, education, and television are subjects for satire; and that we are still interested in the writings of a sixteenth-century poet named Shakespeare. Further, he could deduce that space study is a growing branch of science, that we travel a great deal upon our own continent, and that we are greatly interested in past cultures.

The young adults of today who read are sophisticated and perceptive, and they enjoy controversy and the expression of honest opinion. They have no patience with blandness and safely uncommitted expression. They want to be involved in important issues and to form their own conclusions. Librarians and teachers who respect their students will recognize this desire for involvement and will present a range of adult materials reflecting many areas of knowledge and issues of concern.

ALLEGRO, JOHN MARCO. *Search in the Desert*. Doubleday, 1964 (an account of an archeological expedition in Jordan, with relevant information about the Dead Sea scrolls).

ALLSOP, KENNETH. *Adventure Lit Their Star*. Crown, 1964 (English nature classic about the ringed plover).

ALPERT, HOLLIS. *The Barrymores*. Dial, 1964 (history of the famous family of the theatre).

AMIS, KINGSLEY, and CONQUEST, ROBERT (eds.) *Spectrum III*. Harcourt, 1964 (collection of science-fiction stories for able readers).

ANDERSON, ERICA. *Albert Schweitzer's Gift of Friendship*. Harper, 1964 (photographer tells of her association with Schweitzer in connection with the production of a documentary film).

AUSTING, RONALD. *I Went to the Woods*. Coward, 1964 (autobiography of a nature lover and photographer of birds).

BAGLEY, DESMOND. *The Golden Keel*. Doubleday, 1964 (taut adventure novel about a quest for the lost treasure of Mussolini).

BEATTY, CLYDE, with EDWARD ANTHONY. *Facing the Big Cats: My World of Lions and Tigers*. Doubleday, 1965 (circus animal trainer tells of his varied professional experiences).

BERGER, THOMAS. *Little Big Man*. Dial, 1964 (tongue-in-cheek Western saga on a grand scale).

BOCK, JERRY. *Fiddler on the Roof*. Crown, 1965 (the book of the Broadway musical based on Sholom Aleichem's stories of Jewish life in czarist Russia).

BROWN, IVOR JOHN CARNEGIE. *Shake-*

speare and His World. Walck, 1964 (analysis of Elizabethan society as a background for understanding Shakespeare's plays) .

BUSH, WARREN V. (ed.). *The Dialogues of Archibald MacLeish and Mark Van Doren.* Dutton, 1964 (excerpts from recorded conversations concerning poetry, art, politics, and other matters) .

CARAS, ROGER A. *Dangerous to Man.* Chilton, 1964 (explores myth and reality about wild animals and their reputed dangers to man) .

CARLISLE, HENRY. *Ilyitch Slept Here.* Lippincott, 1964 (comedy revolving about East-West diplomatic representatives in Bern, Switzerland).

CHAPMAN, WALKER. *The Loneliest Continent.* New York Graphic Society, 1964 (annals of Antarctic explorations from Magellan's day to present times).

CHICHESTER, FRANCIS. *The Lonely Sea and the Sky.* Coward, 1964 (adventure-filled autobiography of a pioneer pilot, navigator, and yachtsman) .

CONGDON, DON (ed.). *Combat: World War I.* Delacorte Press, 1964 (firsthand accounts of World War I, selected from various sources) .

CURCIJA-PRODANOVIC, NADA. *Ballerina.* Criterion, 1964 (young ballet student overcomes the handicaps imposed by an injured foot).

DE CAMP, L. SPRAGUE and CATHERINE C. *Ancient Ruins and Archaeology.* Doubleday, 1964 (an examination of theories relating to twelve archeological sites) .

DENNIS, PATRICK. *The Joyous Season.* Harcourt, 1964 (social satire about the problems facing two children when their parents decide to divorce) .

DONOVAN, JAMES BRITT. *Strangers on a Bridge: The Case of Colonel Abel.* Altheneum, 1964 (defense lawyer for Russian spy Rudolf Abel discusses the trial and his unusual client) .

DUBERMAN, MARTIN B. *In White America.* Houghton, 1964 (excerpts from historical documents, organized to form a drama about Negro history in America) .

EHRENBURG, ILYA. *Memoirs: 1921–1941.* World, 1964 (historically revealing autobiography of a Russian writer) .

EPTON, NINA. *Seaweed for Breakfast.* Dodd, 1964 (observations on Japanese culture and customs) .

FERNEA, ELIZABETH. *Guests of the Sheik.* Doubleday, 1965 (anthropologist's wife tells of a visit to a tribal settlement in Iraq) .

GALLICO, PAUL, and SZASZ, SUZANNE. *The Silent Miaow.* Crown, 1964 (new perspectives on cats and humans "translated from the feline").

GATHERU, R. MUGO. *Child of Two Worlds.* Praeger, 1964 (African describes his formative years in Kenya and his later education in America) .

GORDON, DONALD. *Flight of the Bat.* Morrow, 1964 (swiftly paced science-fiction novel) .

HAHN, EMILY. *Africa to Me: Person to Person.* Doubleday, 1964 (collection of articles on aspects of the current African scene) .

HALEVY, DANIEL. *My Friend Degas.* Wesleyan, 1964 (journal kept by a young man who enjoyed a close friendship with Degas) .

HANO, ARNOLD. *Sandy Koufax, Strikeout King.* Putnam's, 1964 (factual sports biography) .

HANSEN, THORKILD. *Arabia Felix.* Harper, 1964 (history of an eventful Danish scientific expedition to the Near East in the 1760's) .

HARRER, HEINRICH. *I Come from the Stone Age.* Dutton, 1965 (German explorer tells of his expedition into the jungles and mountains of New Guinea) .

HOHENBERG, JOHN. *Foreign Correspondence: The Great Reporters and Their Times.* Columbia University Press, 1964 (retelling of historic events in which foreign correspondents played a major role) .

HOLT, RACKHAM. *Mary McLeod Bethune.* Doubleday, 1964 (biography of the Negro leader and educator, with interesting sidelights on southern history and racial traditions) .

HUGHES, LANGSTON (ed.) . *New Negro Poets, U.S.A.* Indiana University Press, 1964 (some of the poems in this collection deal with racial issues; others have universal themes) .

HUXLEY, ELSPETH. *With Forks and Hope: An African Notebook.* Morrow, 1964 (personal travel experiences and discussion of major issues facing Tanganyika, Kenya, and Uganda) .

HUXLEY, JULIETTE. *Wild Lives of Africa.* Harper, 1964 (animal lore and remarks on the destruction of African wildlife) .

IDYLL, C. P. *Abyss.* Crowell, 1964 (study of the ocean and its inhabitants) .

KAUFMAN, BEL. *Up the Down Staircase.* Prentice-Hall, 1964 (satirical novel with pointed observations about conditions in the public school system of a large city) .

KIERAN, JOHN. *Not under Oath.* Houghton, 1964 (witty, digressive autobiography) .

KING, MARTIN LUTHER. *Why We Can't Wait.* Harper, 1964 (explanation of the civil rights movement, its history, means, and aims) .

KLASS, ROSANNE. *Land of the High Flags.* Random House, 1964 (author tells of her two years as a teacher in Afghanistan) .

KLOCHOKO, MIKHAIL A. *Soviet Scientist in Red China.* Praeger, 1964 (Soviet technical advisor to China who later defected to Canada tells about the current status of Chinese science and technology) .

KNEBEL, FLETCHER. *Convention.* Harper, 1964 (fictionalized account of a political convention) .

KRIEG, MARGARET. *Green Medicine.* Rand McNally, 1964 (author tells of new drugs, their properties and unusual sources) .

LA FARGE, OLIVER. *The Door in the Wall.* Houghton, 1965 (well-written stories about anthropologists, Indians, and the Southwest) .

LAWRENCE, MARGARET. *New Wind in a Dry Land.* Knopf, 1964 (writer tells of her long residence in and subsequent affection for Somaliland) .

LEY, WILLY, and BONESTELL, CHESLEY. *Beyond the Solar System.* Viking, 1964 (information about the nature of stars and galaxies and speculation about space travel) .

LISAGOR, PETER, and HIGGINS, MARGUERITE. *Overtime in Heaven: Ad-*

ventures in the Foreign Service. Doubleday, 1964 (studies of nine heroes of the foreign service).

LONGFORD, ELIZABETH. *Queen Victoria.* Harper, 1965 (intimate biography of the long-lived queen).

LUCE, IRIS (ed.). *Letters from the Peace Corps.* Luce, 1964 (selected letters describe the work of the Peace Corps and the problems and pleasures of the young volunteers).

MANTLE, MICKEY. *The Quality of Courage.* Doubleday, 1964 (stories of baseball players in situations when they have shown special courage).

McKNIGHT, GERALD. *Verdict on Schweitzer.* John Day, 1964 (critical observations of the man and the myth).

MEHDEVI, ANNE SINCLAIR. *Persia Revisited.* Knopf, 1964 (an American woman married to a Persian presents her observations of changing patterns of life in her husband's country).

MERTZ, BARBARA. *Temples, Tombs and Hieroglyphs.* Coward, 1964 (Egyptian history as reconstructed from archeological finds).

MILLER, MERLE, and RHODES, EVAN. *Only You, Dick Daring!* Sloane, 1964 (witty exposé of the television industry).

MIRSKY, JEANETTE. *The Great Chinese Travelers.* Pantheon, 1964 (narratives about Chinese travelers over a period of three thousand years).

MOLLOY, PAUL. *A Pennant for the Kremlin.* Doubleday, 1964 (farce involving baseball and American and Russian behavior patterns).

MONTGOMERY, RUTHERFORD GEORGE. *The Living Wilderness.* Dodd, 1964 (the habits of small wild creatures of the woods and fields and suggested methods of observation).

MORGAN, CHARLES. *A Time to Speak.* Harper, 1964 (lawyer tells of his controversial involvement in the civil rights drive in a southern city).

NABOKOV, VLADIMIR. *The Defense.* Putnam's, 1964 (novel translated from the original Russian about a chess player whose total commitment to the game brings about his ultimate destruction).

NARAYAN, R. K. *Gods, Demons, and Others.* Viking, 1964 (retelling of the epic legends and myths of India).

NEWQUIST, ROY. *Counterpoint.* Rand McNally, 1964 (interviews with writers covering their views on many topics).

O'FAOLAIN, SEAN. *Vive Moi!* Little, Brown, 1964 (autobiography of the Irish revolutionary, author, and literary critic).

PAYNE, ROBERT. *The Life and Death of Lenin.* Simon & Schuster, 1964 (a study of the life, thought, and actions of Nikolai Lenin).

PHELPS, GILBERT. *The Winter People.* Simon & Schuster, 1964 (fantasy about an archeologist and his discovery of an unknown Indian tribe in the Andes).

PIAZZA, BEN. *The Exact and Very Strange Truth.* Farrar, Straus, 1964 (the first novel by a young actor; a perceptive study of childhood).

RAUSHENBUSH, ESTHER. *The Student and His Studies.* Wesleyan University Press, 1964 (an examination of the college careers of four students).

RICHARDSON, ROBERT S., and BONE-

STELL, CHESLEY. *Mars.* Harcourt, 1964 (an astronomer and a painter of astronomical scenes have jointly produced this informative book on our nearest planet).

ROBINSON, JACKIE. *Baseball Has Done It.* Lippincott, 1964 (a discussion of integration in baseball).

ROSTEN, LEO. *The Many Worlds of Leo Rosten.* Harper, 1964 (random selection of entertainments, stories, and essays, including some of the original H*Y*M*A*N   K*A*P*L*A*N pieces).

SANDBERG, SARA. *Mama Made Minks.* Doubleday, 1964 (life with a family in the fur business in New York City before the depression).

SAYRE, WOODROW WILSON. *Four against Everest.* Prentice-Hall, 1964 (history of four who attempted to climb Mount Everest with a minimum of supplies and equipment).

SCHAEFER, JACK. *Heroes without Glory: Some Goodmen of the Old West.* Houghton, 1965 (brief biographies of ten forgotten heroes of the West).

SEGAL, LORE. *Other People's Houses.* Harcourt, 1964 (Jewish refugee tells of the years when she had to adapt to a succession of foster families and temporary accommodations).

SHORT, WAYNE. *The Cheechakoes.* Random House, 1964 (true adventure story about a family that migrated to Alaska and learned to live there).

SHRIVER, SARGENT. *Point of the Lance.* Harper, 1964 (a compendium of speeches and articles about the Peace Corps and America's role in finding solutions to world problems).

SILVERBERG, RORERT (ed.). *Great Adventures in Archaeology.* Dial, 1964 (ten archeologists tell of their work and discoveries).

SLESSER, MALCOLM. *Red Peak.* Coward, 1964 (leader of the 1962 British-Soviet Pamir mountaineering expedition presents his personal narrative of the event).

SMITH, HOMER. *Black Man in Russia.* Johnson, 1964 (American Negro tells of his sojourn in the Soviet Union and of his ultimate disillusionment).

SMITH, WILLIE, with GEORGE HOEFER. *Music on My Mind: The Memoirs of an American Pianist.* Doubleday, 1964 (autobiography of a colorful jazz musician).

SOO CHIN-YEE, and LORD, BETTE. *Eighth Moon.* Harper, 1964 (young girl discusses her childhood in Communist China).

STEFANSSON, VILHJALMUR. *Discovery.* McGraw, 1964 (contemporary explorer tells of his experiences in the Arctic).

STEIN, AUREL. *On Ancient Central Asian Tracks.* Pantheon, 1964 (excerpts from the records of the British archeologist who made four expeditions into Central Asia).

STEWART, MARY. *This Rough Magic.* Mill (distributed by Morrow), 1964 (the island of Corfu provides an exotic setting for this suspenseful mystery story).

SULLIVAN, WALTER. *We Are Not Alone.* McGraw, 1964 (a report on the search for intelligent life in other worlds).

THOMAS, LOWELL. *Lowell Thomas'*

Book of the High Mountains. Messner, 1964 (every possible kind of information pertaining to mountains).

TRACY, HONOR. *Spanish Leaves*. Random House, 1964 (impressions noted by a traveler in Spain).

VON HOFFMAN, NICHOLAS. *Mississippi Notebook*. David White, 1964 (a collection of newspaper articles written by a reporter in Mississippi at the time of the 1964 civil rights disturbances).

WAIN, JOHN. *The Living World of Shakespeare*. St. Martin's, 1964 (interpretation and criticism of Shakespeare's dramas).

WALSH, WILLIAM B. *A Ship Called Hope*. Dutton, 1964 (doctor describes the work of the hospital ship "Hope" in Indonesia and Vietnam).

WAUGH, EVELYN. *A Little Learning*. Little, Brown, 1964 (author recollects his early years as a schoolboy and Oxford undergraduate).

WHALEN, RICHARD J. *The Founding Father: The Story of Joseph P. Kennedy*. New American Library, 1964 (an examination of a famous politician, businessman, and father).

WHITE, ROBB. *The Survivor*. Doubleday, 1964 (novel about a Navy pilot in World War II).

WHITE, WILLIAM S. *The Professional: Lyndon B. Johnson*. Houghton, 1964 (a study of our President and his accomplishments).

WHITEHOUSE, ARCH. *The Fledgling*. Duell, 1964 (veteran of World War I tells of his experiences in the British Royal Flying Corps).

WHITESIDE, THOMAS. *Alone through the Dark Sea*. Braziller, 1964 (three episodes from recent history involving unusual voyages).

WICKER, TOM. *Kennedy without Tears*. Morrow, 1964 (biography that emphasizes the human qualities of John F. Kennedy).

ZOLOTOW, MAURICE. *Stagestruck*. Harcourt, 1965 (biography of Alfred Lunt and Lynn Fontanne that is rich in theatre lore).

INDEX

*